We Hold These Truths

The Spiritual Significance of the American Civil War

Murray Lytle

We Hold These Truths:
The Spiritual Significance of the American Civil War

Copyright © 2013 by Murray Lytle

Cover Design: *A portion of Lincoln's Gettysburg Address, A parchment replica and feather quill pen.*
Bonnie Jacobs/iStockphoto.
Digital Composition and enhancement, Jim Deering

All tables in this document were created by the author, Murray Lytle

www.Frameworkproductions.com

Published by: Framework Publishing
1500 14th Ave. Suite B
Vero Beach, Florida 32960

The author would very much appreciate feedback and comment especially if it is to point out errors or to amplify sections of the book. To do so, please write to him at 09civilwar@gmail.com.

Library of Congress Control Number 2013930290

ISBN 978-1-939135-06-3

We Hold These Truths

There is a wonderful scene in the movie *Saving Private Ryan* in which the elderly Private Ryan stands up from the grave of one of his battlefield rescuers, turns to his wife and pleads with tears, "Tell me I was worth it!" Decades before, during World War II, a platoon of soldiers had died to save him and he wanted to be assured that his subsequent life had been worth their spilt blood. It is a great story of redemption. In fact, I sometimes think that all great stories are, at heart, stories of redemption in which something is restored by the sacrifice of a third party.

By the summer of 1865, over three million American men had engaged in one of history's bloodiest conflicts leaving 620,000 of them in graves. The greatest legacy of that conflict was the freedom of four million black slaves, making the Civil War a remarkable story of redemption.

As a lay student of history, I have developed a theory of civi- lizational development which posits that when humans are free to treat one another as equals there are always bursts of creative energy. This is an interesting idea and it is echoed in,

"We hold these truths to be self-evident, that all men are created equal, that they are endowed by their Creator with certain unalienable Rights, that among these are Life, Liberty and the pursuit of Happiness."

With this in mind then, I believe the American Civil War to have been the second most important spiritual (redemptive) moment in the human story. For what other conflict in history was entered into so that one antagonist, in defeating another would redeem the liberty of an unrelated third party? The fact of the Civil War is simply astounding and may be the reason that the United States of America is arguably the most creative nation that has ever existed.

To be sure, the hard fought freedom won by this war was adulterated with the avarice and ill temper of continuing evil. Many more lives would be lost and many more decades would have to pass before anything approaching racial equality would be achieved. But the most difficult first step was taken at horrendous cost and no other nation on earth has ever been willing to pay such a cost for such a prize. On November 4, 2008, Mr. Jefferson's deal was sealed with the election of the first African-American president of the United States of America. His political leanings and my citizenship are irrelevant because his election was an achievement of transcendent importance. However, the singularity of the election of Mr. Obama can only be appreciated in the context of an understanding of the Civil War and one can only judge his desire to be Lincolnesque by knowing something of Mr. Lincoln.

But why write yet another book about the American Civil War? Surely this soil has been well tilled by more erudite authors than myself. Hubris is one reason, of course, but beyond that I want to connect the dots between Thomas Jefferson, Abraham Lincoln and Barack Obama. My belief is that the Civil War could not have happened in the absence of the Declaration of Independence and this was reinforced by President Lincoln himself who started his Gettysburg address with a direct refer- ence to the writing of this document. Perhaps more than any other piece of literature, Mr. Jefferson's prose guided Mr. Lincoln during the most difficult four years of American history. And certainly the stellar rise of Mr. Obama could not have happened without Mr. Lincoln.

This book, then, is written to tell a story that is unique, high- ly significant, and I hope, through its appeal to factoids and character portraits, accessible and relevant to all readers. I am motivated in this endeavour by my grandchildren, all of whom I hope will follow their parents and grandparents into a thorough investigation of the hallways of history. It is a pursuit that pays immediate and rich dividends regardless of what kind of day job one might have. I salute all those historians who have brought much joy into the life of this engineer and so if, in reading my book, the reader is induced to buy and read a book by a real historian then I will be very pleased indeed.

Table of Contents

1: Why Did They Fight? 1

2: Lead up to War: The Antebellum Years 17

3: Secession and the Short, Glorious War 43

4: The Elephant and How He is Known 61

5: 1862 - Death and the End of Innocence 103

6: Union Leaders of the Civil War 147

7: 1863 - Emancipation and the Turning Point 203

8: Confederate Leaders of the Civil War 241

9: War is Hell 295

10: 1865 - The War is Over: Mr. Lincoln Can Rest 327

Afterward: What Makes America Great? 337

Appendix 1: 1860 Census 347

Appendix 2: List of Battles 348

Appendix 2B: 1861 - 1865 351

Appendix 3: Selected Speeches of Abraham Lincoln ... 365

Bibliography 431

1: Why Did They Fight?

It is said that the Civil War was the first war between literate armies. In fact, the literature of the war stands in stark contrast to much of what passes for literature today. Ken Burns' "*Civil War*" series made popular a soldier's letter, written by Sullivan Ballou to his wife. This is what Major Ballou wrote in August 1861 more than 147 years ago.

"My very dear Sarah:

The indications are very strong that we shall move in a few days—perhaps tomorrow. Lest I should not be able to write you again, I feel impelled to write lines that may fall under your eye when I shall be no more.

Our movement may be one of a few days duration and full of pleasure—and it may be one of severe conflict and death to me. Not my will, but thine O God, be done. If it is necessary that I should fall on the battlefield for my country, I am ready. I have no misgivings about, or lack of confidence in, the cause in which I am engaged, and my courage does not halt or falter. I know how strongly American Civilization now leans upon the triumph of the Government, and how great a debt we owe to those who went before us through the blood and suffering of the Revolution. And I am willing—perfectly willing—to lay down all my joys in this life, to help maintain this Government, and to pay that debt.

But, my dear wife, when I know that with my own joys I lay down nearly all of yours, and replace them in this life with cares and sorrows—when, after having eaten for long years the bitter fruit of orphanage myself, I must offer it as their only sustenance to my dear little children—is it weak or dishonorable, while the banner of my purpose floats calmly and proudly in the breeze, that my unbounded love for you, my darling wife and children, should struggle in fierce, though useless, contest with my love of country?

I cannot describe to you my feelings on this calm summer night, when two thousand men are sleeping around me, many of them enjoying the last, perhaps, before that of death—and I, suspicious that Death is creeping behind me with his fatal dart, am communing with God, my country, and thee.

I have sought most closely and diligently, and often in my breast, for a wrong motive in thus hazarding the happiness of those I loved and I could not find one. A pure love of my country and of the principles have often advocated before the people and "the name of honor that I love more than I fear death" have called upon me, and I have obeyed.

Sarah, my love for you is deathless, it seems to bind me to you with mighty cables that nothing but Omnipotence could break; and yet my love of Country comes over me like a strong wind and bears me irresistibly on with all these chains to the battlefield.

The memories of the blissful moments I have spent with you come creeping over me, and I feel most gratified to God and to you that I have enjoyed them so long. And hard it is for me to give them up and burn to ashes the hopes of future years, when God willing, we might still have lived and loved together and seen our sons grow up to honorable manhood around us. I have, I know, but few and small claims upon Divine Providence, but something whispers to me—perhaps it is the wafted prayer of my little Edgar—that I shall return to my loved ones unharmed. If I do not, my dear Sarah, never forget how much I love you, and when my last breath escapes me on the battlefield, it will whisper your name.

Forgive my many faults, and the many pains I have caused you. How thoughtless and foolish I have often been! How gladly would I wash out with my tears every little spot upon your happiness, and struggle with all the misfortune of this world, to shield you and my children from harm. But I cannot. I must watch you from the spirit land and hover near you, while you buffet the storms with your precious little freight, and wait with sad patience till we meet to part no more.

But, O Sarah! If the dead can come back to this earth and flit unseen around those they loved, I shall always be near you; in the garish day and in the darkest night—amidst your happiest scenes and gloomiest hours—always, always; and if there be a soft breeze upon your cheek, it shall be my breath; or the cool air fans your throbbing temple, it shall be my spirit passing by.

Sarah, do not mourn me dead; think I am gone and wait for thee, for we shall meet again. As for my little boys, they will grow as I have done, and never know a father's love and care. Little Willie is too young to remember me long, and my blue-eyed Edgar will keep my frolics with him among the dimmest memories of his childhood. Sarah, I have unlimited confidence in your maternal care and your development of their characters. Tell my two mothers his and hers I call God's blessing upon them. O Sarah, I wait for you there! Come to me, and lead thither my children."

Reading this man's thoughts, one must ask what made him willing to forsake so much? He loved his wife and his children, he revered his God and he felt honour-bound to preserve his nation. But would the life of a young lawyer from Rhode Island have been materially affected by the division of the Union? Would it be so affected that it was worth dying to maintain? That seems hardly possible. Sullivan Ballou was not able to post this letter to his wife and he died a few weeks after he wrote it at the age of 32 from injuries he received at the First Battle of Bull Run.

Perhaps I am so haunted by this young man's letter because I am not an American and cannot understand the deep feelings of patriotic love which are, to me, one of the most endearing features of the American psyche. Some years ago, during one of Canada's spasms of separatist anxiety, I polled my friends to see who was willing to sign up and fight for the preservation of the Confederation. There were no takers. At the same time I asked a simple question of fact about one of the foundational events in the creation of Canada and only 20 percent of my respondents could offer even a partial answer. So was the American Civil War generation an anomaly? Are Americans so different that they would again rush to arms in the event of a modern secessionist movement?

Based on the results of the statistically unrepresentative sample of my Canadian friends and lingering uncertainty about the continued patriotic fervour of my American friends, I conclude that something very unique was taking place in every state and territory of the United States of America in 1861. I further conclude that what motivated Major Sullivan Ballou and the other millions of volunteers and conscripts in the Civil War was deeply spiritual in nature, even if this was not always recognized by those who signed up to fight.

The great Revolutionary generation which preceded Mr. Ballou was revered by Americans living in the antebellum United States. It was almost universally believed by American citizens that the Revolutionary War sparked a unique political experiment that was founded on spiritual principles identified by Thomas Jefferson;

We hold these truths to be self-evident, that all men are created equal, that they are endowed by their Creator with certain unalienable Rights, that among these are Life, Liberty and the pursuit of Happiness.

Other nations have adopted similar creedal statements but no other nation has been willing to pay the price of aligning its society with these principals. The Civil War was that price. Mr. Jefferson and the Founding Fathers were well aware of the glaring irony between their declaration and its practice. While many wanted an end to slavery, Mr. Jefferson saw that the desire for such an end and its implementation would be difficult to reconcile;

"We have the wolf by the ears and can neither hold him nor safely let him go. Justice is in the one scale, and self-preservation in the other."

When there was a failed vote to end slavery, Jefferson voiced his concern in almost poetic terms,

> *"The voice of a single individual . . . would have prevented this abominable crime from spreading itself over the new country. Thus we see the fate of millions unborn hanging on the tongue of one man, and Heaven was silent in that awful moment!"*

> *"Indeed I tremble for my country when I reflect that God is just: that his justice cannot sleep for ever . . . The Almighty has no attribute which can take side with us in such a contest."*

One can discuss forever the quixotic relationship which Jefferson and many of the Founding Fathers had with the issue of slavery but it seems clear that, in the formative stages of the Union, there was a clear recognition that the practice did not match the words and that nothing good could come from this state of affairs. How could a nation founded on such lofty principles maintain the practice of one man owning another as chattel property?

Institution of Slavery

In 1831, Alexis de Tocqueville, a young French aristocrat, was sent to the United States in order to assess its penal system.

As an outsider he was fascinated by the sociology of his host country and took notes on his travels in both the North and South. He compiled his notes into books, the most famous of which is *Democracy in America,* and it remains the most insightful assessment of antebellum American life. His comments on the practice of slavery in the United States are particularly apropos;

> *"[Virginia] was scarcely established when slavery was introduced; this was the capital fact which was to exercise an immense influence on the character, the laws and the whole future of the South. Slavery...dishonors labor; it introduces idleness into society, and with idleness, ignorance and pride, luxury and distress. It enervates the powers of the mind and benumbs the activity of man. On this same English foundation there developed in the North very different characteristics."*

> *"Upon the left bank of the Ohio labour is confounded with the idea of slavery, upon the right bank it is identified with that of prosperity and improvement; on the one side it is degraded, on the other it is honoured; on the former territory no white labourers can be found, for they would be afraid of assimilating themselves to the Negroes; on the latter no one is idle, for the white population extends its activity and its intelligence to every kind of employment. Thus the men whose task it is to cultivate the rich soil of Kentucky are ignorant and lukewarm; whilst those who are active and enlightened either do nothing or pass over into the State of Ohio, where they may work without dishonour."*

Tocqueville was able to see clearly the enervating effects of slavery on the Southern economy and correctly predicted that the more lively and individualistic attitude of the North would overwhelm the South.

And perhaps it has ever been thus.   In his book, *Enemies of Society,* historian Paul Johnson argues that slavery so deadened the economies of both Greece and Rome that it destroyed the middle class from which comes civilizational energy. The abundance of slave labour blunted the need for technological improvement. Indeed, the Emperor Vespasian refused to utilize an innovation which would have greatly reduced the human energy required to move large marble blocks because it would displace the labour of the slaves and the poor leading to civil unrest.

Johnson further argues that the Roman Empire fell when it was unable to expand its economy on the basis of conquest and was forced to resort to heavy taxation of all but the slave and aristocratic classes in order to maintain the empire. When this occurred the impoverished masses were happy to welcome the barbarian hordes who were both Christian and had no slave class. This is not to say that slavery was incompatible with Christianity. It should have been but it took until the late 18th Century for Georgian England to awaken Christendom to the evils of slavery.

With the discovery of the New World came the opportunity for impoverished, persecuted and adventurous Europeans to escape the shackles of their old world and strike out for the new. The vastness and relative lack of population of the new lands called out for agricultural expansion which in turn looked for cheap labour. And cheap labour there was in abundance along the west coast of Africa. For 200 years most of the world was blissfully ignorant of the travails of the African slave who was removed from his village and sent across the "inner passage" to the Americas never to return, never to see family and loved ones, to die as the property of another man.

A picture of the violence done to the African, as well as to those who trafficked in these human lives, slowly began to emerge in the middle of the 18th Century. Slave trader turned anti-slavery activist and evangelical preacher, John Newton, knew first hand both sides of slavery violence. He spent over a year as a white slave owned by black slavers. He witnessed the unbelievable cruelty of the cramped and ill-equipped slave ships. He had heard the stories of how injured and diseased human "cargo" was sent to the bottom of the ocean in order to collect the insurance rather than receive a low price in the New World.

Newton became an influential mentor to a wealthy young parliamentarian named William Wilberforce who, following his conversion to evangelical Christianity in 1785, determined that one of the great occupations of his life would be the eradication of the slave trade. In 1787 he wrote in his journal that,

"God Almighty has set before me two great objects, the suppression of the Slave Trade and the Reformation of Manners."

In company with a small group of anti-slavery advocates (amongst other passions) who called themselves the Clapham Sect, Wilberforce successfully wrote a law to abolish the slave trade in 1807 and, in 1833, a law to abolish slavery throughout the British Empire. It is a testimony to the finality of the work of the Clapham Sect that today it is inconceivable that slavery should ever exist and that William Wilberforce was only resuscitated into public awareness by a recent, popular film.

In the United States, the abolition of slavery remained the quest of comparatively few. Yet recognized or not, slavery was the basis for many monumental political battles. Compromises for the expansion of slavery were developed in the 1820's and it was the breakdown of these compromises that led to war. Even at its outset, few were prepared to accept that slavery was the cause of the Civil War. In 1861, the ex-slave and abolitionist, Frederick Douglass, agreed that not many whites were prepared to discuss slavery but predicted that by the end of the war all would have to admit that "*the war now being waged in this land is work for and against slavery.*"

While President Lincoln agreed with Mr. Douglass, he was fearful of making the war about emancipating the slaves. He was concerned that Northern bigotry would divide support for the war and destroy any chance of restoring the Union. Abolitionists convinced Lincoln that emancipation, as a concept, could be sold as a strategy to win the war. Freeing the slaves in Confederate territory would weaken their effort thus shortening the war. This argument removed the element of civil rights and equality from the debate and made no statement about the morality of slavery. Instead it was sold as a part of the war effort and was heartily endorsed by the army following the Emancipation Proclamation of January 1, 1863.

Another important aspect of emancipation was the impact it would have upon public opinion in Europe, particularly Great Britain. England was working hard to eradicate slavery and, with emancipation in the rebel states, it would be difficult for her to side with the Confederate South thus promoting re-enslavement of the freed slaves. Nor was Lincoln ignorant of the fact that huge sacrifices need something to ennoble them and emancipation would bring a higher purpose to the awful sacrifices of the war. And finally, if slavery was not dealt with during this war, the chances of another war within 20 years were high.

Why Did They Fight?

On one level, the Civil War is a thrilling story of adventure and battle in a hundred different places. It is the story of young farm boys from the North and South discovering their country for the first time and of passing their young adulthood in the company of a Band of Brothers. Interestingly enough, it is also the story of up to 600 young women who pretended to be young men so that they could join that band as well. 'Band of Brothers' refers to that unique fraternity which is forged in combat and was first coined by Shakespeare (Henry V) but was popularized by those sea captains who served with Admiral Horatio Nelson during the Napoleonic Wars. But, as with all Bands of Brothers, the intensity of feeling amongst those living is directly proportional to the amount of bloodshed and destruction experienced. The price in bloodshed and destruction was particularly high for those who experienced the Civil War.

The casualty rate for the 2.5 million men who served in the Union Army during the Civil War was 25 percent with about 360,000 dying from wounds and disease and an additional 280,000 men wounded. Casualties in the Confederate Army were even worse - 33 percent of Southern soldiers were killed or wounded from an enlistment of 780,000 men. These are the highest casualty ratios of any war in which America has been involved. By comparison, the casualty rate in the Second World War was 6 percent and the rate for the Vietnam War was less than 5 percent. Looked at another way; 620,000 American soldiers died during the Civil War coming from a total population of 31 million. Therefore, roughly 6 percent of all American males died in the Civil War. This is the equivalent of almost 9 million American men dying in a 4 year war if such were to occur today.

Why indeed did they fight? Why was the country, both North and South, willing to offer so great a sacrifice? So that young men could seek adventure and belong to a Band of Brothers? Did they fight to preserve the Union and vouchsafe a trust from previous generations? Was it to protect slavery as a social and economic way of life? Is it possible to conceive of today's citizens of the United States tolerating the daily arrival of over 6,000 coffins filled with dead young men? That these men and boys (and girls) fought, and fought hard, is beyond question. But... why?

The most complete and direct attempt to answer this question is an interesting study by historian James McPherson described in his book, *For Cause and Comrades; Why Men Fought in the Civil War.* By examining more than 25,000 letters and diaries of 1,076 men who fought in the Civil War - 647 Union soldiers and 429 Confederate soldiers – McPherson obtained insights into the thoughts of these men which had been honed in the debates that raged in army camps on both sides of the battlefields. It is very clear that these soldiers personalized the question and made continued attempts to answer for themselves and their loved ones why they were doing what they were doing. His research very effectively debunks the notion that soldiers, from privates to generals, were naively ignorant of what it was all about.

Before examining this question, it bears stating that the over three million Americans who fought each other in the Civil War did not uniformly set their teeth and march grimly into the storm of flying lead that awaited anyone standing upright.

Most battles were fought with regiments weakened by no-shows, skulkers, beats and stragglers. As many as one third of the regimental soldiers would break off and hide in foliage, help their wounded friends to the rear and not return or sign off sick on "special" days. Once having "seen the elephant," as Civil War soldiers so poetically called the first battle experience, many were not anxious to see it again. McPherson quotes one soldier;

> *"The sneaks in the army are Legion... When you read of the number of men engaged on our side, strike out at least one third as never having struck a blow."*

He suggests that the initial impulse to sign up for the war was based on the rage militaire that has engaged the enthusiasms of young men from time immemorial. When the consequences of this decision became obvious, every soldier needed to provide a satisfactory answer to their mothers, wives and betrothed. For many in the North, the fighting in the opening stages of the war, was driven by love of country and flag. It was to maintain the Union and keep faith with the Founding Fathers who had shed their blood to create the Republic in the first place. Many of those fighting for the South simply wanted to drive the "Northern mudsills" and "Black Republicans" from their land. They too appealed to their Founding Fathers and saw the war as a re-enactment of the War of Independence. They could repeat the words of Patrick Henry, *"Give me Liberty or give me Death!"* apparently unaware of the irony involved in fighting for the freedom of one race of people to remove the liberty of another race of people.

McPherson also points out the role of religion in the establishment and maintenance of both armies. He cogently argues that, in the final two years of the war, the Northern soldier was fighting to end slavery just as the Southern soldier was fighting to maintain it. And in an irony noted by President Lincoln in his Second Inaugural Address, both sides were motivated by a faith that convinced them that God was on their side. Hear the words of one soldier as quoted by McPherson,

"...the hand of God is in this, and that in spite of victories and advantages He will deny us Peace until we grant to others the liberties we ask for ourselves..."

President Lincoln delayed issuing the Emancipation Proclamation for fear that his soldiers would leave the battlefield rather than fight for abolition. The document was carefully and cleverly crafted to ensure his Union coalition held together and that his armies continued to fight. McPherson's research led him to conclude that, at its onset, 30 percent of Northern soldiers saw slavery as the over-riding issue of the war and this rose to over 50 percent by the war's end. But there were many who felt betrayed by the Proclamation and the New York riots of August 1863 were likely in response to the fear of many, that emancipation would result in increased competition for jobs. However, as more ex-slaves fought and died alongside white soldiers, the more respect they gained and the greater the acceptance of abolition as the primary reason for the war. This was more than born out by the 1864 presidential election results in which Northern soldiers voted overwhelmingly for Lincoln (78 per cent).

***

The Civil War is remembered for the large battles in its two main theatres. However, it must be remembered that there were pitched battles all across the United States. For example, when the Confederate government sought to open ports on the Pacific Ocean by conquering California, the war was taken to Santa Fe in what is now New Mexico. Few single volume stories of the war encompass the entire breadth of the fighting and this one is no exception.

With these deficiencies then, this is that story and almost everyone who participated thought it would be a little war....

2: Lead up to War: The Antebellum Years

Historian Shelby Foote stated that the Civil War resulted from a failure of the American genius for compromise. And indeed this is so - but perhaps some issues cannot survive a compromise.

The history of the Civil War really begins in 1776 with the Declaration of Independence and the nascent fight to end slavery. There was a strong feeling that slavery could not be abolished in the slave colonies of the South. Many of the Founding Fathers were themselves slave owners; they represented slave owners; and they had no mandate to change the basis of their economies. The coming revolution was designed to end English meddling in their colonial affairs and the Southern colonists weren't about to replace the English meddlers with New England Puritans. There was a strong push for prohibiting slavery in new territories and states but the compromise resolution of 1784 failed by one vote prompting Thomas Jefferson to state,

"The fate of millions unborn hung on the tongue of one man, and Heaven was silent in that awful moment."

Fortunately for the posterity of that one man, few remember his name.

It is tempting to view the years between the successful revolution and the Civil War as being riotous in the fortunes made as the new nation expanded to fill the available land and in the political battles fought to put meaning behind the words of the Constitution. But this period was also a time of significant artistic expression as writers and painters gained maturity and confidence. These were exciting times of development and, with the Louisiana Purchase of 1803 vast new areas of land, some with a unique French flavour, became part of the new nation.

Antebellum Arts

The pulse of creativity generated by Mr. Jefferson's Declaration was felt in the arts although much of the literature written in the antebellum years was not fully recognized at the time and tastes continued to be established by European trends. The short story was the first American innovation to gain local acceptance as were biographies of the heroes of the Revolutionary War.

By 1828, after 25 years of compilation, Noah Webster published his *American Dictionary of the English Language* which, to this Canadian, so distorted the spelling of English words that the US suffers for his innovations to this day. In his 1837 Harvard address, Ralph Waldo Emerson argued for a particular American literature noting that the nation needed to assert its growing independence in the arts as well as politics. Perhaps his "American Scholar" speech merely reflected what was already taking place but it was also a strong encouragement to other indigenous writers and artists.

George Bancroft published his ten volume *History of the United States,* in 1834 and one wonders how massive would be his work were it written 232 rather than 58 years after independence.

In many respects antebellum America was a seedbed for prolific and unique writers. Writers from New England, in particular, produced a large body of important fiction and non-fiction. William Prescott, though legally blind, wrote his impressive conquest histories of Mexico and Peru in the 1840's. Henry Wadsworth Longfellow (*Evangeline, The Song of Hiawatha*), John Greenleaf Whittier (*Ichabod*), Oliver Wendell Holmes (*Old Ironsides*), Nathaniel Hawthorne (*Scarlet Letter, House of Seven Gables*), Henry David Thoreau (*On Walden Pond*) and Margaret Fuller all wrote from a New England perspective. New York alone produced Washington Irving (*The Legend of Sleepy Hollow, Rip Van Winkl*e), James Fenimore Cooper (*Last of the Mohicans, Deer Slayer*), Herman Melville *(Moby Dick)* and Walt Whitman (*Leaves of Grass*). Edgar Allen Poe *(Fall of the House of Usher, Murders of the Rue Morgue)* did most of his writing in New York although he was born in Virginia.

The war itself produced remarkable music with lyrics expressing optimism in the midst of the darkest of days. During Christmas 1864, Henry Longfellow wrote the words to, *I Heard the Bells on Christmas Day*. This was the first Christmas he celebrated following the death of his wife in an 1861 fire and the wounding of his son on December 1, 1863 during the Battle of New Hope Church. On Christmas day, 1864, with returned optimism, Longfellow penned "God is not dead, nor does He sleep."

Julia Ward Howe wrote the poem *The Battle Hymn of the Republic,* in order to give loftier meaning to the popular ditty "John Brown's Body" and it was composed in a couple of sleepless hours during the summer of 1862. The poem was sold to Atlantic Monthly for the princely sum of $5.

One of the greatest writers produced during the antebellum years was Abraham Lincoln himself and he was not recognized for his prose until his wartime pronouncements began to make an impact in Europe. His style was sparse but his arguments were both coherent and compelling Witness his closing arguments to Congress in December, 1862:

> *"The fiery trial through which we pass will light us down, in honour or dishonour, to the last generation. We say we are for the Union. The world will not forget that we say this.... In giving freedom to the slave, we assure freedom to the free – honourable alike in what we give and what we preserve. We shall nobly save or*

meanly lose the last, best hope of earth. Other means may succeed; this could not fail. The way is plain, peaceful, generous, just - a way which, if followed, the world will forever applaud, and God must forever bless."

Slavery was never far from the surface. Under the terms of the Constitution, each State determined whether slavery would exist within its boundaries. However, the issue of slavery in territories and new states was very much open to question and, for the next 77 years, resolving the issue involved a number of debates and compromises.

Slavery in an International Setting

The issue of slavery had many interesting distortions as people tried to rationalize an assumed economic need with crushing moral reality. For example, in the 1787 debate on the poll tax liability calculation, the Southern states argued that slaves are people for the purposes of determining representation in Congress but are not people in calculating taxes. Northern states preferred a reversal of this thinking. In the genius of compromise, the result was that five slaves were deemed equivalent to three non-slaves; that is each slave was 3/5 of a person. Poll taxes are always difficult issues, as Margaret Thatcher more recently discovered, but poll taxes in the context of slavery leads to insanity.

It is well to understand the tenor of the times. The American War of Independence was the first successful modern revolution and it upset European alliances. The singular success of the Revolutionary generation gave it an impact that reached to the Civil War generation. This first generation of US citizens was revered and honoured by all succeeding generations. The success of the war reinforced an existing wave of religious and economic confidence which arose during the First Great Awakening (1730 – 1760) and this confidence was reinforced once again by the Second Great Awakening which followed the Revolutionary War in the opening years of the 19th Century. These were times of profound religious movements, which resulted in perhaps 30 percent of the population becoming actively evangelistic.

The waves of the religious revivals were felt on foreign shores and England was also swept by evangelical fervour. The preaching of the Wesleys, John Newton and others led parliamentarian William Wilberforce to join an abolitionist group and dedicate his life to ending slavery. It is of interest that Wilberforce was a leading parliamentarian at age 21 and his best friend, William Pitt, was Prime Minister at age 24. You can get rather a lot done when you start early.

Most people did not own slaves and, in the early years, its practice was neither understood nor its excesses recognized. The issue, then, was not that people were for or against slavery. The fact is that very few people even thought about slavery.

But for those who did think about it, the lines of battle were becoming well developed. In 1807 the first break came with a British law to end the slave trade. The next year the U.S.A. prohibited the importation of slaves based on a 1788 law which had placed a 20 year time limit on the inter-oceanic trade in slaves. Building on this success, Wilberforce and his group would have persuaded Czar Alexander to abolish serfdom had it not been for an ill-timed attempt on the Czar's life. The refusal of France to abolish slavery under the pressure of the Council of Vienna was a terrible blow to Wilberforce and his group but they were most pleased when Napoleon returned rather unexpectedly from exile in 1815 for a short spin about the country and, in an effort to curry favour with England, immediately abolished slavery. Most of the former Spanish colonies also abolished slavery upon achieving their independence. In England those who participated in slavery and the slave trade were gradually being excluded from polite company and the institution was being dismantled. The slave economy in the American South was beginning to feel the pressure of public censure.

But there were other pressures to which Southern slave owners were subject. The development of the cotton gin (engine) demanded cheap labour. As the slave population increased, it was felt that slaves would have to be spread out over more territory or the rising density could result in a violent explosion similar to the 1791 Haitian slave rebellion. There were economic pressures as well. Slaves represented a large portion of Southern wealth and intransigent Southern views had a material basis. At an average price of $1,000, slaves represented a significant portion of the patrimony of the Southern states ($3.5 billion). Abolition, it was correctly felt, would impact the Southern economy by "letting the wolf go" as it were. This point is worth considering when studying the prolonged economic depression of the South in the post bellum years.

Compromise – Politics up to 1850

Tensions over slavery and other issues grew due to the increasing differences in state populations. The faster growing Northern states were given proportionately more representation in the House of Representatives and House bills were often overturned in the Senate where, under the Constitution, each state had two representatives and so there were as many Southern as Northern senators. The bill to bring Missouri into the Union was an example of the wrangling. Under the terms of a compromise bill, the new state, which was largely settled by people from the South, did not allow the importation of slaves and enforced the emancipation of existing slaves. The bill passed the House of Representatives in 1819 but was voted down in the Senate. The admission of Alabama in 1819 as a slave state balanced the Senate and it was agreed that the admission of Maine as a non-slave state and Missouri as a slave state would maintain the balance. It was finally determined in

1821 that Missouri would join the Union with no restrictions on slavery. The Missouri Compromise of 1820-21, authored by Representative Henry Clay and Senator Jesse Thomas, restricted slavery to new states which were south of latitude 36° 30'N, an extension of the Mason-Dixon Line, and the compromise remained in effect until 1854.

A tariff crisis between 1828 and 1833 tested many of the issues that would arise in the Civil War. People who are elected to govern have a tendency to do just that, and when a Federal tariff was imposed on the external sale of cotton, South Carolina threatened to secede from the Union if they were not made exempt. When President Andrew Jackson (from the South) upheld the national government's right to collect the tax "even at the point of a gun," and none of the other cotton states came to its aid, the government of South Carolina was forced to back down. Perhaps this issue was still festering when South Carolina became the first state to secede from the Union.

The early decades of the 19th Century were good ones for the new nation. Huge tracts of land were available to be settled, immigrants were pouring in from Europe and fortunes were being made. With rapid economic expansion and population growth the American people began to believe in their "Manifest Destiny" as a nation blessed by God.

In 1835, Americans living in Texas rebelled against the Mexican government with the expectation that they would be invited to join the United States. In 1844, James Polk was elected president on a platform of expansion into Texas, but Northern fears of upsetting the legislative balance in the Senate by including another slave state prevented this inclusion until not only Texas but also California, and Oregon, could be brought into the Union. The Mexican-American War of 1846-48 was fought to obtain more land south of the latitude specified by the Missouri Compromise so that the Senate would remain in balance as the Union expanded. Not surprisingly, support for the Mexican-American War was split along sectional lines with Southern states offering enthusiastic support and Northern states denouncing it as an unjust aggression.

By 1848 there were three proposed solutions to the question of slavery; the "Free Soil" position which allowed for no slavery; unrestricted slavery in all new states; and extending the Missouri Compromise to the Pacific Ocean. To these was added a fourth position called "Popular Sovereignty" which held that people in each territory should decide the slavery question for themselves prior to entering the Union. At the time, people thought the expansion of slavery was a moot point because nobody would want to move to the newly won states and territories of the hot, dry southwest. This view changed dramatically with the discovery of California gold in 1849. People began to flood into the new territories and slavery once again became a divisive issue.

The admission of California to the Union in 1850 re-ignited the secession fuse. Henry Clay created compromise legislation which was moved through Congress by Senators Stephen Douglas and Daniel Webster in order to avert a national disaster. In the compromise, California was admitted as a free state, the Territory of New Mexico was bought from Texas and was not required to prohibit slavery, the slave trade was abolished in the District of Columbia and the Fugitive Slave Act, requiring all citizens to return runaway slaves, was passed. The complicated Compromise of 1850 was unpopular but effective until the Kansas-Nebraska Act of 1854. Success sometimes comes with its own costs and the heated rhetoric used to get to this compromise destroyed enough relationships that Southern states were now suspicious of the motives of the Northern states on any issue much less that of slavery. These hardened attitudes created a divide that was becoming too wide to bridge and an eventual rupture was inevitable.

Abolition Movement

As in the case of many social/moral causes, support for abolition was never particularly strong anywhere in the United States prior to the Civil War. All great ideas - and abolition was a great idea - take time to soak into the national psyche and support for abolition changed largely as a result of the untiring and gradually expanding efforts of the abolition movement in the North. The movement had begun with the 1775 formation of a Quaker abolitionist society which had the tacit support of many Baptists and Methodists. These latter churches, however, subsequently adopted a compromise position which accommodated slavery in order to improve living conditions and bring Christianity to the slaves. The compromise allowed these churches to attract Southern adherents to their denominations making it a less than morally courageous stand.

The Second Great Awakening, a Christian revival movement which lasted until the 1840s, motivated many reform movements, including that of abolition. In 1831 William Lloyd Garrison of Massachusetts began publishing "The Liberator" and in 1833 founded the American Antislavery Society which included ex-President John Quincy Adams. Garrison's was to be a constant, nagging voice of conscience. His non-compromise position argued that slave owners were not good Christians and that slavery threatened the moral and economic future of the United States.

Major inflection points in the progress of civilization often come from the arts. Wilberforce moved England with handbills showing the inhuman crowding of slave ships and in 1852, Harriet Beecher Stowe moved the Northern States and created an international sensation with the publication of *Uncle Tom's Cabin*. Her father (Lyman) and brother (Henry Ward) were well-known abolitionist preachers and the popular novel dramatically affected Northern attitudes towards slavery.

But the greatest impact of the Northern abolition movement was in the South where citizens were mobilized against the North in general and abolition in particular. People in the South had inherited slavery and felt honor-bound to maintain it. Proslavery arguments were largely based on the belief that blacks and whites could not live together and that slavery was necessary to maintain peace and racial harmony. Southern whites pointed to black preacher Nat Turner who, in 1831 with a small group of followers, killed 60 whites on a 36 hour spree of indiscriminate violence. As always happens, the retaliation was out of proportion to the event and in this case over 200 slaves, most of whom had nothing to do with the original violence, were killed. Rightly or wrongly, many Southerners tied the Nat Turner violence to the rise of William Lloyd Garrison's abolition movement. The particular hatred for abolitionists was quickly generalized to all Yankees and the potential for compromise slowly eroded away.

The Fugitive Slave Act from the 1850 compromise, which required citizen participation in the capture and return of runaway slaves, galvanized anti-slavery feeling in the North. Often the slave catchers, who were paid by the number of "units" returned, were less than scrupulous about the exact identity of their targets and would grab black men and women, slave or free, and send them back into slavery. The unfairness and lack of justice of this one-sided legislation was universally decried in the North. Not surprisingly, the effect of the Fugitive

Save Act was to create vigilante committees to frustrate the capture of runaway slaves.

Pressure for abolition came not only from the Northern states. By the 1850s all western nations had banned slavery and it was left to the English navy to stomp out what embers of malice continued to exist. The sole exception to universal abolition was in the American South. Feeling under siege, Southerners changed their argument from one of "necessary evil" to one of "positive good" and began to advocate for the spread of slavery. Southern churches supported and defended the institution of slavery using Biblical proof texts to support their position. They argued that their slave-based economy was stronger than a wage-based economy by confusing a cotton shortage, and concomitant Southern economic boom, with the virtues of a slave-based economy. They held that black people were not as intelligent or as self-disciplined as white people and thus needed to be under the protective custody of a benevolent owner. Forgetting that freedom is an issue of personal dignity, Southerners argued that the material situation of the black slave was better than that of an impoverished Northern worker. But they failed to explain the "irrational" desire of their slaves to face execution by running away to become "impoverished Northern workers."

The Role of the Church

In his book, *Both Prayed to the Same God; Religion and Faith in the American Civil War*, author Robert Miller presents a closely argued case that the churches in the antebellum United States missed the opportunity to influence the slavery debate by a stronger appeal to the "better angels of their nature." Most of what follows is a summary of his argument.

The 13 colonies were originally created out of religious impulses and, by 1776, the spiritual revival of the First Great Awakening (1730 – 1770) markedly changed both the United States and England. As many as 90 percent of Americans were Calvinists and bore the "Stamp of Geneva" in their understanding of faith. He demonstrates that the Second Great Awakening (1800 – 1840) had a compounding impact on the spiritual life of the nation with rapid church growth in both the North and South. In the antebellum years, Christianity was the overwhelming world view and the Bible was a trusted guide to understand and interpret that world view. Unfortunately the issues of race and slavery could not be resolved by Biblical exegesis. Both sides in the slavery dispute could point to passages which "proved" their argument.

Pulpit preaching followed the fault lines of the slavery debate and became more strident in churches both in the North and the South. Only the black churches could understand the basic fallacy of the arguments expounded by their white Christian brothers. Nowhere in the North and certainly not in the South did it occur to anyone in the church that God's image peered out from under black eyelids as surely as it did from under white ones. Racism was not limited to the South and Biblical arguments against slavery had no traction because they were consistently based on an incorrect premise; that blacks were mentally and morally inferior. Frederick Douglass recognized this blind spot in the arguments of both sides and, during the Civil War, argued eloquently for the enlistment of blacks so that the inherent racism of people from the North could be effectively stifled. Blacks were required to spill their blood in order to prove their humanity and thus win their equality Douglass argued,

> "... colour makes all the difference in the application of our American Christianity... the same Book which is full of the Gospel of Liberty to one race, is crowded with arguments in justification of the slavery of another."

The church was unable or unwilling to be faithful to its role of reconciliation and so settled for the sword. The preacher, Henry Ward Beecher, went so far as to raise money for the purchase of rifled muskets for those willing to fight in Kansas – John Brown among them - and they became known as "Beecher's Bibles." One wonders if the radicalizing, abolitionist sentiment of many Northern churches is what kept Abraham Lincoln from joining one of them.

Unable to find a point of reconciliation and unwilling to give up racist prejudices, American churches completely missed the significance of being made in God's image and the slavery issue took its toll on the institutional nature of the church. In 1837, the Presbyterian Church split over slavery and the divided parts each split again in 1857 and 1861. When Baptist clergy from the North appealed to their Southern brethren to repeal slavery, they were warned that any more affronts to the Southern character would lead to a split in the church. Apparently the Northern Baptists could not leave well enough alone and in 1845 the Southern Baptist Convention was formed. The Methodist Church of John Wesley was not immune to the slavery issue. Wesley himself was opposed to slavery calling it "the execrable sum of all villainies... the vilest that ever saw the sun..." Nevertheless, in 1845 the Methodist church in the United States split over whether church leaders could own slaves.

Could the church have brokered a compromise on slavery or developed a winning argument to allow for voluntary manumission? Absent a compelling belief in the inherent equality of all mankind, it is hard to see how American society, or any society, can free itself from its prejudices; racial and otherwise. That the antebellum church was not able to articulate this argument demonstrates that important spiritual truths must sometimes be sought outside the walls of organized religion.

Political Developments of the 1850's

One of the more significant developments of the 1850s was the dissolution of old political parties and the creation of new ones – primarily the Republican Party. The raging debate over slavery and the rapidly expanding Union required old parties to be adaptive and thrive or to wither and die. The truncated remains of the Whigs and other parties became the seed bed for a new political generation. Amongst the new leaders of this changing political landscape was a successful lawyer from Illinois named Abraham Lincoln.

In the 30 years prior to 1860, two million Irish and one and a half million German-speaking immigrants came to the United States resulting in rising employment competition and fear of being overwhelmed by the mostly Catholic newcomers. This resulted in protective "nativism" and a hatred of immigrant culture. Underground clubs and parties were formed to confront the "growing menace" proving that there is nothing new under the sun. In 1855 the American Party, or "Know Nothings," was formed to blunt the political influence of the new immigrants and ensure preferential treatment of non-immigrants. Unable to blunt this rise of xenophobia, the Whig party collapsed leaving fallow ground for the less choleric Republicans.

In 1854 Democratic Senator Douglas, who had been instrumental in the 1850 Compromise, shepherded a law through

Congress granting statehood to Kansas and Nebraska on the basis of Popular Sovereignty. In order to influence the coming vote, both proslavery Southerners and Free Soil Northerners poured into Kansas and violent clashes erupted. Two illegal legislatures were eventually created in the state, one espousing Free Soil and the other proslavery and by the end of 1856 the escalating violence resulted in over 200 deaths. Prominent in the anti-slavery violence was John Brown who, with accomplices, killed five proslavery settlers by hacking them to pieces. And the violence was not restricted to Kansas. In Washington, an abolitionist leader from Massachusetts, Senator Charles Sumner, gave a speech in 1856 which was insulting to the South and he was later physically attacked in the Senate by Congressman Preston Brooks. His convalescence took several months and he never fully recovered from the attack. Predictably the attack was applauded in the South and abhorred in the North.

In 1856 the Republican Party nominated John C. Fremont as their presidential candidate to run against James Buchanan of the Democratic Party and Millard Fillmore of the American party. Buchanan won the election but the Republicans had a strong showing across the North. The Republican Free Soil platform was not as morally pure as might be thought, however. Its support for keeping slavery out of the West extended to also keeping black people out of the West and when Oregon became a state in 1858, black people were banned from living there. Giving up any pretense of looking for Southern votes, the party argued that a West free of slavery would injure the strong cotton economy of the South and that too many presidents had come from the South bleeding power away from the North. Immigrants largely supported the Democratic Party and so the xenophobes and abolitionists drifted toward the Republican Party.

In 1857 Chief Supreme Court Justice Roger Taney ruled that black men have no rights which the white man is bound to respect and sent Mr. Dredd Scott back into slavery. The Republican Party protested that the Southern-dominated Supreme Court was in error and that this decision threatened Constitutional checks and balances. The adoption of a proslavery constitution by the Kansas Legislature in 1858 caused even Senator Douglas to break with his party thus destroying his political appeal in the South. In a series of debates with Senator Douglas during the 1858 midterm elections, Abraham Lincoln argued that the black man has,

> *"the right to eat the bread which his own hand earns."* and maintained, *"for although volume upon volume is written to prove slavery a very good thing, we never hear of the man who wishes to take the good of it, by being a slave himself."*

The Douglas-Lincoln debates of 1858 cemented Abraham Lincoln as the hope and ambition of the Republican Party and he came to be recognized as its intellectual leader.

In October 1859 abolitionist John Brown seized the federal military arsenal at Harpers Ferry, Virginia with the intention of arming slaves and starting a rebellion. The slaves, however, had a more realistic view of things and took a pass on the rebellion allowing Brown and his men to be quickly surrounded. Brown declined to surrender to army Lieutenant J.E.B. Stuart and so Colonel Robert E. Lee gave the order to end the insurrection. Brown was judged and hanged for treason on December 2 immediately converting himself into a Northern martyr. People in the South did not share this view and were incensed with both Brown and those who made him a hero. Throughout the Union anger gave way to incipient violence and Congressman and Senators started to carry weapons.

The presidential election of 1860 was the tipping point for the Union. Most Northerners believed that Southerners were bluffing about their threats to secede but everyone recognized that secession meant war. At the Democratic presidential nominating convention, the party was split on the issue of slavery and was unable to mount a significant campaign against the Republicans. The Republicans held their presidential nominating convention in Chicago where the moderate Abraham Lincoln won on the third ballot over William Seward (New York), Salmon Chase (Ohio) and Simon Cameron (Pennsylvania).

Secession and the Failure of Compromise

The subsequent presidential election was actually two independent campaigns: Lincoln versus Douglas in the North and
Breckinridge versus Bell in the South. In ten of the slave states,
Lincoln was not even on the ballot. Douglas campaigned
courageously and traveled throughout the South denouncing
secession. Though he only lived until June 1861, Douglas was
to be a stout support for his one time opponent, President
Lincoln. Early polls in Indiana, Ohio and Pennsylvania gave
the lead to Lincoln and this momentum drove him to a final
result of 40 percent of the popular vote and 65 percent of the
electoral vote. Ominously, he ran last in all of the slave states
in which his name appeared on the ballot. Unhappy with the
election of a "Black Republican," the slave states created
conventions to consider secession and by February 1, 1861
seven states, led by South Carolina, had declared themselves
sovereign nations. John Crittenden of Kentucky led efforts to
reach a nonviolent compromise but the terms were unacceptable
to President Lincoln and it never came to a vote. The Crittend-
en family was to become emblematic of the painful struggle to
come and during the war his sons George and Thomas, both
with the rank of major general, fought on opposite sides and
almost fought against each other at Shiloh.

The Confederate States of America was created at Montgomery, Alabama in February 1861 and its founders adopted a
Constitution almost identical to that of the United States. The

first choice as president for many of the delegates was Robert Toombs of Georgia. Fortunately for him, as it turned out, he was inebriated at the moment of his proposed ascension and the convention elected Jefferson Davis of Mississippi instead. Toombs was appointed Secretary of State but quickly resigned to become one of the many "political" generals in the war who served with less than great distinction. President-elect Davis was a graduate of the US Military Academy, had fought in the Mexican-American war, served as Secretary of War for President Franklin Pierce and was a currently serving United States Senator. He was not well liked and many considered him to be aloof, cold and haughty. But nor was he a big fan of secession.

President-elect Abraham Lincoln left his home in Springfield, Illinois traveling by train with his family and 7 friends. For 10 days he whistle-stopped towards Washington taking the final leg of the journey under a cloak of security due to a death threat that had been received. Arriving safely in Washington he took the oath of office on March 4, 1861 and delivered a conciliatory speech suggesting to Southerners that dissolution of the Union was in their hands and not his. If there was to be war, they must strike the first blow.

> *"I hold that in contemplation of universal law and of the Constitution the Union of these States is perpetual. Perpetuity is implied, if not expressed, in the fundamental law of all national governments... One section of our country believes slavery is right and ought to be extended, while the other believes it is wrong and ought not to be extended.*

This is the only substantial dispute ... In your hands, my dis-satisfied fellow-countrymen, and not in mine, is the momen-tous issue of civil war. The Government will not assail you. You can have no conflict without being yourselves the ag-gressors. You have no oath registered in heaven to destroy the Government, while I shall have the most solemn one to "preserve, protect, and defend it." I am loath to close. We are not enemies, but friends. We must not be enemies. Though passion may have strained it must not break our bonds of affection. The mystic chords of memory, stretching from every battlefield and patriot grave to every living heart and hearthstone all over this broad land, will yet swell the chorus of the Union, when again touched, as sure-ly they will be, by the better angels of our nature."

Lincoln faced a greater crisis than any president before or since. Many from his own party thought that he was an unedu-cated, uncultured buffoon and few were convinced of his ability to lead. He and his country were about to face the most chal-lenging of circumstances and the President willingly conceded they were mostly out of his power to control. Of his cabinet, William Seward (State) and Edwin Stanton (War) were to become trusted advisors and close friends as Lincoln demon-strated his remarkable leadership and poise during the most trying of times.

In spite of the gathering darkness, most continued to believe it would be a short and glorious war...

Status of Secession – May 1861

3: Secession and the Short, Glorious War

The precise beginning of the Civil War depends upon one's philosophy of war. Some would argue that the secession of South Carolina on December 20, 1860 pushed the hostilities inexorably forward. Negotiations and attempts at compromise solutions to maintain the Union continued throughout the remaining days of the presidency of James Buchanan but no accord could be found. By February 7, 1861, seven secessionist states met at Montgomery, Alabama to draft a provisional constitution for the Confederate States of America. Several forts within the boundaries of the Confederate States were captured and President Buchanan made no effort to recapture them. War was on everyone's mind and some Union states began building and supplying their militias.

It must have been grimly satisfying to President Lincoln when five Southern states voted against secession on the day of his inauguration. In his March 4 inaugural speech President Lincoln constructed a legal and constitutional argument that secession, to be legal, required all states to jointly abrogate the constitutional contract. Like President Davis he wanted to consolidate the loyalty of those five states. He then closed with an impassioned plea directed towards the dissenting Southern states,

> *"In your hands, my dissatisfied fellow-countrymen, and not in mine, is the momentous issue of civil war. The Government will not assail you. You can have no conflict without being yourselves the aggressors. You have no oath registered in heaven to destroy the Government, while I shall have the most solemn one to "preserve, protect, and defend it." I am loath to close. We are not enemies, but friends. We must not be enemies. Though passion may have strained it must not break our bonds of affection."*

At the outset of the war, the Union had a population of 22 million people while the Confederacy contained 9 million, of which 3.5 million were slaves. This meant that for every fighting man from the South there were four from the North. However, it also meant that in the South, 85 percent of eligible white men could fight while the slaves did the work with the corollary that the provisioning of the Southern armies was left to the people who would most benefit from a Southern failure. This fact was not lost on either President Davis or the slaves. The Union produced over 90 percent of the manufactured goods of the United States as the war began and, in the South, only the Tredegar Ironworks in Richmond, Virginia was able to produce armaments. In spite of these disadvantages the South remained convinced of victory and predicated their success on the pattern of the Revolutionary War in which a small economy defeated a much larger one. The strategy of the South was to remain in the war long enough for European nations to recognize them as a new nation state.

In the first half of 1861, most people felt that the war would be short with limited casualties. It took both sides several months to develop the logistics, train the personnel and accumulate the war materiel required for the glorious battle to come. It did not escape notice that American citizens would be killing American citizens. When the true nature of the war was revealed, citizens on both sides blamed their leaders for incompetence and for misrepresenting what was happening.

For the first six months of the war both sides were sustained by inventories of material and food that existed at the outbreak of hostilities. The Northern economy greatly profited from the war as more equipment and materiel was required. In April 1861, for example, the U.S. Navy had only 40 ships in service but by the end of 1861 there were nearly 250. Efficiently and effectively spending a lot of money quickly is difficult to do at the best of times and is always a magnet for corruption. And corruption was rampant in the first year of the war. The word "shoddy" which, prior to the war, was a type of poor quality cloth, took on its more generalized meaning as a result of the criminally low quality of material being sold to the US government. Secretary of War, Simon Cameron, was eventually replaced by Edwin Stanton who was urged to bring order to government procurement.

US Army Major Robert Anderson had been an artillery instructor at the US Military Academy and in 1861 commanded Forts Moultrie and Sumter in the harbor of Charleston, South

Carolina. As tensions mounted, he attempted to improve the defenses at Fort Moultrie until his efforts provoked an angry response from the community. On December 26, 1860, Anderson destroyed the armaments of Fort Moultrie and led his men to the newly completed Fort Sumter. In a "states rights" debate that was to recur throughout the war and was one of the fatal flaws in the Confederate proposition, the state government of South Carolina and the new provisional Confederate government argued over who enjoyed jurisdiction over Fort Sumter. President Davis won the argument and in March, he appointed Brigadier General Pierre Toutant Beauregard to command the forces confronting Fort Sumter. Ironically Beauregard had been a favoured student of Anderson at West Point. When supplies at the fort became dangerously low, President Lincoln informed the South Carolina government that he was sending a boat to re-provision the garrison with food only. The Confederate government decided to force the surrender of Fort Sumter before the relief provisions would arrive. Confederate Secretary of State Robert Toombs protested the decision,

> *"[the attack] will lose us every friend at the North. You will wantonly strike a hornet's nest. ... Legions now quiet will swarm out and sting us to death. It is unnecessary. It puts us in the wrong. It is fatal."*

At 4:30 a.m. on the morning of April 12, Confederate batteries began the bombardment of Fort Sumter. The fort was built to protect against an assault from the sea and any attempt to fire back onto land placed the gun crews in peril of the

Confederate gunners. The Union troops inside the fort withstood a 34 hour shelling and then accepted a cease fire in the early afternoon of April 13 finally surrendering at 2:30 pm on April 14. During Anderson's 100 gun salute to the flag upon capitulation (a condition of his surrender) an errant spark set off a premature explosion resulting in the death of two gunners, the only casualties of the battle. All Union soldiers were transferred to the North the next day and the flag they carried with them became emblematic of the coming struggle. On April 14, 1865 it was again raised over Fort Sumter by Anderson, now a major general, even though he sat out most of the war on sick leave.

With the war now officially underway, both sides began to plan their strategies to win it. Union General-in-Chief Winfield Scott, and hero of the Mexican-America War, devised the Anaconda Plan to squeeze the South by blockading the commerce of its seaports, control the Mississippi River and take its capital at Richmond, Virginia. Lincoln wanted the war to be as bloodless as possible and to minimize the destruction of Southern property. However, the general public and the press ridiculed Scott's plan and demanded quick action irrespective of the degree of preparedness of the army. In fact, both Lincoln and Davis were somewhat constrained in their strategic planning by the need to address public opinion.

Jefferson Davis was forced to formulate a strategy which was at odds with the natural advantages of the Confederacy. He needed to drag out the war as long as possible so that European nations would intervene and so that public opinion in the North would turn against the war. However, he did not have the resources required for a long war and he knew that as it progressed Union generals would gain needed experience. He considered the idea of a massive attack on Washington but decided that the low probability of success did not outweigh the risk of wasting resources.

By July 1861 Lincoln was under increasing pressure to start the war and he instructed his commander of the Army of the Potomac, Major General Irvin McDowell to march against Richmond. McDowell's plan was to attack the Confederate army at Manassas Junction south of Washington and contain the Confederate forces that were in the Shenandoah Valley. It was a sensible plan but McDowell and his army were both untested and it was not well executed. General Joseph Johnston of the Confederate Army was allowed to bring his troops from the Shenandoah Valley and reinforce those of Major General Beauregard at Manassas Junction. The First Battle of Bull Run was fought on July 21, 1861 and after an initial drive forward, the Army of the Potomac was pushed back largely due to the efforts of General Thomas Jackson who was henceforth known as "Stonewall" Jackson. It was also on this battlefield that the "rebel yell" was born as General Johnston's troops rushed into the battle. The Northern soldiers fell back in total confusion and became mixed with the civilians who had come out to watch the great event giving it the name of the "Great Skedaddle."

The First Battle of Bull Run

When McDowell led his army of 35,000 men across the Potomac River in July 8, 1861 it was the largest army ever seen in North America. Beauregard had positioned his troops along a stream known as Bull Run protecting the fords and covering the bridge which crossed it. He borrowed heavily from Napoleonic strategies and consciously patterned his campaign after the Battle of Austerlitz.

When McDowell surveyed the battlefield at Manassas Junction he was forced to revise his battle plans opting for a diversionary attack on the stone bridge while the main force of his army crossed Bull Run at Sudley Ford - the only ford unprotected by Beauregard's men. Unfortunately the Union army was late arriving at the ford on July 20 and the Confederate Army quickly recognized that the attack on the stone bridge was just a diversion. Confederate reinforcements arrived in time to meet the Union attack and the outnumbered Southerners made the first charge. Union reinforcements, led by William Tecumseh Sherman, slammed into the side of the Southern attackers inflicting heavy losses on the units commanded by Thomas Jackson. Jackson and his men refused to retreat prompting Confederate Brigadier General Barnard Bee to rally his men by calling out, "There is Jackson; standing like a stone wall! Let us determine to die here, and we will conquer. Follow me." From this point forward Thomas Jackson was known as "Stonewall" Jackson and Brigadier General Bee, good to his word, died on the field that afternoon. Confederate General Joseph Johnston then brought his reserves onto the battlefield to support Jackson by having his men lie on the ground and pour heavy fire into the Union troops.

Anticipating victory, Major General McDowell brought up his heavy artillery and positioned his cannons, without cavalry support and in front of his troops. Rather than deploying overwhelming force, McDowell sent his army into action unit by unit thus allowing the smaller Confederate army to fight a more balanced force. By 4:30 p.m. the concentrated Confederate forces advanced against the collapsing Union ranks and became occupied with the logistics of handling large numbers of Union prisoners, material of war, and camp equipment. Beauregard ended the forward movement of his army at 7 p.m. fearing a counterattack on his weakened flank but there was little to fear from the "Great Skedaddle" of the Union troops.

This first battle showed that the Civil War would be a long, bloody affair, that the impact of the long distance accuracy of the rifled musket rendered infantry charges over open ground suicidal and that small numbers of trained riflemen could hold off large advancing forces. In 1855, George McClellan and two others had been sent to observe the Crimean War and his report detailing the events of that war neglected to mention the devastating impact of the newly introduced rifled musket. Unfortunately battlefield tactics in the Crimea and northern Virginia were not changed to reflect the new reality.

The Confederate Army acquitted itself very well and the battle failure, a significant embarrassment for the North, was blamed on Lincoln. Almost nine hundred men died in the battle and another 2,600 were injured - nearly equaling the casualties of the Mexican-American war. The psychological damage to the Northern soldiers in the Eastern Theatre lasted for the next 18 months. McDowell was relieved of his post and a 31 year old West Point graduate named George Brinton McClellan was put in his place. McClellan immediately set about to train the Army, instill discipline and improve its morale.

Apart from their differences in age, George McClellan and Robert E. Lee shared a common past. Both graduated from the US Military Academy; both returned to the academy (McClellan as an instructor in 1848 and Lee as the Superintendent in 1851); both served in engineering companies; both held cavalry commands; both served in the Mexican-American War as staff officers.

In April 1861, Lee had been offered command of the Union army but he declined and followed Virginia out of the Union taking command of her militia units. He was responsible for the defense of the four accesses to his state from the North and at the outset of the war controlled only the routes through Harper's Ferry and the Shenandoah Valley. Union forces controlled Fort Monroe opposite Norfolk and thus access up the peninsula and the routes through western Virginia were completely uncontrolled.

In sealing the accesses through western Virginia, Lee did not appreciate the pro-Union sentiment that existed in this part of the state. While most of Virginia raised troops for the Confederate army, the western region raised troops for the Union. In fact, the strong pro-Union sentiment led to the secession of West Virginia from Virginia on June 20, 1863. With the massing of Union troops in Washington, Lee was forced to concentrate his efforts around Manassas Junction and he paid little attention to what was happening in the west.

It became confusing when Jefferson Davis formed army units from Virginia without consulting Lee. Adding to the confusion, Davis then authorized two other leaders, former Governor Henry Wise and former Secretary of War John B. Floyd, to raise militias in Virginia, again without apprising Lee of this decision. The Southern forces in western Virginia were never consolidated or coordinated as neither Wise nor Floyd would concede control.

In the North, George McClellan accepted a commission to command the forces of Ohio on the same day that Lee took his commission in Virginia. He presented to General Winfield Scott an invasion plan through the western passes of Virginia and promoted having a single commander to make this happen – both ideas were accepted by Scott. When Virginia seceded from the Union on May 23, 1861 McClellan acted by moving his army into western Virginia with a view to gaining access to the western passes and reinforcing pro-Union sentiment in Kentucky. As he moved into the state, the Virginia militia forces retreated in what was to become known as the Philippi Races.

Fortunately there was limited action in the Kanawha valley of western Virginia as the armies jockeyed for position. McClellan's larger forces pushed the Confederates out of the way and he wrote glowing reports of successful military engagements to enhance his credibility in the North. When Lee was given command of the Kanawha Valley (Joseph Johnston had turned it down), McClellan, asserting that his work in western Virginia was complete, was offered the generalship of the Army of the Potomac. Robert E. Lee, without a coordinated command, now faced William Rosecrans.

August 1861 was a wet, cold month and both armies were demoralized and in poor fighting shape. While Wise and Floyd argued and worked against one another, Rosecrans consolidated the gains made by McClellan and supported the pro-secessionist sentiment in anticipation of a plebiscite to be held October 24. Lee spent August assessing the situation until the command structure was put in order. His constant presence with the troops endeared them to him so that when he was promoted to general he had willing followers. On September 12, Lee determined to attack the Northern troops at Cheat Mountain assessing that if he did not attack, the illnesses affecting his men would force him to retreat. His battle plan was effective but complex and totally unsuited to the raw recruits and untrained commanders. Five columns of men were to move to different targets and then attack at the same time. The key column did not attack as directed and this caused confusion and eventual loss of surprise resulting in the remaining Confederate forces pulling back rather than attacking as planned.

Union forces occupied all of what was to become West Virginia but were blocked from the Shenandoah Valley by the Allegheny Mountains. It was a bitter opening to the war for Robert E. Lee and he was roundly criticized for his lack of action or results. To his credit he refused to defend himself by pointing out that the problem was an unworkable command structure and two ego-driven, rival generals. As a result, from the start of the war Lee had a reputation to redeem after learning all of the hard lessons of command and strategy. McClellan, on the other hand, had an ill-gotten reputation to protect and had learned none of the necessary lessons.

In the months following the Confederate victory at Bull Run in July 1861 the Union armies were reorganized and retrained under George McClellan. In Richmond, the Confederate army was reorganized under provisional President Jefferson Davis. The hero of Fort Sumter and Bull Run, Pierre Gustav Toutant Beauregard, was considering a run for the presidency of the Confederate states and so Davis sent him west to join the army of Albert Sidney Johnston. This left Joseph Johnston to command the Army of Northern Virginia and he pulled his forces back to protect Richmond allowing Union forces to retake some of their positions south of Washington.

The Battle of Ball's Bluff

In order to drive all Confederate troops from northern Virginia, McClellan planned a diversionary action at Leesburg. Brigadier General Charles Stone sent a 20 man patrol to scout around Leesburg and report on any Confederate activity. They erroneously reported that the Confederates were retreating and in the morning of October 20 Stone's forces ferried across the Potomac River into Virginia at Ball's Bluff. Again the Union soldiers saw no sign of Confederate activity and were unaware that just below the horizon was a significant concentration of rebel forces.

A scouting party of Confederates ran into the Union soldiers and retreated to report that there were incursions into the Virginia countryside. The Union forces were being directed by Colonel Edward Baker who had, at one time, been a law partner of President Lincoln. Unfortunately he was a better lawyer than he was military strategist and instead of taking the high ground he established his position below the bluff and in full view of the Confederate soldiers who quickly formed their line above. Baker moved mountain howitzers into position and commenced an effective bombardment of the Confederate line. However, he did not secure the placements and the gun crews were quickly killed by Confederate snipers. Attempting to lead his men in a charge against the Confederate line, Colonel Baker stood up and was immediately killed. The Union troops were then left to retreat as best they could leaving behind over 800 men taken prisoner, killed or wounded. As effective as the Confederate side fought, this was to be their last victory for most of the next year.

This battle, which should not have taken place, was a great embarrassment to Major General McClellan whose vague orders were misunderstood by the Union commanders. As a result of this fiasco, Congress decided to establish the "Joint Committee on the Conduct of the War" to investigate and assess blame for all Union army failures. In fact, the committee became a hated star chamber which met in secret and was used as often to punish political enemies as to understand battlefield tactical errors.

One such "enemy" was Brigadier General Charles Stone who was brought before the committee in January 1862. Stone was not popular with his soldiers and some felt that his luke-warm praise for the fallen Colonel Baker was inadequate. As a result, Stone was accused of consorting with the enemy, arrest-ed and held at Fort Lafayette in New York Harbor. General McClellan recognized that Stone was not guilty but acquiesced to Stone's treatment in order to protect his own reputation.

Stone retained counsel and awaited the charges to be pressed against him; charges which were never made. Politically, it was in everybody's best interest to hold Stone in prison and not allow his case to come to trial. President Lincoln stated, "*to hold one commander in prison and tried is less harmful in times of great national distress than to withdraw several good officers from active battlefields to give him a trial.*" Under pressure from his friends, including the now retired General Winfield Scott, Stone was released on August 16, 1862. In September 1862 George McClellan requested that Stone be reinstated but the request was denied. In 1863 Joseph Hooker named Stone to be his chief of staff and again the request was denied.

Although he was eventually reinstated, Stone was considered a pariah and not given a new command. In 1870 he left for Egypt and was made chief of staff in the Egyptian army. In 1882, he supervised the construction of the foundation for the Statue of Liberty and only after his death on January 24, 1887 was Stone's service finally recognized.

Apart from the First Battle of Bull Run, there were few large land engagements during 1861. The unexpected bloodiness of that battle was a shock to those who believed that the war would be short and glorious. It was becoming clear that this would not be the case. Southerners were encouraged by the showing of their gallant army and support for secession increased. Government calls for additional men and material were widely supported and most thought the war would bring glory and success. In the North, the Great Skedaddle stunned and humbled the Union. Disenchanted and demoralized soldiers were bivouacked all about Washington and it was the role of George McClellan, the new commander of the Army of the Potomac, to mould the volunteers into an efficient army.

A Civil War story that is often inadequately told was quietly taking place along the coastline of the Confederate states. A significant part of the Anaconda Plan, favoured by President Lincoln, involved the blockading of Southern ports and the US Navy was making good progress towards this goal throughout the latter half of the year. Secretary of the Navy Gideon Welles recognized that he needed ports in the South to provision his fleet. In October he determined that Port Royal (Fort Walker and Fort Beauregard) on Cape Hatteras in South Carolina would provide a base and coaling station. He chose Samuel DuPont to lead the naval assault which had to be timed for the tides and to strike the two opposing batteries simultaneously.

The Battle of Port Royal

The Southern batteries were manned by Thomas Drayton whose father, a fierce anti-secessionist, had moved his family from Virginia to Pennsylvania prior to the Nat Turner problems of 1832. Thomas attended the US Military Academy with Jefferson Davis and, with the outbreak in hostilities, opted for the Confederacy and was appointed to command the defense of Cape Hatteras on the strength of this friendship. His brother,

Percival, attended the naval academy at Annapolis and by the late 1850's was a commander who remained loyal to the Union when hostilities broke out.

After having been blown out to sea by a storm, the Union fleet attacked the Confederate installations in October 1861. The batteries were abandoned by the artillery officers and Thomas Drayton's untrained reserve soldiers were unable to reinforce the position. As a result the attack was a complete success for the North and resulted in recovered prestige after the ignominious defeat of the First Battle of Bull Run. The only ship to be significantly damaged was the *Pocahontas*, commanded by Percival Drayton, which took a direct hit on its main mast. This was not the first nor the last time that brothers fired on each other during the Civil War.

As 1861 ended it was becoming obvious that the war was not going to be short and glorious but rather long and glorious. The new year would finally end the notion of a glorious war. It was ugly, bloody and awful and the citizens of both republics would soon learn this by seeing the pictures and reading the casualty lists. By the end of 1862 few communities were exempt from the effects of the war.

The Major Battles of the Eastern Theatre

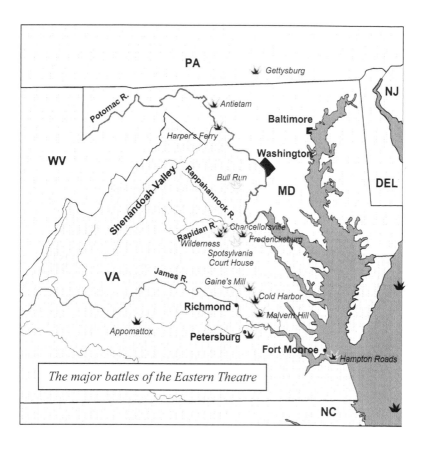

The major battles of the Eastern Theatre

4: The Elephant and How He is Known

Overview

"To know the elephant" is to know the horror of war and was a popular phrase during the Civil War. It is one thing to describe an elephant; it is quite another to see, smell and touch an elephant. It is easy for those who have never known the "elephant" to analyze the errors of those to whom it is all too real. The reaction of soldiers to the confusion, fear and physiological arousal that attends battles great and small are unknowable beforehand and these imponderables render outcomes unpredictable. Napoleon said that *"the general who makes no mistakes, never goes to war"* and his truism certainly holds for the Civil War. Evaluating Civil War battles long after the fact clearly demonstrates that some of the mistakes were obvious and catastrophic. But is it the role of historians and others to provide value judgments? Or is it to simply observe and draw lessons? What follows provides an insight into the forces and circumstances which sculpted the strategies and tactics of the Civil War.

These forces and circumstances were, for the most part, political, psychological and geographic. The influence of the Napoleonic wars resulted in an almost universal belief that wars are won by great battles which destroy great armies and there was a political demand from both republics that the war be epic, glorious, profitable and short. In many respects the Civil War opened according to the blood lust of the press rather than the calculation of the generals. Both armies felt that success would ultimately come when they over-ran the capital city of their opponent. When this proved more difficult than expected it resulted in the creation of two huge theatres of war often in undeveloped areas with sparse populations. The productive capacity of the North dwarfed that of the South but, in a short, glorious war, this would have little impact. Unfortunately, the military tactics of the Civil War were often superceded by technology and hidebound ideas sometimes resulted in a lot of unnecessary spilled blood.

The census of 1860, as shown in Appendix 1, demonstrates that the Northern states had a population of 22 million while the Southern states had a population of 9 million of whom 3.5 million were slaves. The economies of the two republics were even more unmatched and the much greater capacity of the Northern states to make war must be born in mind. It was this basic socio-economic fact which animated the successful strategy of the North. Wars are won by men and materiel and the developed North had a population and industrial economy that far outstripped that of the more rural South.

Apart from destroying the Union forces in a big, winner-take-all battle in northern Virginia, the Confederate strategy was to prolong the war sufficiently to restrict cotton sales to English mills. By this thinking, the resulting economic depriva-tion in England should force support for the Confederacy. This

"King Cotton" strategy had a rational and understandable economic appeal. Additionally, the experience and lessons of the Revolutionary War, in which a Southern gentleman led a much smaller country to victory over a larger invader, bolstered Southern spirits and animated their strategic councils. But war is the calamity of the unexpected.

Big battles slaked the blood thirst of both republics and it seems churlish to criticize generals who answered to politicians who answered to an, at times, rabid public. The first Battle of Bull Run was fought to assuage political pressure and the general staff of both republics knew their armies were not ready to take the field.

As the war was prolonged and it became obvious that neither side was capable delivering the knock-out blow, strategies began to accommodate themselves to reality. The Confederacy was driven to fight a largely defensive war on its own soil and the Union was required to fight a largely offensive war with longer supply and logistics lines. The numerically smaller Southern armies strove towards the principle of "concentrating masses against fractions." That is, they would focus their available troops on targets chosen to bring the sizes of the engaging armies into equilibrium. This demanded fast moving divisions and rapid deployment in combat. General Jackson's Shenandoah campaign is the best example of this strategy.

Although not recognized until 1864, when Major General Grant was promoted to General-in-Chief, it became a war of attrition that would affect populations on both sides. In the attrition war the Union forces had a very distinct advantage. They could replace their losses of men and equipment from a much larger pool of both requisites. Lincoln, in issuing the Emancipation Proclamation, also added to the pool of soldiers by opening his army to former slaves. In the slave-based economy of the South, a higher percentage of men were available to fight while the slaves provided the agricultural and factory labour. But everyone was keenly aware that the slaves had the most to gain by a Southern defeat and their attention to this task was diffident at best. Nevertheless, some slaves fought for ex-slave trader, Nathan Bedford Forrest under the promise of manumission if the South was successful.

The effect of his greatly superior access to resources allowed Grant to doggedly pursue a nasty and costly drive into Virginia in 1864. In the months leading to the siege of Petersburg, the Army of the Potomac suffered 100,000 casualties. His losses, in fact, were larger than Lee's army and, while it earned Grant the epithet of "Butcher," it was the price to be paid for winning the war and bringing the bloodshed to an end.

In wars of attrition, strategy is often formulated to obtain longer term gain at the expense of short term loss. The South invaded the North on three significant occasions more to demonstrate its power to Europe than to deliver the secondary goal of a knock-out blow. When, for example, Jubal Early brought his troops to within rifle shot of Washington it was to gain relief for Richmond and impress Europe rather than to conquer the Northern capital. But attrition favours the side with the greatest resources of manpower and materiel. It also favours that side whose population is least affected by the warfare and whose demands to end the bloodshed can be most easily ignored. By 1863, every Southern family knew firsthand the horrors of war and many had lost homes and farms to Northern invaders. By the end of the war, the Southern population was destitute from inflation and high taxation.

The politics of the Confederacy and the Union both played significant roles in strategic formulations as well. The strength of those Northern groups advocating a negotiated settlement were a significant problem for the Lincoln administration and the President needed battlefield successes if only to curb the erosive impact of the chanting peaceniks. Merely exiling the Peace Democrat or "Copperhead" leadership was insufficient. The battles at Fredericksburg and Chancellorsville were driven by political rather than military need. On the Confederate side, the population was more easily convinced to support the war as most of the dying occurred on Southern property. However, as inflation, economic privation and the death toll rose, President Jefferson Davis had the more difficult problem. He was called upon to stop the rioting of Southern wives and mothers who had nothing to eat and, in the latter stages of the war, he was unable to stop the flow of letters urging soldiers to abandon their army posts in favour of their familial posts. When wives and children are starving it is difficult for husbands and fathers to remain at war.

Ultimately wars are won or lost by generals and the deployment of these generals, given their strengths and weaknesses, is a significant part of strategic planning. It took Confederate President Davis only a year to find his general for the Eastern Theatre and, by installing Robert E. Lee as General of the Army of North Virginia, he stuck a strategic blow from which it took Lincoln 30 months to recover. Lee was a master at knowing not only what his opponent would do but also what his own generals would do. This reliance on psychic knowledge was to rarely let him down and, with uncanny accuracy, he was able to confound the Northern armies with his unusual tactics while predicting precisely how they would respond. To a large extent, Confederate strategy had a name - General Robert E. Lee.

The Union army in the Eastern Theatre, by contrast, took a long time to find its general. General McDowell, who was defeated by the idiosyncratic stubbornness of Thomas Jackson at the First Battle of Bull Run, was replaced by the "Little Napoleon," George McClellan who rebuilt the shattered Army of the Potomac. Major General McClellan, the brilliant tactician and reluctant fighter, was nominated twice to the post and both times removed by a disgusted and impatient President Lincoln. Lincoln tried another four generals before finally finding Lieutenant General Grant. Major General Pope was caught in a nasty political battle with the deposed McClellan and was sent to fight Indians following the second embarrassing loss at Bull Run; Major General Ambrose Burnside, who took the post with reluctance, was removed after the debacle at Fredericksburg and ignominious Mud March; the ambitious and profane Joseph Hooker was knocked senseless at Chancellorsville and removed from the post after a quarrel with the War Department; and the steady and popular Major General George Meade, who won the day at Gettysburg, was effectively replaced for allowing Lee and his bruised army to safely slip back across the Potomac. This, at least, was the case in the Eastern Theatre of northern Virginia.

The situation was reversed in the Western Theatre where the Union armies of the North were able to count on the dogged genius of their primary strategist – Ulysses S. Grant. Like Lee, Grant was confident of his field staff and was content to allow his generals to devise their own tactics safe in the knowledge that they would do the right thing. Rarely was he disappointed. It was not so with the Confederate army in the west. Generals were changed and not one of them came to the stature of Robert E. Lee. As with Northern general John Pope, politics eventually claimed the career of Southern general Braxton Bragg.

President Davis faltered by personally maintaining control of the Southern strategy. Unlike Lincoln, Davis had military training and some experience of war but he was also prone to judging his generals on the basis of friendship rather than capability. Lincoln, on the other hand, was egalitarian in the treatment of his generals and they were judged on the basis of performance rather than political ties. When Lincoln did find his man he was happy to give complete control of the military effort to him. As in most of his endeavours, Lincoln was self-taught in the art of war and hubris was never an impediment. When Grant took the reins of military control of the Union army, the Northern troops were able to fight in a coordinated fashion towards a single goal. It was the first time either side had allowed such coordination and it was to be a decisive act.

Both sides attempted, with mixed results, the deep, penetrating horse – and in the slightly ludicrous case of Abel Streight – mule cavalry raids. These drives were an embarrassment to the defensive side when they worked and a disaster to the offensive side when they didn't. Mostly they scored public relations points. However, they appealed to a more romantic notion of war and so were desirable appointments for those in the cavalry. The punishing and effective work of the war, as always, fell to the infantry. Civil War battles almost always proved the importance of good intelligence and communications in making complicated infantry maneuvers. They likewise proved how characteristically absent good intelligence and communications are from complicated infantry maneuvers.

The early battles, in particular, were brilliantly planned and abysmally executed largely due to the level of training of the infantry units in general and their commanders in particular. The wooded terrain in which the armies often fought, the general confusion of the combat maelstrom and the rapid changes and shifts due to unpredictable events made battlefield command a difficult assignment. Battlefield maps gave inadequate assessments of the depth of the mud, the temperature of the swamp water, the impenetrability of the woods or the density of rifle smoke. And who knew that the hot coffee and personal effects of an overrun camp could effectively stop the full scale attack of hungry soldiers who needed to send some plunder home to loved ones?

Such confusion was not unique to the citizen armies of the Civil War. One need only recall the charge of the Light Brigade by a professional British army during the Crimean War. The charge was ordered by a general who could see the entire field and yet the cavalry still managed to capture the wrong objective and was forced to return under the same heavy shelling that killed so many of them during the attack. As futile and devoid of meaning as the charge was, it did not diminish Lord Cardigan's appetite for the French cuisine served on his yacht that night and it provided a rare opportunity for the French to die supporting the British.

Commanding generals in both armies often issued vague instructions to compensate for the chaotic movements on the battlefield thus releasing their subordinates to take appropriate action as conditions changed. This, of course, has created a cottage industry of armchair generals who have the time and vastly enhanced information to issue moment by moment critiques of the decisions made during the heat of the battle. Perhaps it is best to conclude that the combatant decision-makers were intelligent people who had to make awful decisions under conditions of great uncertainty. Sometimes these decisions led to happy outcomes and often times they led to appalling results.

Major General William Tecumseh Sherman famously said from Atlanta that he would "make Georgia howl." Bringing war to civilians to destroy infrastructure and morale is hardly a new strategy. One need only think of the Assyrian King Sennecharib hauling off the northern tribes of Israel to see how routinely civilians have been historically brutalized by war. But following the Thirty Years War in Europe (1618 – 1648) and the resultant Treaty of Westphalia, the crushing burden of war had generally been lifted from the civilian populace. Major General Pope recommended punishing non-combatants but Sherman turned the recommendation into action. The devastation on his trek north to join Grant and defeat Robert E. Lee has earned Sherman special disapprobation in the South. Targeting civilians, while an odious tactic, is certainly not a relic of the Civil War. Dresden, Hiroshima and New York are but a few of the cities which have suffered in more modern hostilities.

The role of the navy during the Civil War was very much ancillary to that of the army. Naval activity on the James,

Mississippi and Tennessee Rivers was generally in conjunction with army battles. Exceptions were the Battle of Hampton Roads, which pitted two ironclad ships in a knock-down battle that ushered in the end of wooden tall ships in the world's navies, and Union Captain Ferragut's defeat of New Orleans to open up the Mississippi River to Northern transportation. But for the most part, naval activity during the war consisted of the Union navy blockading Southern ports.

Military Organization

At the outbreak of the Civil War the U.S. Army had only 16,000 regular troops who provided a policing function and these men, with their officers, had to make an election between loyalty to their units or to their states. Many chose the latter and both the Confederate and Union armies started the war with trained army regulars. Both armies also had officers trained at the U.S. Military Academy at West Point, New York. Although many had combat experience in the Mexican-American War they did not have the experience to command divisions much less armies. The opening months of the Civil War were a trial by fire and the rate of making mistakes did not begin to attenuate until well into 1863. In fact, in the opening months of the war, the armies fought much better than they were led.

Both of the combatants initially anticipated a one battle war with limited losses. Union Major General Winfield Scott chose to keep his regular forces intact and allowed the volunteer units to train without the influence of trained soldiers. The Confederate army took the opposite, and some have argued, better approach of inserting trained soldiers into volunteer units. Their initial successes certainly add strength to that argument. The volunteer forces were often commanded by untrained senior officers who were political as opposed to military appointments. In the egalitarian spirit of the volunteer army, all officers were elected to their positions rather than appointed on the basis of merit. Sometimes there was a happy coincidence of election with merit. More often, battlefield events identified the capable leaders.

A short, glorious war was a very attractive draw to farm boys who looked for adventure. In response to President Lincoln's initial call for 75,000 volunteers, 92,000 responded from every remaining state of the Union. The situation was mirrored in the Confederacy and the biggest hindrance to forming the army was the lack of arms and equipment to supply the volunteers. The bright-eyed volunteerism of the opening months of the war soon dimmed, of course, with the increasing losses and realization that the war would be long, hard fought and very bloody. Both sides eventually resorted to unpopular conscription laws in order to fill their regiments.

Never had such large armies been formed. Approximately 2.5 million men served in the Union army and half of them were in uniform at the close of hostilities. The Confederate army enlisted 780,000 men with a peak strength of 450,000.

Building, training and equipping such massive military buildups is perhaps one of the enduring legacies of the Civil War. In every essential element of logistics it was an enormous undertaking and for the most part, successfully executed.

In any reading of the Civil War it is important to understand the formation of the armies which did the fighting or there is a tendency to glaze over at the nomenclature. The land battles were comprised of three combat units; the infantry, cavalry and the artillery. The cavalry and the artillery were only used in support of the infantry but required a higher level of training. About 80 percent of the army was comprised of infantry units.

The commanding ranks shown in parenthesis in the table below are applicable to the Confederate forces which included a rank of "general" not used in the Union army. The highest

Infantry Organization

*Confederate designations in parenthesis

Unit	Size	Commander	Total
Squad	12 men	Corporal	12
Section	25 men	Sergeant	25
Platoon	50 men	Lieutenant	50
Company	100 men	Captain	100
Regiment	10 companies	Colonel	1,000
Brigade	4 - 6 regiments	Brigadier General	4 – 6,000
Division	3 - 4 brigades	Major (Lieut.) General	12 – 24K
Corps	3 divisions	Major General	36 – 48K
Army	3 – 5 divisions	Major General (General)	100,000+
All forces		Lieutenant General	500,000+

Union rank was lieutenant general held by Winfield Scott as a brevet rank. Ulysses S. Grant was the only commissioned lieutenant general in the Union army and was the first such general since George Washington.

The ordering of the different ranks of general creates confusion because major general is a lower rank than lieutenant general reversing the pattern of the lower ranks. The ranking system used by the Civil war armies was adopted from the British army which had ranks of sergeant-major general, lieutenant general and captain general. Common usage dropped "sergeant" from sergeant-major general thus creating the confusion.

Remember that the table above deals with an optimum condition and results in the field were much different. Most units during the Civil War were fortunate if they were staffed to 40 percent of their full strength. When reading of the battles, then, it is prudent to think of significantly undermanned companies and regiments. Likewise it must be remembered that casualty rates amongst officers were high and often units went to battle with leaders whose commissions had not caught up to their functions. And commissions came rapidly enough. Philip Sheridan, for example, rose from being a captain to being a major general and not all of the rapid rise was due to his leadership capabilities and courage. The density of Minnie balls in battle cleared the path for his promotions with great efficiency. Battlefield promotions did not always end in glory, however. When Buell chased the Confederate Bragg into Kentucky, Captain C. C. Gilbert was promoted to Major General of Volunteers subject to presidential approval. The president saw fit to promote him only to Brigadier General of Volunteers subject to congressional approval and Congress saw fit to limit him to his captaincy. For a time, at least, he had fun charging around on the battlefield with his men and new commission.

The various types of ranks used during the Civil War also can cause confusion. Brevet ranks were awarded for courage or in recognition of meritorious service and have since been replaced by battlefield medals. They were honourary and were not reflected in salary, job function or uniform. An officer could use his brevet rank in correspondence and could not be tried by anyone lower than his brevet rank if involved in a court martial. When regular army and militia units were mixed, the officer with the highest brevet rank would be given command. In an added twist, the structure of the regular army units was distinct from that of volunteer units. Therefore, an officer could have 4 ranks; a Volunteer rank, brevet Volunteer rank, Regular rank and brevet Regular rank. It would be a safe guess that the pay scale was based on the lowest of the four ranks.

On March 13, 1865 the War Department brevetted almost every officer in the army destroying the value of those brevets earned on the battlefield. The brevet rank, thus cheapened, was discontinued in 1869. During the Spanish-American war the system was revived and discontinued again at the close of World War I.

Role of Artillery

The role and organization of the artillery is less understood than the infantry and yet it almost always played a part in Civil War battles. The infantry "company" is called a battery in the artillery and generally included 6 cannons. Each battery required 3 officers and up to 100 men to operate and maintain the field pieces and as many as 90 horses to move the cannons and associated equipment. When the cannons were deployed, of course, they were not surrounded by horses and men other than those required to load and fire. The remaining members of the battery were held behind the lines to provide maintenance and logistical support following the battles.

The key role of the cannon batteries was to rain down death and destruction upon the heads of the opposite infantry units. This they were able to do with ghastly consequences using solid and explosive projectiles for long range killing and cans full of scrap metal and small ball bearings for short range killing. As a result of their ability to destroy, batteries became important targets for the opposing forces and often suffered dispropor-tionate casualty rates. The capture of a battery by the infantry was a moment of great rejoicing and the guns were immediately turned to empty their barrels into the bodies of their erstwhile owners who would then try to recapture them. Think of this as "capture the flag" with lethal consequences.

Like the cavalry, the artillery units were organized and trained independently of the infantry and were assigned to brigades according to tactical need. It has been calculated that the average army in the Civil War was just over 50,000 men with 1 battery unit for every two regiments (2,000 men).

Army and Battlefield Nomenclature

The organization of both armies followed a pattern of Military Divisions (similar to theatres of war), Departments and Districts. The Military Divisions encompassed large geographical areas (e.g. Military Division of the Pacific) and were subdivided into Military Departments which were generally named for the predominant river within the department's boundaries (e.g. Department of the Cumberland). In the case of the Union army, the Departments were sometimes named after occupied Southern States (Department of Mississippi). Military Departments were further sub-divided into Military Districts and sub-districts.

The military commander of a department often had an army with the same name. Therefore, the military commander of the Department of the Cumberland would command an army named the Army of the Cumberland. This system was unambiguous until a military commander crossed his army into a different military department and then you just had to be there to figure it out.

Another source of confusion in studying the Civil War is the practice of giving different names to the same battles. The differences in battle nomenclature was explained by Southern general D.H. Hill who suggested that Union soldiers were more highly urbanized than Confederate soldiers and so tended to name their battles according to a local and obvious physical feature near the battlefield. Confederate soldiers, for their part, picked names based on the nearest community. The table below shows the most important battles with two names.

Date of Battle	Confederate Name	Federal Name
July 21, 1861	First Manassas	First Bull Run
Aug. 10, 1861	Oak Hills	Wilson's Creek
Oct. 21, 1861	Leesburg	Ball's Bluff
Jan. 19, 1862	Mill Springs	Logan's Cross Rds
Mar. 7-8, 1862	Elkhorn Tavern	Pea Ridge
Apr. 6-7, 1862	Shiloh	Pittsburg Landing
June 27, 1862	Gaines's Mill	Chickahominy
Aug. 29-30,1862	Second Manassas	Second Bull Run
Sept. 1, 1862	Ox Hill	Chantilly
Sept. 14, 1862	Boonsboro	South Mountain
Sept. 17, 1862	Sharpsburg	Antietam
Oct. 8, 1862	Perryville	Chaplin Hills
Dec. 31-Jan 2, 1863	Murfreesboro	Stones River
Apr. 8, 1864	Mansfield	Sabine Cross Roads
Sept. 19, 1864	Winchester	Opequon Creek

The convention used throughout this book is to generally follow the Union nomenclature. The use of "Shiloh" and "Gaines's Mill" are exceptions to this norm.

Confederate Rebel Yell

In the pre-Christian, Punic Wars, the Roman soldiers were devastated and demoralized by the charging elephants of Hannibal's Carthaginian troops. It wasn't until Scipio, the Roman general, was able to demonstrate how elephant charges could be deflected that order was restored in the Roman ranks. It is said that the Roman troops of a few centuries later never did become accustomed to the screaming charges of the long haired, bearded and naked Germanic hordes. It would seem that, for some time, soldiers have known that advantages can be gained by overloading the sensory processing capability of their opponents. Screaming, naked guys running at you with really sharp weapons qualifies as sensory overload. Major General Thomas Jackson of the Confederate Army certainly understood this.

No one really knows what the Confederate "Rebel Yell" sounded like although Confederate soldier, Thomas Alexander, was recorded giving his version of the rebel yell in 1935 when he was 90 years old Listening to the recording, one wonders why so much was made of the yell. But then one must remember that they are listening to a 90 year old man without the sustaining

1 http://www.26nc.org/History/Rebel-Yell/rebel-yell.html

accompaniment of an army of such yells. Several thousand men with sharp weapons running at you and yelling like this would certainly have resulted in some sensory overload.

It is likely that there were many versions of the rebel yell and perhaps they changed with terrain and the breathlessness of their hard charging lung carriers. But, however it sounded, it frightened the Union soldiers who witnessed the spectacle. Some even claimed that,

> *"If you claim you heard it and weren't scared that means you never heard it."*

The source of the yell is disputed and there are theories that it came from some North American Indians who fought with the South; that it was a modified fox hunting call similar to the baying of the dogs; and that it was an ancient Celtic yell perhaps used to scare Roman soldiers who were unused to the sight of naked combatants. Its first use was at the First Battle of Bull Run when Stonewall Jackson urged his men to charge and "yell like the furies." One of the best descriptions of its effect was offered by Lieutenant Ambrose Bierce who heard it while defending Horseshoe Ridge during the Battle of Chickamauga,

> *"At last it grew too dark to fight. Then away to our left and rear some of Bragg's people set up 'the rebel yell'. It was taken up successively and passed around to our front, along our right and in behind us again, until it seemed almost to*

have got to the point whence it started. It was the ugliest sound that any mortal ever heard – even a mortal exhausted by two days of hard fighting, without sleep, without rest, without food and without hope."

Flags and Uniforms

The uniform of the United States Army, immediately prior to the Civil War, was defined by a general order issued in 1851. The new design was a radical change from previous uniforms and was based on a single breasted, dark blue frock coat (extending to one half the distance between the waist and the knee) for enlisted men, lieutenants and captains and double breasted for all other ranks. The pants were a sky blue colour with a dark blue stripe or welt sewn into the outside trouser leg and styled to fit comfortably over boots. The cap or kepis was also made of dark blue cloth with a flat leather brim or visor and a leather strap which passed under the chin. Alterations to the standard uniform were made to account for the wearer's service unit (army, artillery or cavalry) and other variations and insignia were added to identify rank. A complete description of the uniform would necessarily identify all of the variations but, in general, this was the uniform of the Union soldier from the beginning until the end of the Civil War.

In many units, a dark blue sack coat was included in the enlisted soldier's dress kit to be used for campaigning purposes. Overcoats for officers were dark blue and sky blue for enlisted men. It is very evident from pictures of the era that most men who could, wore beards and little attention appears to have been paid to the length and condition of either hair or beards.

At the onset of the war, the Confederate soldiers were dressed in whatever seemed appropriate. And for many regiments, dark blue jackets with sky blue pants seemed appropriate. The obvious confusion this caused on the battlefield resulted in an immediate rethink of Southern sartorial trends. By 1863 all troops were required to meet a standard regulation of grey, double breasted frock coats with sky blue pants. Grey was chosen for the army due to the relative abundance of these dyes. By the end of the war even grey dyes were hard to find and all ranks were forced to use undyed, butternut coloured uniforms. For some reason the cloth chosen by both sides was a heavy wool which was suitable for winter campaign quarters but stifling in the Southern summer heat resulting in health issues for soldiers on both sides.

While both armies had official requirements for their uniforms throughout the war, it was not uncommon for companies and regiments to maintain locally designed uniforms. More to the point, as the war dragged on and the Southern economy faltered, uniforms for the Southern soldiers became whatever clothing wasn't reduced to rags.

One of the more colourful uniforms to find its way onto Civil War battlefields was the Zouave uniform patterned off the North African troops who served in the French army in the early 1800's. Instead of a cap, the soldiers wore a fez or turban, the pants were generally red and baggy, gathered at the ankles or wrapped with leggings. The brightly decorated coats were short and the original Zouave units were noted for their bravery under fire. Zouave units also fought in the Crimean war and the popularity of their uniforms became "feverish" in antebellum militia units. By some estimates there were over 200 Zouave units from 32 states and as uniforms became tattered and frayed during the course of the war most units opted for the regular army dress.

Flags and banners have always been an important element in military life and battles were considered as good as won if regimental and divisional standards were captured. When the Jews captured the Eagle of the Roman 12th Legion in 66 AD, it so embarrassed and infuriated the Roman generals that they destroyed Jerusalem four years later. During the Civil War the most dangerous place on any battle field was near a flag or banner.

The Confederate government moved quickly to develop its own flag and, receiving instructions from Southerners to not deviate from "Old Glory," settled on the "Stars and Bars" which was similar to the Union flag. However, confusion between the flags on the battlefield during the First Bull Run resulted in modifications. Confederate general P.G.T. Beauregarde is widely credited for pushing to develop a new flag. It was finally decided that the stars would remain and the bars would move from horizontal to diagonal. Some early versions proposed bars which were horizontal and vertical but the resulting cross was deemed too ecclesiastic to be practical.

The second flag was a white background with the new Confederate "jack" placed in the upper left corner. While the white background might have been emblematic of the purity of the Southern cause, on a windless day it appeared that the armies across the South had capitulated and were seeking a truce. As a result, a broad, vertical red stripe was used to break the white background and was known as the "blood stained banner." Ever optimistic, the Confederate government adopted this flag on March 4, 1865. The battle flag was comprised of the Confederate "jack," two diagonal blue stripes, bordered with white on a red background and as many white stars as states along the diagonal blue stripes.

Battlefield Equipment

Many historians believe that the rifled musket was a technological innovation that was not matched during the Civil War by a complementary strategic innovation. Napoleon marched his massed columns into deadly fire knowing that the rate of fire of a relatively inaccurate musket was such that his columns would reach the enemy prior to all of his men being killed. When it was demonstrated that a musket firing 3 shots per minute (instead of Napoleon's assumption of two shots per minute) could destroy the French columns the tactics needed an upgrade. The weapons of the Civil War included rifled muskets and repeater rifles which were much more accurate and faster loading and it was demonstrated in many battles that a small army, well entrenched could hold off a much larger force attacking from an open field. The extremely high casualty rates of the Civil War were due to this mismatch between technology and tactics. Certainly those who were mowed down by the concentrated barrage tended to this view.

It was also the more accurate muskets and rifles which curtailed the role of the cavalry in the Civil War. There were some important cavalry skirmishes during the war but they were of limited strategic importance and the more usual role of the cavalry was to be the "eyes of the army" as an angry General Lee explained to J.E.B. Stuart at Gettysburg – in a loud voice. When the cavalry was deployed on the battlefield, the horsemen typically rode to their assigned position, dismounted and fought as infantry often with very pleasing results. The days of the saber charge had come to an end as had been demonstrated by the Light Brigade at Balaclava in 1854.

There were essentially three types of firearms used in the Civil War and there were significant technological improvements made to them throughout the duration of the war. The musket was the weapon of a previous generation and by the onset of hostilities it had been improved by rifling, which is a spiral groove inscribed onto the inside of the barrel causing the bullet to spin thus gaining both distance and accuracy. The rifled musket was the most common infantry weapon and it came in a variety of calibers which often caused logistical headaches for both armies, neither of which had standardized their armaments. For example, it did little good to receive a supply of .57 mm shot if your gun had a .54 mm barrel. All muskets required the powder, wadding and projectile to be pushed into the barrel from the muzzle end and tapped into place with a tamping rod. Percussion caps were then placed under the hammer making the gun ready to fire. Soldiers were typically given 40 rounds of ammunition per day and if they ran out during the course of the battle they could only hope that the dead guys next to them had been using similar ammunition.

The range of a rifle or musket is determined by the velocity of the explosive used and the length of the barrel. The black powder explosives of the early Civil War battles were relatively slow burning and so longer barrels meant greater range. Long barrels were a significant impediment to the cavalry and, by opting for the recently developed carbine ("carabins" – cavalry trooper), the troopers traded range for comfort and weight. With the advent of faster burning and more explosive gunpowder the carbine was able to recover the lost range and accuracy. More importantly the better gunpowder allowed the use of jacketed bullets which fed into the breech rather than the muzzle of a rifle resulting in faster firing times.

The projectile of choice for both armies was the Minié ball (Minnie ball) named after its inventor Claude-Étienne Minié. The bullet was made of lead and conically shaped with a diameter slightly smaller than the bore of the rifle. When it was properly tamped the bullet would deform to fill the entire bore preventing the loss of explosive gases (thus increasing the range) and filling the gun rifling to provide spin for accuracy. In theory, at least, each shot cleaned the barrel of unspent powder from the shot before. Some claim that the minié loaded rifle was accurate up to 750 yards but success at this range would likely have resulted in a heart attack of the surprised sharpshooter. Its predictable accuracy was likely closer to 500 yards and the bullet would smash its way through any soft tissue it encountered. Wounds from this ammunition were horrific and bones were not merely broken but were destroyed. Civil War surgeons, therefore, made little effort to save limbs but opted for rapid amputation. Historian Shelby Foote noted that the pictures of Civil War dead often showed shirts and jackets torn open. This was because the injured soldier knew that if he had suffered a gut shot his intestines would be mostly on the ground behind him and he was about to die. The opened clothing was silent testimony to the undaunted nature of human curiosity.

Artillery weaponry also included rifled and non-rifled barrels. Field guns included short-range howitzers for firing explosive shells to destroy fortifications and smooth-bore cannons which were favoured for their reliability and relative ease of use. Rifled cannons, like rifled muskets, were very accurate because the ammunition was caused to spin thus enhancing its aerodynamics. Rifling a cannon barrel is not an easy procedure and the metallurgical technology of the day often resulted in devastating breakage of the cast iron barrels and instant death to anyone located nearby. The projectiles fired by the artillery were specific to the type of field piece. Smoothbore cannons fired round iron balls and rifled cannons fired cylindrical bolts. The impact force of the cannon balls and bolts was designed to destroy whatever impeded its path. The projectiles would skip across dry ground destroying men and equipment until their kinetic energy was spent.

Explosive shells were fired from both smooth-bored and rifled cannons and they would either explode from impact or based on a timing fuse. In both cases the intent was to send shrapnel from the exploding shell into a conical kill zone. Most shells would break into only a few large pieces and so the destructive impact was often muted in relation to the emotional impact on the soldier past whose head the red hot metal flew. Confederate General Johnson, injured by shrapnel during the Battle of Seven Pines, could attest to the fearsome impact of the explosive shell. Case or shrapnel, shells were designed to explode above or in front of an advancing enemy and were loaded with lead or iron balls that were ejected at speed following the shell explosion. These early cluster bombs, when properly timed and charged, had a devastating impact on longevity and morale.

The most reliably lethal projectile from an artillery piece was canister. This projectile was a thin-walled container filled with small balls packed in sawdust. As the projectile exited the muzzle, the pressure drop ripped it open and the small iron balls sprayed out at high velocity destroying whatever lay in their path. The range of canister was less than 400 yards but the killing rate on a close-spaced, advancing column of men was very high. At the Battle of Cold Harbor, Confederate canister killed and wounded 7,000 men in 20 minutes or 6 men per second.

Field guns were always accompanied by both a caisson and a limber. The limber was a two-wheeled ammunition carrier which was attached to the front of the two-wheeled artillery carriage. The articulating characteristics of the joined carriages made them more maneuverable than a four-wheeled unit. Likewise the caisson was a two-wheeled unit also carrying ammunition and a spare wheel. Additional to these carriages were supply wagons and a portable forge to repair over-stressed cannon barrels at the conclusion of battle.

Influence of Napoleon on Civil War Tactics and Strategy

The significance of the Napoleonic period on the development of subsequent warfare cannot be overstated. Napoleon's success in fighting over 99 battles in the space of 19 years resulted in a density of warfare that ensured his tactics would be studied ever after. Who, after all, had more experience in warfare than the little Corsican?

As inevitably happens, someone codified the military operations of Napoleon and reduced his tactics to a manual, ignoring that each battle presents its own idiosyncracies and difficulties. Antoine Henri Jomini was that someone and his writing was translated by Henry Halleck, *Elements of Military Art and Science*, for use at the US Military Academy. Most of the leadership in the Confederate and Union armies were trained at West Point and were thus well-steeped in Napoleon's battlefield tactics.

There were two problems with strict adherence to Napoleonic tactics during the Civil War and both had more to do with the application of the tactics than with the tactics themselves. European battlefields, with large open spaces, dense populations and access from all quarters of the compass, were different from American battlefields which were densely wooded with only narrow pathways. In dust or mud you didn't want to be the last of 40,000 men who walked down a narrow wagon track. Regiments and divisions often got lost on the way to the battlefield and ground depressions sometimes caused acoustic shadows resulting in adjacent divisions being unaware that their neighbour was fighting for its life. As a result, when commanders of the Civil War attempted complex battle formations, their programs often went awry. Battle plans became confused and misunderstood as untrained and undisciplined soldiers left the battlefield. And the reason they left the battlefield was because they were being shot at by more accurate weaponry.

The muskets of Borodino were not the rifles of Gettysburg and the saber attack was to become a dying skill.

The Napoleonic frontal assault was another staple of battlefield tactics for both the Northern and Southern armies. In this case massed columns of men would charge what was perceived to be the weakest position of the defensive line and attempt to break through in order to turn and roll up the enemy's line from the point of the breakthrough. This tactic rarely worked but was continually attempted.

Battlefield Strategies

We do well to remember that war, like all human activity, is a summation of the foibles and personalities of those called upon to make the dreadful decisions. The decisions of Civil War generals played out in strategies and tactics which, understood, enhance one's appreciation of the monumental consequences of the war.

On the political level, the war was conducted by a reserved Confederate Davis who was trained in war and felt he understood the game and an amiable Union Lincoln who learned as he went. The Northern president had long adopted the "Anaconda Plan" devised by Major General Winfield Scott in which the navy would blockade the Southern ports and the Mississippi would be controlled by Northern gunboats. The resulting economic squeeze would ultimately destroy the ability of the

Confederacy to maintain the war and it would have to capitulate as Northern armies moved on Southern targets. He knew that the superior resources of the North would allow his armies to stay on the field longer than their adversaries.

Southern President Davis' preferred a strategy of protecting the key population centers and maintaining the integrity of the Confederacy by controlling the Mississippi River. By staying in the war, he reasoned, there was a chance of gaining European support and thus a negotiated settlement. Unfortunately, he ruled 11 states which had seceded on the basis of state rights and they, doggedly pursuing this notion, required that armies be located across the breadth and width of the Confederacy instead of being focused in strategic locations.

On the military front the war eventually became a battle of wits between Robert E. Lee and Ulysses S. Grant. There are those who find the career of Robert E. Lee to be devoid of mistakes and that, of course, is to fly in the face of Mr. Bona-parte's dictum. General Lee certainly did fight and he certainly did make mistakes but he also made brilliant tactical decisions that were startling at the time and have lost little of their shine with the passage of years. His ingenious mangling of the rules of war resulted in many unlikely victories. Lieutenant General Grant was created in the mould of Lee and registered brilliant successes and less brilliant defeats. His Vicksburg campaign re-wrote several rules of war and it was his determination to press on irrespective of his casualties that finally brought an end to the conflict.

Both armies used guerrilla tactics and extensive spy networks to procure information about the enemy and seed incorrect information about themselves. The wildly inaccurate assessment of the Confederate forces provided to Major General George McClellan suggests that the Confederate forces were the most accomplished at this art. Colonel McGruder's use of fake artillery and creative parading of his limited forces to give the effect of a much larger army was instrumental in stalling the Union advance from Fort Monroe to Richmond. McClellan was robbed of the element of surprise and the Confederate forces were able to prepare defensive battlements and plan the expulsion of the Union army.

The role of improved communications and logistical support in the Civil War cannot be understated. When McClellan assumed command of the disorganized and dispirited Army of the Potomac he instituted a new regimen of training and communications infrastructure which paid dividends throughout the remainder of the war. Whatever his failings as a battlefield general, he earned appropriate respect for his understanding of the new exigencies of battlefield warfare.

Infantry Tactics

The campaign season in the Civil War was somewhat varia-
ble but typically was constrained by the rainy winter season
when roads and paths became impassable to large regiments of
soldiers. This was not always the case and many battles were
fought in the cold and wet. The infantry was typically capable
of marching 10 to 20 miles per day but the brigades under
Stonewall Jackson accomplished remarkable feats of movement
and repeatedly confused the Union generals sent to flush his
army from the Shenandoah Valley.

Battles typically began with the converging of opposing
forces on a suitable battlefield. Both sides rushed to take the
high ground with a view to building defensive battlements from
which to repulse an assault in the hope that the offensive army
would be so weakened that the defenders would then be able to
attack and destroy it. The armies would arrive in columns
normally following different routes. One of the problems of the
Civil War were the restricted accesses and narrow roads which
prevented bringing large groups of soldiers into position
quickly. Often the failure to coordinate brigade arrivals led to
confusion and defeat. Sometimes armies would unexpectedly
encounter their enemy and unplanned hostilities would break
out. The Battle of Gettysburg broke out when a group of
Southern soldiers, looking for shoes in the small town of
Gettysburg, were surprised by Buford's Union cavalry and an
ad hoc encounter grew into a major conflagration.

In the opening phases of a battle the combatants would send out skirmishing forces to test the strength of the enemy line by probing for points of weakness and provide a screen for flanking maneuvers and battery emplacement. Once the artillery was deployed, a period of bombardment would ensue – particularly if one side was dug into a defensive position. Rarely did artillery bombardment affect the outcome of a battle. The intense fight of the Hornet's Nest during the Battle of Shiloh in which the Union forces retired from an artillery barrage was a notable exception.

The infantry brigades would then spread out into a battle line usually two men deep in order that firepower could be maximized. This diluted the effect of the shooting and extended the battle lines but it also reduced the impact of the artillery. The offensive army would typically attempt an "end run" or turning maneuver to bring their troops behind the defensive position and thus "crack the nut" in a pincer movement. It was up to the battlefield commanders to move their brigades to strengthen their lines where the enemy was strongest always keeping a close eye on their flanks to ensure they were anchored and could not be bypassed.

In those cases when armies met and one side did not seek a battle or when one army was forced to retreat in disarray from the field, the stronger army would have to decide whether to give chase. It was a great frustration to President Lincoln that his successful generals did not pursue the defeated army. McClellan did not pursue Lee following Antietam nor did Meade pursue Lee after Gettysburg. But nor did Lee pursue McClellan after the Seven Days Battles or Bragg pursue Rosecrans after Chickamauga. In fact, the only time a chase was successful was at Appomattox Court House. One can only speculate that the horrors of the battle so enervated the battle-field commanders that they could not move themselves to pursue.

Naval Strategy

Naval strategy is often given little attention in discussions of the Civil War and this is likely because there were no Trafalgar-like sea battles. The Northern strategy was to cork the Southern bottle by creating an effective blockade of all Southern ports and the strategy was very successful. Southern trade and commerce wilted during the war and the resulting economic privation in the Confederacy was a significant factor in the weakening of the rebellion. There were blockade runners, of course, and the Confederate navy did win some important gains at sea but nothing the South did was able to overcome the strangulation of their trade by the Northern navy.

What is also often overlooked were the significant naval technological advances that resulted from the war. The steam driven, ironclad ship was first introduced during the strangely named Battle of Hampton Roads. The CSS *Virginia*, built on the frame of the USS *Merrimac*, was well on the way to destroying the Northern fleet at Fort Monroe when the USS *Monitor* entered the fray, evened the fight and drove off the Southern attack. Had the *Monitor* not been successful, the war undoubtedly would have had a much different ending. Later in the war Southern engineers introduced the submarine into naval warfare. Perhaps the most important innovation in naval participation was the much enhanced coordination that the Union armies were able to achieve with their navy partners. Grant made good use of army-navy cooperation in taking Forts Henry and Donelson and in pursuing the Vicksburg campaign. Perhaps the army/navy coordination of D-Day was a logical outcome of the Civil War.

Military Innovations from the Civil War

In 1849, Abraham Lincoln, having previously spent a year lifting his barge over innumerable Mississippi sandbars, devised a machine for lifting shipping vessels over shoals. With this background in technological curiosity, it is not surprising that Mr. Lincoln encouraged inventions to facilitate the conduct of the war. Civilizations have always paid a high premium for creativity in efficient killing and the Civil War was remarkable by this measure as well. It is true that while many of the innovations had first been proposed in the Crimean War, they were implemented and tested in the Civil War.

Coming at a time of unparalleled scientific enquiry, when even the origins of humanity were being questioned, it is perhaps logical that the Civil War would provoke such inventiveness. Not only the implements of war but also the way of doing war was improved and made efficient during those four years.

Certainly the allocation of resources and the goal-setting of the industrialized North surprised the world with the efficiency in which factories and supply systems were quickly altered to supply the needs of its army. Some say that this was largely driven by the great possibilities for new ways to defraud the U.S. government. As previously stated, the word "shoddy," which used to mean a type of cloth, was given its current meaning during the Civil War as an expression of incomplete or low quality manufacture. Nevertheless, the marshaling of resources to support the war effort was an impressive Northern achievement.

The sale of war bonds by Treasury Secretary Chase and banker Jay Gould was a significant factor in the ultimate success of the Union army. The sale of bonds was not unusual in government finance but the sophisticated network of 2,500 sales agents who raised over three billion dollars from more than one million, middle class purchasers was very creative and this sales practice continues to this day.

Tactical inventions thrived during the war as well. The use of rifle trenches to shield defensive positions and protect against long range sharpshooters resulted in honeycombed battlefields and the practice of one column exchanging fusillades with another soon ended. Tactical deception was honed to a finer art as well. The use of "Quaker" guns, logs blackened and positioned to look like field artillery, companies marching in circles to give the appearance of a larger than actual army, use of campfires in abandoned positions and bands playing to empty tents gave the illusion of an occupied camp. General Beauregarde even used a shunting train, complete with whistles and cheering men, to give the illusion of arriving reinforcements. Strangely, these tactics always seemed to work best on the gullible Northern armies – or at least on their commander George McClellan.

The graduates of the U.S. Military Academy were well trained in engineering and many of them worked as surveyors, engineers and construction managers during the antebellum years. It is not surprising, therefore, that the Civil War tactics placed such a heavy reliance on army engineers to facilitate the movement of troops and construct both defensive and offensive embattlements. They were instrumental in placing artillery batteries, installing pontoon bridges, providing telegraph communications, repairing logistical lines such as railroads and building camp facilities to stop the spread of disease through poor sanitation facilities.

Railroad science was well advanced and the Lincoln government approved the first transcontinental railroad. Herman Haupt was employed by President Lincoln during the war to reorganize the Union railroads in order to improve the logistics of getting armaments and war materiel from the foundries and factories to the battle fronts and his success maximized the use of railroads to bring in materials and to remove wounded soldiers from battlefield hospitals to convalesce in larger hospitals behind the battle lines.

In innovation, the navy was certainly not outdone by the army. There were several patents taken out on the USS *Monitor* alone. It was the first boat to have a Timby rotating turret allowing the gun to be actively engaged irrespective of the boat's orientation to its target. It was the first ship to be powered by a screw propeller rotating on a longitudinal shaft rather than a paddlewheel rotating on an axial shaft. The boat presented a very small target by virtue of its semi-submersible nature and only the cylinder of steel which protected the gun was above the water line. That the boat was designed, built, tested and placed in service within 100 days is a testament to the genius of its architect John Ericsson.

Due to the economic strangulation being felt by the Northern blockade, the Confederacy invested a considerable amount of time and money in the search for ways of dislodging the Union ships. Perhaps the most unique approach was the submarine which was an idea resurrected from the Revolutionary War. Only one unit was ever produced and it killed more Confederate than Union sailors but the CSS *Hunley* was a significant achievement. It unfortunately sank on its first and only contact with the enemy, the USS *Housatonic*, but not before destroying the Union vessel.

Floating mines made their first debut as part of the Southern defence against the Northern blockade and these were followed by the towable torpedo. It was an easy jump from a mine floating in the water to one buried in the earth – and nations have been trying to dig them up ever since.

A more prosaic but much appreciated innovation was the differentiated boot – a boot designed to fit either a left or right foot (but not both). These Northern boots were in high demand and photos from Civil War battlefields are a testament to their comfort showing the dead Union soldiers with their boots stripped off. In fact, it was a Confederate excursion to investigate a rumoured supply of such boots at Gettysburg which touched off that historic confrontation.

While hot air and gas balloons were not novelties, their use as observation posts was greatly extended during the Civil War. The Union army in particular dedicated rail cars to the transport and tethering of balloons which were inflated with hydrogen produced from iron filings in water doused with sulfuric acid and then cooled in a retort. The observer would rise to 500 feet on a tether and telegraph his observations to a ground receiver.

The development of rifled guns accelerated during the Civil War as both sides could see the advantages of rapid firing, accurate weaponry. The breech loading rifle, developed by

Christopher Spencer, was a significant development especially when coupled with jacketed bullets. B. Tyler Henry developed a lever-action rifle that could fire 25 shots a minute and Richard Gatling developed the first rapid fire machine gun. Fortunately for those being fired on, the gun had restricted mobility and a tendency to heat up and jam, and the guns saw limited battle-field action.

Bringing large groups of men together in unhygienic conditions with less than adequate sewage treatment is always a recipe for disaster. During the Civil War men lived in such conditions with the added stresses of fatigue and cold weather and it is estimated that twice as many men were felled by bugs than bullets. Much had been learned about the importance of camp and hospital hygiene during the Crimean War of 1853-56 and more was to be learned from the Civil War. The voluntary Sanitation Commission inspected camps and suggested improvements to hygiene, cooking, hospitals and latrine systems. The construction of large, airy, heated and "clean" hospitals reduced the mortality rates for injured Union soldiers. On the battlefield, of course, medical sanitation was unknown and surgeons would simply wipe their saws on bloodied aprons before starting on the next patient.

The little war would become a gruesome nightmare.

5: 1862 - Death and the End of Innocence

If there were doubts about the horrors of war in 1861 they were disavowed in 1862. Significant battles in which thousands died were fought and the North tightened its stranglehold on the Southern economy. Replacing the fallen troops became a pressing issue for both sides.

When Major General McClellan finally encamped his army outside of Richmond, the Confederate Army volunteers were just completing their one-year term of service. As a result, the Confederate Congress passed the first conscription law in American history requiring all men between the ages of 18 and 35 to serve for the duration of the war. At most, Davis could count on only 1.1 million white men of military age compared to a Union population of more than four times that. The conscription law of the South was widely hated and created division within communities and even families. It was made worse by a clause which allowed any man who owned 20 or more slaves to avoid the draft. It was "*a rich man's war but a poor man's fight*" and, as in the North, substitutes could be hired to fight in the place of those who were drafted. This law led to a decline in support for Jefferson Davis and the war effort.

The Northern blockade of Southern ports became more efficient and shortages of material and food became widespread throughout the South creating inflationary pressures. Southern farmers misjudged the effectiveness of the Northern blockade and did not rotate their crops from cotton to foodstuffs. The popular view was that cotton could not be blockaded by the North without destroying the economy of England and drawing them into the war. What everyone failed to consider was that England would find alternative sources for its cotton in India and Egypt. This miscalculation resulted in food shortages and a lack of foreign currency to finance the war.

While George McClellan was rebuilding the Union forces in the Eastern Theatre, Ulysses S. Grant began his rise from obscurity to national prominence. Grant graduated from the U.S. Military Academy in 1843 and fought with valor in the Mexican war. In 1862, under the command of Major General Henry Halleck, he commanded Union forces west of the Tennessee and Cumberland Rivers and determined that Forts Henry and Donelson could be taken from the Confederates commanded by Major General Albert Sidney Johnston, also a West Point graduate.

Johnston was a close friend and confidant of President Davis and was given the job of organizing the Confederate positions in the west to ensure that Kentucky and Tennessee earned their stars in the Confederate flag. Leaving Richmond amidst great fanfare, Johnston was horrified by what he found in the west. He was required to maintain the Confederate presence with very few soldiers and less materiel of war. His was to be a battle of wits as he attempted to bluff the Northern armies into thinking that he was better provisioned than he was. The strategy worked - but only for a time.

Fame and glory result from action and the Union generals, eager for the rewards of war, began testing the Southern lines preparatory to an all-out attack. The results of such testing by Don Carlos Buell in eastern Tennessee had not been propitious. Further west, Henry Halleck seized the opportunity to make his name by unfastening the traces on Ulysses Grant.

With Halleck's permission, Grant and Andrew Foote of the Navy planned a coordinated attack on Fort Henry. The naval attack was so successful, however, that the battle was over before Grant arrived. Grant then destroyed a railroad bridge south of Fort Henry allowing the Union Navy to control the Tennessee River through to northern Alabama thus placing Johnston and his army in a precarious position.

The Battle of Fort Donelson

Some of the Confederate defenders of Fort Henry escaped overland 12 miles to Fort Donelson on the Cumberland River. To prevent the breech in the Confederate line protecting Tennessee from expanding, Albert Sidney Johnston decided to increase the forces in Fort Donelson from 5,000 to 12,000 and moved his other forces to south of the Cumberland River rather than await an attack which might destroy his army. Confederate Brigadier General John Floyd, who had been Secretary of War in the Buchanan administration and had caused much confusion in western Virginia, was given command of Fort Donelson.

Union Major General Halleck was nervous of a campaign against Fort Donelson and, believing Grant to be a reckless alcoholic, invited Major General Don Carlos Buell to lead the attack. Grant was unaware of Halleck's efforts to replace him and insisted that speed was of the essence. On February 11, 1861, for the first and last time in the Civil War, Grant held a counsel of war with his subordinates to formulate a plan. The Confederates at Fort Donelson recognized that their position was untenable and attempted a failed breakout. On February 14 an additional 10,000 Union troops arrived with the six gunboats which had fought successfully at Fort Henry. At Grant's urging, Foote opened fire on the shore batteries of the fort and they responded by damaging the fleet and driving it off. Fort Donelson was not to be a repeat of Fort Henry.

On the morning of February 15, the Confederate soldiers attempted another breakout and successfully surprised the Union soldiers who were focused on their breakfast. Grant had left the field without appointing a commander in his absence and instructed that no decisions were to be made prior to his return. It was a mistake he was to repeat but it was in the recovery from moments like these that he earned his reputation for cool headedness.

The Confederate forces pushed the Union line back almost 2 miles and might have made good their escape but for confusion amongst their generals. When Grant arrived he brought the naval guns to bear in order to create a diversion and, noting the provisions being carried by the Confederate soldiers, correctly interpreted their intention to flee. His massed build-up of forces in front of the stalled Confederate line caused them to retreat to the fort.

Both sides had lost 1,000 dead with another 3,000 wounded left on the battlefield, many of whom froze to death during the night. The Confederate generals, while pleased with the activities of the day, recognized that they would have to surrender. One after the other, the senior commanders slipped across the river rather than face prison in the North and finally Brigadier General Simon Bolivar Buchner petitioned for an armistice assuming that Grant would offer generous terms to an old friend. Grant's response earned him his nickname of "Unconditional Surrender" Grant and was ironic in its cordiality,

"Sir: Yours of this date proposing Armistice, and appointment of Commissioners, to settle terms of Capitulation is just received. No terms except unconditional and immediate surrender can be accepted. I propose to move immediately upon your works.

I am Sir: very respectfully
Your obt. sevt.
U.S. Grant
Brig. Gen."

The capture of Fort Donelson with the surrender of over 12,000 Confederate soldiers was hailed in the North and the Confederate army under Albert Sidney Johnson was forced to retreat to south of Nashville placing most of Kentucky and Tennessee under Union control.

Following the capture of Fort Donelson, the Confederate forces began preparations to strike at Grant before he could be reinforced by the 50,000 man army of Don Carlos Buell thus destroying the two armies in detail. The Northern forces were mustered at Pittsburg Landing near a small Methodist Church known as Shiloh ("place of peace"). For three weeks Grant drilled his men in the large, open space while awaiting reinforcements from Don Carlos Buell. The Union army was not expecting an engagement and did not build defensive installations. The Confederate troops, located 35 km to the south at Corinth, Mississippi, were also receiving reinforcements and training their troops. Albert Sidney Johnston did not want to take command of the Southern forces as he was shaken by the collapse of his efforts in Kentucky. General Beauregard, newly arrived from the Eastern Theatre, also refused command because he was sick and he felt that Johnston was the better officer. In the end Beauregard led the attack under Johnston's orders.

The Battle of Shiloh

The Union army was bivouacked in a triangular encampment pressed up against a creek on one side with the Tennessee River on another. Access to the camp was open to the south. His least experienced troops were encamped on the southern edge of the field and Grant himself was headquartered at Savannah almost 9 miles away. As at Fort Donelson, Grant failed to appoint a camp commander in his absence and early on the morning of Sunday, April 6 Confederate forward units encountered the Union Army (again) preparing their breakfast. William Tecumseh Sherman was shot in the hand when he rode out to see what was happening and one of his orderlies was killed. Recognizing that the Union camp was under attack, he organized the other divisional commanders to establish a defensive position and the Confederates were held for almost 90 minutes before forcing the Union line to retreat. Grant reached the battlefield between 8:30 and 9:00 in the morning and found almost 3,000 soldiers huddling under the protection of the river bank.

The Union troops were falling back in a disorganized fashion and their commanders were having a difficult time coordinating any kind of counteroffensive. Grant established defensive lines amongst the trees and forced the Confederates to attack from across open ground. Fortunately for the Union, the Confederate commanders were also having difficulty managing the battle as their line was raggedly pushing forward as their soldiers, tired and hungry from their long march, were delighted to pause and finish the uneaten Northern breakfast. By the time the Confederate attack had reorganized, many of the soldiers were out of ammunition. Johnston took some of his men to the center of the Union line for a final push across a 300 yard clearing known as Duncan Field and into a thicket of trees which is remembered by the descriptive name of the "Hornet's Nest." Here the Northern troops had successfully held off the Confederate soldiers for over 7 hours and, as Johnston led the final, successful charge into the right flank of the Union troops, he was injured by friendly fire. A bullet passing through the back of his knee cut the femoral artery and he quickly died from blood loss.

The Confederates brought fifty cannons to bear on the Hornet's Nest and unleashed a barrage which shattered the will of the Union soldiers. The 2,200 remaining Northern troops surrendered but their brave action saved Grant's army from total destruction.

By nightfall Buell's army arrived and began disembarking at Pittsburg Landing. The Union line was in complete shambles and the Confederate commanders knew that victory would be theirs with one last push. However, their men were tired, hungry, and thirsty from the battle. The Confederate troops lined up at 5:30 p.m. for a final charge but this was called off by Beauregard who was convinced that Buell was marching into

Alabama and that Grant was safely across the river. As the Northern troops lay huddled along the banks of the Tennessee River, the Confederate soldiers ransacked their camp and enjoyed the better Northern food, convinced that the Southern victory at Shiloh would end the war. Not all of the Southerners were convinced of victory.

Cavalry leader Nathan Bedford Forrest knew that Buell was, in fact, reinforcing Grant and in the counterattack, the Southerners would be destroyed. At 5 a.m. the reinforced Union troops formed a line and pressed into the Confederates. The fighting was ragged but fierce and by 3:30 p.m. Beauregard moved his men back and, as they retreated, the Northerners were happy to let them go. Forrest, in protecting the retreating army with one last charge, narrowly missed capture and was the last to be injured in the Battle of Shiloh, a minnie ball lodging next to his spine. Just under 25,000 men were killed or wounded at Shiloh making it the bloodiest battle of the Civil War up to that point in time and families and communities across the North and South knew that the nation was at war.

The Southerners nevertheless claimed a victory; although a victory at a high price. Likewise, the Union troops interpreted the battle as their most brilliant victory. Victors don't usually change their leaders but, following the battle, Major General Halleck replaced Grant with George Thomas and took personal control of the three armies in the Western Theatre. Six weeks later he was reassigned to Washington and elevated to general-in-chief. Grant, who had considered resigning his commission, returned to his position as commander for the District of West Tennessee. William Tecumseh Sherman was also blamed for his lack of preparedness but those who fought with him were effusive in praising his efforts. In the end he was promoted. In assessing blame following the Battle of Shiloh, President Lincoln came down on the side of Grant stating, *"I can't spare this man; he fights."*

The Battle of Shiloh was a significant missed opportunity for the Confederate forces and there was blame enough for all. Albert Sidney Johnston, rather than remaining as the commanding general, decided to redeem his reputation by playing the role of a gallant captain and it cost him his life. Braxton Bragg was obsessed with taking the Hornet's Nest when it could easily have been outflanked and Pierre Beauregard called off the attack before the Union army had been destroyed.

As a result of his continued poor health, P.G. T. Beauregard took a leave of absence without permission and was reassigned by an angry Jefferson Davis. Braxton Bragg was given command of the Army of Tennessee and determined that Shiloh was a failure due to a lack of organization and discipline. His efforts to remedy these shortcomings resulted in him becoming the most despised commander of the best disciplined army in the Confederate states.

The loss of 25,000 men resulted in little more than a continued stalemate; nothing was gained by either side and the violence of the battle shocked the armies involved and stunned the people of both the Confederate and Union republics. It was now clear that the Civil War would last much longer and consume more lives than anyone had anticipated. Anyone, that is, except William Tecumseh Sherman who had almost driven himself mad with his clear understanding of what the war would be.

***

The Union Navy continued to successfully blockade Southern ports, capturing Jacksonville, Pensacola, Biloxi, Norfolk and finally New Orleans. New Orleans was guarded by two intimidating fortresses at Jackson and St. Philip near the mouth of the Mississippi River. Union navy captain David Farragut, coaxed out of retirement, led his naval forces past these forts during a midnight, high risk dash up the river. Thousands of shells were traded but the effort was successful and only one Union boat was lost. The next day, April 24, New Orleans surrendered and Farragut continued upriver to capture Baton Rouge. On June 6 a separate Union flotilla captured Memphis, Tennessee placing most of the Mississippi River under Union control. Only Vicksburg remained to hold the Confederacy together. Controlling the Mississippi River was a high priority for Abraham Lincoln and maintaining Vicksburg was critical to Jefferson Davis.

Naval battles were not a big part of the Civil War but it was a naval battle which had the most profound effect on the future of warfare. The battle of the ironsides, on March 9, 1862, was a showcase of American creativity and ingenuity and it has gone down in history as one of the great battles of all time. The USS *Merrimack* had been constructed in the Norfolk shipyards in the summer of 1861 and then scuttled by Federalist forces when they left after the secession of Virginia. The Confederacy raised the ship, rechristened it the CSS *Virginia*, covered it with 3 inch thick iron plates and planned to use it to drive off the Union blockaders and open Southern ports to shipping.

Navy Secretary Gideon Welles recognized the danger of this ironclad and countered with an ironside of his own. He hired John Ericsson, a Swedish-American naval designer, to build a boat in 100 days or forfeit any payment. On January 30, 1862 the USS *Monitor* made its maiden voyage in the New York harbour. It was 124 feet long with 1 inch plating over heavy oak beams and planking. It sat low in the water and could fire on an enemy, from any orientation, with a revolving turret containing two, 11 inch Dahlgren guns.

The Battle of Hampton Roads: Monitor vs Merrimac

On March 8 the CSS *Virginia* set out on a testing voyage off the coast of Virginia with a full complement of 300 sailors. Sighting Union warships, Captain Franklin Buchanan declared the test a success and steered directly for the USS *Cumberland* oblivious to the shells being fired at him. The *Virginia* hit the *Cumberland* and pushed its ram deep into the wooden boat. When the Southern ironclad reversed, the *Cumberland* quickly sank. Buchanan's next target was the USS *Congress* which quickly raised a white flag. As the *Virginia* set out to assist the sailors of the wounded *Congress*, Union shooters from the shore batteries continued to fire and so an angry Buchanan resumed his bombardment of the *Congress* with hot shot leaving it to finally sink. The *Virginia* next turned to the USS *Minnesota* which had run aground while trying to escape. Fortunately the Confederate ship could not get close enough to destroy it and so broke off the engagement to await the morning tide. At midnight the USS *Monitor* arrived at the battle scene.

On March 9, as the *Virginia* returned to destroy the *Minnesota*, the *Monitor* sailed into view and the two ironclads opened fire on each other. The crew of the *Monitor* was told to prime its guns with small powder charges because no one could predict the impact on the ship's frame of the guns recoiling from a full charge. As it was, the internal structure of the *Monitor* suffered little damage while the *Virginia* was cracked by the incessant pounding. A full charge from the *Monitor's* guns may, in fact, have destroyed the *Virginia*. While the fight was a draw and neither side gained any strategic advantage, the battle changed forever the design of naval ships and destroyed Confederate hopes of breaking the Union blockade.

***

Grant's successes in the Western Theatre had raised the spirits of the Northern forces and the Union blockade was beginning to have a telling effect on the Southern economy. But flagging Confederate spirits soon changed as a result of a series of battles in Virginia. Major General McClellan had reorganized and re-energized the Army of the Potomac. His ego was monumental as a result of minor successes in western Virginia and his troops hailed him as the "Little Napoleon." Writing to his wife he proudly stated,

> *"I almost think that were I to win some small success now I could become dictator or anything else that might please me - but nothing of the kind would please me - therefore I won't be dictator. Admirable self-denial!"*

He described Lincoln as a well-meaning baboon and regularly refused to meet with the Secretary of War. Everyone grew anxious and impatient as he refused to move his army onto the field of battle.

Finally, in late March, McClellan, under increasing pressure from President Lincoln, launched his invasion of Virginia. After a false start in northern Virginia, where he had been fooled by "Quaker cannon" (logs painted to look like cannon), he shipped his men and war materials by boat to Fort Monroe and then moved northwest up the peninsula towards Richmond. The plan was to link with Irvin McDowell who was simultaneously moving his army of 35,000 men south from Washington.

As often happened, a good plan was rendered inoperable in its execution. McClellan was convinced that he faced an army two or three times as large as his own and he stopped at Yorktown due to a Confederate subterfuge. Brigadier General John Bankhead MacGruder used Quaker cannons to suggest a large artillery force and rotated his men to give the appearance of a much larger infantry force. After a month of preparation, during which time Confederate forces prepared the defenses of Richmond, McClellan was finally ready to fight. Magruder and his forces, however, simply melted away to Richmond. McClellan finally established a camp in a swampy region of the Chickahominy River, east of Richmond in late May and faced the 60,000 men under Confederate General Joseph E. Johnston.

To bring additional pressure on Richmond, McClellan attempted to move his navy up the James River. After the Battle of Hampton Roads, the USS *Monitor* idled at Fort Monroe and chose its fights with care. When Confederate troops moved inland from Norfolk and Portsmouth in early May, the warship *Virginia* was refitted to sail to Richmond. Unfortunately, it was caught in a low tide, abandoned and sunk on May 11, two months after its maiden voyage. Emboldened and unimpeded, the Union navy sailed upriver and was stopped by the Fort Darling battery on Drewry's Bluff located 7 miles downstream from Richmond. During the ensuing battle, it became obvious that ironclad wooden ships could not withstand a concentrated attack and that the *Monitor* had to be able to elevate its guns in order to engage shore batteries. The Union navy was not able

to penetrate to Richmond, an event which, if it had been successful, may have ended the war.

With McClellan and his army encamped on the outskirts of
Richmond, Confederate General Joseph Johnston (with advice
from Lee) took a calculated risk by reducing his strength and
sending Stonewall Jackson to the Shenandoah Valley with
17,000 men to create a diversion and draw off the army of
Irving McDowell. President Lincoln, sensing an opportunity to
destroy Jackson's army, also mobilized 30,000 men in two
armies under Nathaniel Banks and John Frémont.

Jackson was born poor but graduated from the US Military
Academy and was decorated for bravery in Mexico. He had
been a stern teacher at the Virginia Military Institute, was a
fanatical Presbyterian with many eccentric behaviors and was
perhaps the best battlefield general produced during the Civil
War. By taking advantage of the local geography and by
marching his men in the Shenandoah Valley beyond what any
thought possible, he kept the Union forces occupied, thus
saving Richmond and the Southern Confederacy.

General Johnston, with his back to Richmond, recognized
the weak position into which McClellan had put himself by
placing his army on both sides of the swampy Chickahominy
River. An attack on one half of the Union army could not be
supported by the isolated other half. On May 31, 1862 he
planned a coordinated, three pronged attack on Union forces
south of the Chickahominy. Typically, the attack was uncoor-

dinated. The Battle of Seven Pines was repelled by the Union forces but they nonetheless moved back from Richmond. More importantly, command passed to General Robert E. Lee when Johnston was injured by shrapnel.

Lee's father had been a Revolutionary war hero and he, a graduate of the US Military Academy, had served with distinction in the Mexican war. He was not in favor of secession but he was a patriot to his state and came to be the embodiment of the Southern warrior gentleman. The new Confederate General, whom McClellan believed to be timid and irresolute, now demonstrated his military genius.

The Seven Days Battles

Lee refurbished and trained his army for one month while McClellan idled his troops. He then broke out against the Union forces in what is known as the Seven Days Battles. The plan of battle was appropriate to a professional army but became hopelessly uncoordinated in the hands of the inexperienced commanders. The first Battle of Oak Grove on June 25, 1862 was preparatory to the larger phase of the battle on June 26. In the Battle of Beaver Dam Creek, Major General Thomas Jackson, with support from Major General A. P. Hill, was to outflank Union commander John Pope on the north side of the Chickahominy. A. P. Hill had more than military reasons for driving hard at McClellan's Northern armies. Years before, his offer of marriage to the daughter of his then commanding officer had been spurned for the better terms offered by George McClellan. In the heat of battle, Hill's men could be forgiven for wishing that the young lady had accepted the first offer.

In the ensuing battle, the two Southern generals lost contact and their attacks were uncoordinated. Although the result was a tactical victory for the Union army, Major General McClellan interpreted the action as proof that he was heavily outnumbered and retreated from his positions.

The following day, June 27, Lee launched his largest offensive at the Battle of Gaines's Mill. It was during this battle that Stonewall Jackson's proclivity to becoming lost was manifest and his forces did not arrive on the battlefield until late in the afternoon. The battle had been long and bloody with no obvious breakthrough by either side. McClellan again withdrew his forces and established a base at Harrison's Landing on the James River. McClellan's timidity on the battlefield has consumed the attention of historians since the Civil War. He was convinced that Lee had a force several times the size of his own and he placed the blame for his retreat on the lack of support from the War Department.

The subsequent battles were largely pushes by the Confederates and slow retreats by the Union army. The Battles of Garnett's Farm and Savage's Station on June 28 and 29 pushed the Union army across the White Oak Swamp Creek. In an attempt to cut off a Union salient, Lee ordered an all out assault that again became uncoordinated and the Battle of Glendale on June 30 did not deliver the blow that he had intended. The Union army escaped to within sight of the James River.

Both armies were preparing to annihilate the other and the miscues and communications errors of previous battles were now considered in battle planning. McClellan regrouped on Malvern Hill which was a flat plateau rising 150 feet above the surrounding swamps and accessible only from the north. McClellan opted to leave command of the battle in the hands of Fitz John Porter and spent the day on a boat in the James River.

The battle opened on July 1 with battery barrages from both armies. The Union batteries were better placed and coordinated and were able to drive off some of the Southern batteries as well as the first tentative attempts at forward infantry movements.   Again the Confederate field commanders received mixed signals and the order to attack was interpreted differently by different units. Magruder led 5,000 men in an attack that was harried by Union sharpshooters and the noise induced D. H. Hill to send his 8,200 men into the Union right flank. Both generals had assumed that a general attack had commenced only to realize too late that they were alone on the field and were decimated by the Union counter attack. The Union cannons, firing grapeshot at almost point blank range, delivered unimaginable carnage. The Southerners fought on but in piecemeal fashion rather than in a concentrated attack and the wounded soldiers walking back from the front impeded the forward progress of the new attackers.

The next day Porter sent word of his success to McClellan and appealed for an advance against the Confederates. McClellan instead ordered his army to retreat to Harrison's Landing. The poor coordination of the Confederate army resulted in heavy losses but an even more significant characteristic of battle was the imbalance between the artillery units. The Northern gun commanders were almost all West Point-trained and had battle experience. Their Southern adversaries had almost no experience and acquitted themselves very poorly. Nevertheless, McClellan was not willing or able to follow up on this success and his absence from the battlefield was noted by his men and his president.

While the Seven Days Battles resulted in 20,000 Confederate losses to 16,000 Union losses it represented an ignominious defeat for the Army of the Potomac. Unhappy with McClellan, President Lincoln decided to split the Army of the Potomac into the Army of Virginia led by Major General John Pope and the Army of the Potomac led by McClellan. A dispirited George McClellan withdrew his much-reduced army from Harrison's Landing on August 16, 1862 and moved towards Washington. The political intrigues subsequently arising from his demotion almost destroyed the Northern command structure in the Eastern Theatre.

Confederate General Lee was concerned that McClellan was going to join up with Pope in a renewed attack on Richmond from the north and decided to strike the Northern forces first. When a copy of General Lee's orders fell into Union hands (along with the plumed hat favoured by J.E.B. Stuart) he was forced to change his battle strategy and instead of crushing the Union troops between the Rapidan and Rappahannock rivers, the battlefield was once again established at Manassas Junction.

The Second Battle of Bull Run was perhaps the most controversial battle of the Civil War from the Union perspective and it took decades to unravel what went wrong. The splitting of McClellan's army resulted in many dispirited field commanders fighting under Major General Pope but remaining loyal to Major General McClellan. For his part, McClellan was not interested in a Northern success by Pope and remained on the sidelines.

The Second Battle of Bull Run

The Confederate army was organized into two wings led by Major Generals Longstreet and Jackson. With the debacle of McClellan's Peninsula Campaign, Major General John Pope was told to protect Washington, plug the entrance to the Shenandoah Valley and create a diversion to protect the forces of George McClellan from further Confederate attacks. Having proven his point, General Lee saw no need to counter a threat from McClellan and instead concentrated his forces against Pope hoping to destroy him and then McClellan. Sensing what was coming, General-in-Chief Henry Halleck ordered McClellan to start his withdrawal.

Jackson was sent by Lee on a fast moving flanking maneuver to approach Manassas Junction from the west, attack it and then retire to draw the Union forces towards him. It was a high risk strategy but Lee knew his adversary. Hostilities commenced on August 9th at the Battle of Cedar Mountain where Union forces under Nathaniel Banks were pushed back by a Confederate counter-attack under Brigadier General A. P. Hill. The two armies skirmished on the banks of the Rappahannock River and on August 27, when Pope was driven off his defensive line, the Confederates advanced to Manassas Junction, capturing the Union supply depot located there and setting the stage for a repeat of the First Battle of Bull Run. Jackson and his troops retreated to a defensive line along an abandoned railway grade which gave a good view of the battlefield. The next day Confederate artillery commenced the battle.

In one of the singular actions of the battle, a Wisconsin regiment faced the Virginian Stonewall Brigade and for two hours in the fading twilight traded volleys from a distance of 80 yards. Jackson, in understated irony, described it as "fierce and sanguinary." When Union forces advanced against Jackson his line would sag and then return in a strong counter attack. No ground was gained or lost and Pope felt that he had Jackson in a trap ready to be sprung the following morning.

Pope then sent a confusing and controversial joint order to Major Generals Porter and McDowell suggesting they attack Jackson's flanks. Assuming that Jackson's flanks were being pummeled, Pope ordered frontal assaults which met with some success but were not supported and fell back. When it became apparent that Jackson was not being attacked, Pope sent an explicit order for Porter to attack but the courier got lost and the order arrived two hours late resulting in another unsupported assault.

With considerable evidence to the contrary, Pope refused to believe that Lee's second wing under Major General Longstreet was on the battlefield and advancing from the east. Without knowing it, Pope was now the nut in the nutcracker. When he finally acceded to this development, he assumed that Longstreet's presence was intended to cover a retreat and prepared for a renewed assault. This had catastrophic results as now the Confederate forces outnumbered the Union army and had the geographical advantages. When part of Longstreet's wing fell back to a more protected position early on August 30, Pope's belief in his impending success was reinforced. Against the advice of his subordinates to move forward cautiously, Pope ordered a new offensive against the "retreating" army. His enveloping tactics were precisely what General Robert E. Lee had anticipated and as the Union troops attacked, the Confederate artillery opened up on them.

The Confederate battle plans called for a broad attack by Longstreet with support from Jackson to roll up the Union army towards Henry Hill Farm thus sweeping the field. In another inexplicably and seemingly random battleground event, the two armies were completely uncoordinated and attacked at different times. Pope was able to reinforce his Henry Hill Farm position and complete an orderly withdrawal of his army from the field. It was not the "great skedaddle" of the previous year but it was a bitter defeat nevertheless. From the Confederate perspective it was a great success but it did not achieve the overarching objective of destroying Pope's army.

The unwillingness of Major General McClellan to support Pope is one of the many controversies of the Civil War and it appears, from a letter written to his wife, that he wanted the battle to result in a Union defeat. McClellan was a proslavery Democrat who believed in limited war while Pope was a radical Republican who was antislavery and favored total war. Lincoln had moved from McClellan's position to that of Pope and approved the decision to lay waste to Northern Virginia dealing harshly with its population.

Unfortunately, this political schism began growing in the Union Army. The animosity felt by commanders loyal to McClellan towards those who wanted his removal became a political issue of consuming importance to President Lincoln and he was not free of McClellan's lingering influence until he appointed Lieutenant General Grant to the position of General-in-Chief in late 1864.

As a result of his failure, General Pope was reassigned to the west but he blamed his failure at Bull Run on Fitz John Porter. Porter had been a favorite of George McClellan and he was vocal about his unhappiness at being reassigned to the Army of Virginia under Major General Pope. His dispatches were filled with disparaging comments about what he perceived to be the inadequacies of his new commanding officer and those reading the dispatches concluded that the Army of the Potomac suffered a viral infection of political rivalries amongst its senior staff. In December 3, 1862 a court of inquiry was opened to investigate Pope's claims. In order to save his career, Irvin McDowell asserted that a Union victory was prevented by the inactivity of Porter. McDowell's career was not salvaged and Fitz John Porter was relieved of his military position and disqualified from holding any office of trust in the government of the United States.

Porter fought to restore his reputation and it was reversed in the Schofield report of 1876. In August 1886, Democratic president Grover Cleveland restored Porter's rank as of May 14, 1861. In those 25 years, the Second Battle of Bull Run was fought and re-fought in the press and in courtrooms. It is likely that his court-martial had been rendered too quickly and unjustly but Porter, by his many indiscretions and slavish dedication to Major General McClellan, did the Union Army a great disservice.

The Civil War began to be felt all across the South as Pope's actions were copied by other Northern generals and the war was taken to the civilians of the South. Confederate soldiers who were husbands and fathers now worried about their wives and daughters. Southern men trapped behind Northern lines were no longer eligible for the draft and there was increasing concern about the position of the slaves - would they remain placid or would they rise in rebellion?

After his successes in Virginia, Robert E. Lee decided that his best option was to continue north and invade the Union. He intended to feed his army of 45,000 on Northern crops and hoped that a major battlefield success would convince European nations to support the Confederate South and apply pressure on Lincoln to sue for peace. Recognizing that the newly re-instated George McClellan would not advance in strength, Lee split his forces and sent Longstreet ahead into Maryland along the Hagerstown Turnpike.

On September 11, 1861 Confederate forces under the command of Thomas Jackson approached the Union depot at Harper's Ferry, Virginia on the south bank of the Potomac River. The town was located in a deep valley and its defense relied upon controlling the hills rising 1,500 feet above it. The

Confederate army needed Harper's Ferry to secure their supply lines and when the Union garrison did not evacuate, a three day battle ensued. Skirmishing troops from Harper's Ferry met the advancing Confederates at Maryland Heights on September 12 and were able to hold their positions until September 13. Under a concentrated Confederate attack, the inexperienced New York regiment collapsed and retreated to Harper's Ferry after spiking their guns. The 14,000 man garrison remained in the town susceptible to Confederate shelling.

In an attempt to break out of the town, the Union cavalry commander, Benjamin Davis of Mississippi, led his 1,400 troopers across the river and straight into a Confederate wagon train heading north. They tricked the wagoneers into believing they were Southern soldiers and led them back to Union lines capturing 40 wagons with Longstreet's ammunition. With no casualties, it was the first cavalry success of the Army of the Potomac.

On September 15 the artillery barrage on Harper's Ferry commenced and the garrison commander refused to evacuate. When a bursting shell injured his leg, no one volunteered to take him to the hospital and it has been speculated that his death the next day was from "friendly fire." The Union garrison of 12,500 men surrendered, giving up 73 field artillery pieces and vast stores of equipment, making it the largest Union capitulation of the war. For famished and poorly equipped Confederate soldiers it was a most welcome victory.

The Battle of South Mountain occurred simultaneously with the capture of Harper's Ferry. The mountain is a continuation of Virginia's Blue Ridge Mountains and separates the Hagerstown Valley from eastern Maryland. The battle was initiated when two Union soldiers found a copy of Order 191, Robert E. Lee's battle plans for the invasion of Maryland, which had been sent to Major General D.H. Hill from his brother-in-law Stonewall Jackson. Knowing that Lee had split his army, McClellan moved into South Mountain to prevent the Confederate armies from concentrating against him. When Lee discovered the loss of his order, he reinforced the passes through the mountain to block McClellan's advance.

The battle occurred in three mountain passes and by nightfall on September 14 the Confederate lines were about to collapse. McClellan failed to push to victory the next day allowing Harper's Ferry to be taken and the Confederate army to reunite at the small town of Sharpsburg, Maryland. Once again McClellan was plagued by the belief that Lee had an army twice the size of his own and failed to take decisive action to bring the war to an end. With Lee's forces split there is little doubt that the much larger Union army could have won a total victory.

The Battle of Antietam

The Battle of Antietam lasted a single day and resulted in the bloodiest day of fighting in US history, eclipsing even the losses of the D-Day landing in Normandy.

Lee arrived at Sharpsburg with only 18,000 troops and, had McClellan attacked in force, the Civil War would have been brought to an early conclusion. As it was, McClellan did not move his divisions until the evening of September 16 by which time Lee received reinforcements from Major General Longstreet and was able to consolidate his defenses. The Northern attack, when it came on September 17, was uncoordinated. McClellan had not briefed his subordinates and as field commanders fell their replacements did not know the plan of battle.

General Lee positioned his troops along the Hagerstown turnpike which was situated on a low plateau above the small community. It was separated from the advancing Union forces by the broad (80 to 100 feet) but shallow Antietam Creek over which there were 3 bridges and several fords. While Lee's position allowed for adequate defenses it was not difficult to outflank from either the north or the south and the only escape across the Potomac was to the south at Boteler's Ford.

The top of the plateau was comprised of dense bush which opened into a corn field flanked by the Hagerstown Turnpike.

At the south end of the cornfield was a small Dunker church which became the focus of the first phase of the battle. From 6 a.m. until after 10 a.m. the battle was waged over the cornfield in a titanic struggle between Northern commander Joseph Hooker and Southern commander Thomas Jackson. Possession of the field changed hands 15 times with the dead of both sides piled in windrows, falling either to canister or minnie balls. The Northern troops did eventually make it to the Dunker Church and threatened the Confederate center. The advance was not supported, however, and they were forced to retreat taking high casualties. Many consider the fight over the cornfield to have been the most horrific slaughter of the Civil War and that is saying a great ghastly lot. When the rifles finally fell silent on this phase of the battle nothing had been gained by either side and a total of 13,000 men were dead, dying or captured.

The second phase of the battle commenced at about 9:30 a.m. and involved a frontal assault on the Confederate line on the east-facing slope rising from Antietam creek. The Confederate troops were positioned in a wagon trail worn into the side of the hill and which provided a well-protected defensive position from which they fired down upon the attacking Union soldiers. Multiple attacks were made against this track which came to be known as "Bloody Lane" and each time the Union troops were forced to retreat with massive casualties. In one attack, the Irish Brigade approached under emerald standards as their chaplain shouted out the final unction from which 540

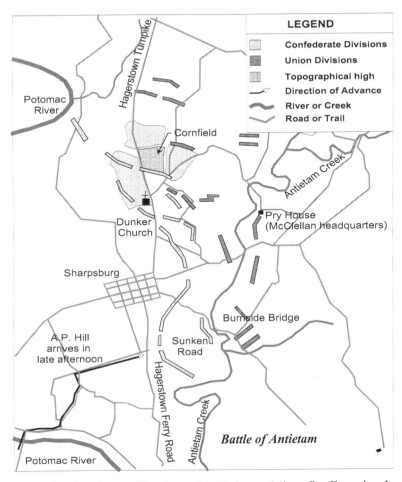

Battle of Antietam

men gained an immediate benefit. Union soldiers finally gained control of a position which allowed enfilading fire into the Bloody Lane and the defensive position was immediately turned into a slaughter pit. McClellan opted not to support the resulting breech in the Confederate center and another opportunity to destroy Lee's army was lost.

In the final phase of the battle, four Union divisions totaling 12,500 men and 50 field guns were to cross Antietam Creek to the south of Sharpsburg and flank the Confederate line rolling it towards the north. Demonstrating an astonishing lack of creativity, Major General Ambrose Burnside insisted on crossing over a stone bridge thus funneling his men into a concentrated mass rather than wading across in a well-spaced, diffused line. The Confederate soldiers were positioned above the bridge on steep slopes overlooking the exposed Northern troops struggling to cross. It was an ideal defensive position.

Shortly after noon, the Union armies blasted their way across the bridge with artillery support and created a salient on the far side. Other troops had finally crossed at a ford a mile downstream and the Confederate defenders, with their ammunition running low, began to retreat from their positions. Rather than attack immediately, Burnside paused for two hours to replenish ammunition. The Union attack finally drove the panicking Southern soldiers north into the streets of Sharpsburg but the Confederates brought in fresh soldiers and counter attacked at 3:30 p.m. A combination of untrained soldiers, confusion caused by Confederate soldiers wearing Union uniforms taken from Harper's Ferry and exhaustion from heat and exertion resulted in a rout of the unsupported Union forces and, as some of them returned to the bridge, Burnside ordered a general withdrawal until he could obtain reinforcements. McClellan chose to not support Burnside and the advance was lost.

General Lee anticipated renewed attacks the following day but the ever cautious McClellan, fearing a massive Confederate counter-attack, did nothing. The two armies collected their dead and wounded and Lee straggled unimpeded back to Virginia. General Lee's foray onto Union territory had been a disaster and his army of 45,000 was now reduced to 30,000. McClellan, by not pursuing the Confederate forces, missed yet another opportunity to end the war.

President Lincoln declared the Battle of Antietam to be a Union victory and on September 22 used the occasion to announce the Emancipation Proclamation. Lincoln said that the war was killing slavery by "*friction and abrasion*" and as more slaves became free it became increasingly difficult to maintain slavery in any of the states, Confederate or Union. The Proclamation was received joyously by abolitionists, accepted by Republicans, and opposed vehemently by Democrats.

In the midterm elections of 1862 Lincoln was attacked for being inexperienced and incompetent – attributes, it was argued, which allowed the war to continue long past a reasonable conclusion. McClellan, with an eye to his post-military career, advertised his view that Lincoln had undermined his ability to conquer Virginia. The Democrats, in giving the English language the word "miscegenation," argued that freeing slaves would result in unfair labor competition and the mixing of the races would result in a weakening of intellectual feedstock. They made large gains in the elections and controlled the legislatures of five states formerly Republican. Lincoln, astonished at McClellan's continued insistence on more troops, removed him from command on November 7 following the elections and McClellan never commanded another army.

For all his lethargy on the field, the removal of McClellan from command infuriated the Army of the Potomac and the lamentations over his removal were both long and loud. He could, had he wished it, have turned the army around and marched it against Washington. But he didn't wish it and it was "admirable self-denial." George Brinton McClellan remains one of the most enigmatic of the Civil War leaders and Robert E. Lee was right when, years after the war, he named McClellan as his most competent adversary.

The Emancipation Proclamation must be viewed as a shrewd political document rather than as a moral statement. It had the effect of freeing slaves only in Confederate-held territory which, in turn, meant that European support for the Confederate cause was tantamount to an acceptance of slavery and the re-enslavement of those who had been freed. However much European politicians and newspaper columnists might wish to support the South, their populations would not allow it. By not freeing slaves in the border states, Lincoln was able to maintain their support for the Union cause. Most importantly, the proclamation injected moral clarity onto the battlefield. Many Northern soldiers were unhappy with this turn of events but most felt the awful losses were now justified by a higher cause. Rather than lose his army, Lincoln had consolidated its support and his bet paid out.

***

Like Confederate President Davis, Lincoln was convinced that Kentucky was strategic to success. It had become a battle-ground during the slave debates of the antebellum period and both sides rushed troops into Kentucky at the outbreak of the war. While it never seceded from the Union, the Confederates considered it a Southern state and included the star of Kentucky on their flag. When the Confederate troops under Albert Sydney Johnston retreated from Kentucky earlier in the year, it was with a view to eventually returning. In July a Southern cavalry raid into Kentucky was well supported by the local population and Colonel John Hunt Morgan, who led the raid, was confident that 25,000 men from Kentucky would join the Confederate army if invited.

In order to issue this invitation, the Confederate armies of Kirby Smith and Braxton Bragg planned to combine and defeat the Union army of Don Carlos Buell. The Confederates would then march into Kentucky and place the state under the Confed-erate flag. If Major General Grant attempted to reinforce Buell he would be defeated before leaving Mississippi. The plan was bold and required careful coordination between geographically separated armies that did not have a unified command. Civil War plans often had a short shelf life and this one immediately disintegrated when Kirby Smith decided to take Kentucky alone thus garnering the unadulterated praise of the Confederacy. On August 27 he reached Lexington, Kentucky as Bragg moved out of Chattanooga, Tennessee. Buell immediately set out to protect the Union-controlled city of Louisville, Kentucky.

In order to prevent Major General Ulysses S. Grant from joining Buell, the Confederate Army of West Tennessee under Major General Earl Van Dorn was sent to intercept Grant at Iuka, Mississippi. The army of Major General William Rosecrans was consequently ordered to converge on Iuka in order to support Grant.

The Battles of Iuka and Chaplin Hills

The two Northern generals decided that when Rosecrans engaged the enemy, the other units would engage upon hearing the sounds of the battle. At 4:30 p.m. on September 19, Rosecrans closed with Confederate units who overran the Union position and captured a 6 gun battery. Due to an atmospheric effect called an "acoustic shadow" none of the other Union divisions heard the noise from the raging battle and did not enter the field. When they were made aware of the fighting they closed ranks and prepared for a subsequent battle the next day. The Confederates however had retreated during the night.

Bragg, meanwhile, made a strategic decision to reinforce Smith at Lexington rather than continue towards Louisville.

This allowed Buell unimpeded access to Louisville and once there he replenished his supplies and inducted thousands of new recruits into his army. His enlarged army met the Confederates at Perryville (Chaplin Hills) and preliminary action commenced on October 7 for control of the small town and its valuable water supplies. The first shots were fired early on October 8 when the newly promoted Brigadier General Philip Sheridan was dispatched to ensure that Union armies controlled a small, stagnant pool in a dried-up creek bed. The Confederate attack began later that afternoon following an artillery barrage. As at Iuka, an acoustic shadow prevented the sounds of the battle from reaching Buell's headquarters and he was unaware of the fighting until the evening. The first attack was repulsed but the second moved the Union line beyond its batteries and six of twelve Union guns were captured. The Union army formed a new line on a parallel ridge and the Confederates, in three bloody assaults, were unable to dislodge them. At one point in the action Confederate Brigadier General Leonidas Polk rode out to see who was firing on his men and ran into a Union regiment. He saved himself by racing down the line pretending to be a Northern general and calling for the men to stop firing.

The Battle of Chaplin Hills was a tactical win for Bragg but it exposed his precarious position. With no expectation of a large intake of new recruits and no logistical support, he decided to retreat out of Kentucky to Knoxville, Tennessee. Bragg was sharply criticized for his conduct during the campaign and his command was severely compromised but President Davis decided to leave him in place. Don Carlos Buell returned to Nashville rather than pursuing Bragg and was demoted for this dereliction when the armies of the Western Theatre were reorganized.

***

McClellan's replacement in the East was Major General Ambrose Burnside who unwillingly accepted the assignment. Burnside was devoted to McClellan and, by his own admission, was not a decisive battlefield general and had never led an army into battle. Under pressure to take to the field he planned to make a feint towards Culpeper Court House and then, assuming that Lee would be frozen by uncertainty, move to Fredericksburg and from there use the railroad to advance against Richmond. The plan was hotly contested and finally approved by Lincoln with the condition that he move with all haste.

The Battle of Fredericksburg

On November 17, with the onset of winter rains, Burnside delayed his attack to await the arrival of pontoon bridges, fearing that by advancing part of his army across the Rappahannock he risked it being cut off by rising waters. The delay destroyed any hope of surprise and by November 21 both Jackson and Longstreet were moving their men into place at Fredericksburg. Ignoring his original plan, Burnside assembled his troops directly across the river from the town and ringed the hills behind them with 220 field guns. He was certain that he could drive out the Confederate soldiers protecting the town and, with superior numbers, destroy Lee's army gathered on the hills above.

A small team of Union skirmishers was sent across the river in boats to clear the town and create a beachhead. The looting of the town by these Union soldiers infuriated the Confederates and contributed to the subsequent vigor of their fighting. By December 13, Burnside had moved his army into Fredericksburg and was ready to launch his attack. What had started out as a surprise move based on a tactical feint had become a set-piece battle with Lee enjoying all the advantages of fighting from a defensive position located on the high ground.

The assaults began at 11 a.m. and to engage the Confederate line, Union soldiers had to cross a drainage ditch and move 400 yards across an open field that was dominated from the heights by Confederate artillery and infantry who were dug in behind a sunken road and stone wall at the crest of a hill known as Marye's Heights. Union artillery from across the river were hampered, in the opening stages, from engaging their Confederate counterparts by a thick fog. In all, sixteen assaults were hurled at the Confederate line on Marye's Heights with 8,000 Union casualties. Watching the carnage from the center of the Confederate line, General Lee famously observed,

"It is well that war is so terrible, or we should grow too fond of it."

Burnside was finally convinced that the assaults were futile and the fighting ended as darkness approached. Many of the Union soldiers who were injured or pinned down during the assaults spent a cold night on the exposed field and, in the morning, Burnside considered personally leading another assault. Fortunately he was talked out of it and instead sued for a truce in order to retrieve the dead and wounded. The Union army then moved back across the Rappahannock and the campaign came to an end. Burnside lost 12,600 casualties to Lee's 5,400 and a month later, following the "Mud March" - a disastrous attempt to penetrate into Virginia on impassable roads - lost his command.

Marye's Heights saw more than just carnage on December 13. In an overwhelming display of moral courage and generosity of spirit, South Carolina Sergeant Richard Kirkland continually left the safety of the rock wall to provide water to the injured Union soldiers whose cries so piteously appealed to the "angels of his better nature." Union soldiers ceased their fire when it became obvious what he was doing. For this, Kirkland won his place in history as the "Angel of Marye's Heights."

Predictably, the South was enormously buoyed by the victory and success once more seemed within reach. In the North, a despondent President Lincoln concluded, *"If there is a worse place than hell, I am in it."*

***

Following the Battle of Chaplin Hills, Confederate Braxton Bragg retreated to Chattanooga, Tennessee and then to Murfreesboro where he joined the army of Kirby Smith in a defensive position on the banks of Stones River. The Confederate strength was reduced to 30,000 soldiers when 7,500 men were dispatched on December 16 to assist in the defense of Vicksburg. Bragg continued to have significant morale problems due to complaints from his subordinates who wanted him replaced. Once again President Davis evaluated the situation and decided to take no action.

For his sluggish action, Don Carlos Buell was replaced by Major General William Rosecrans who was instructed to move quickly against Bragg in eastern Tennessee. Rosecrans re-equipped and trained his army before setting off after Bragg and arrived at Stones River on December 29 after being harassed by Bragg's cavalry who had circumnavigated the Union army capturing 4 wagon trains and taking 1,000 prisoners.

Battle of Stones River

During the night the two armies, camped within 800 yards of each other, started a "battle of the bands" and soldiers from both sides were treated to a different kind of war. The "battle" ended with one band playing Home Sweet Home and both armies nostalgically sang together across the battlefield. The bonhomie of the moment was lost in a very few hours.

Having still not learned from Fort Donelson and Shiloh, the Northern army was completing its breakfast when the Confederates slammed into their right flank hoping to turn it and begin the roll up. Perhaps the only Union commander to learn from mistakes was newly promoted Major General Philip Sheridan who placed his men on the line at 4 a.m. and prepared them for the attack. His men were able to repel the first three assaults but when both his flanks were attacked simultaneously they began to fall back. Their stand was an expensive one in which all three brigade commanders were killed and casualties in a cedar forest known as the "Slaughter Pen" were 33 percent. By 10 a.m. the Confederates had taken 3,000 prisoners and 28 field guns.

The Union line, re-formed behind and roughly parallel to their original position, was strengthened as Rosecrans plugged holes and rallied his troops. In the afternoon the Union army repulsed all subsequent attacks and the fight ended by 4:30 p.m. Bragg's battlefield tactics had worked at cross-purposes to his primary objective. Instead of exposing the Union supply line he drove the Union line back onto it. New Years Day 1863 was quiet and Rosecrans used the time to prepare for the next assault which came at 4 p.m. on January 2. The Confederates drove the Union line back while exposing themselves to the Union artillery which opened fire and decimated the Confederate ranks. The Union counter-attack was successful and when reinforcements arrived on January 3 the Confederate center was driven back. Believing that more Union reinforcements were coming Bragg retreated and moved south unimpeded by Rosecrans. Following the disaster at Fredericksburg, this tactical Union victory was important to Northern morale and Rosecrans was recognized by the White House for having consolidated central Tennessee. Extensive defensive fortifications were built around the town of Murfreesboro and it served as a Union supply depot for the remainder of the war.

As the effects of the war became personal to towns across the North and South, civilian opposition began to mount. The cost of the war escalated dramatically and the Southern economy teetered on bankruptcy. In the North, peace demonstrations and anger over emancipation led to rioting. Both presidents found it difficult to replace their fallen and by the end of 1863 it was finally understood that war is never glorious.

Major Battles of the Western Theatre

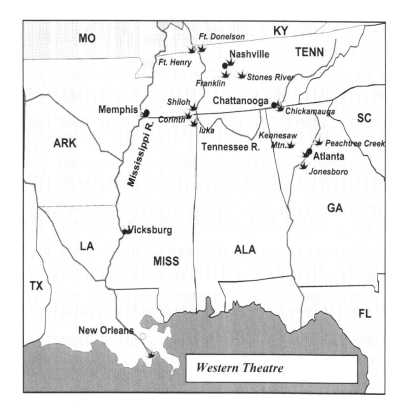

6: Union Leaders of the Civil War

Wars are remembered for the leaders who took their men into battle and, except for displays of outstanding valor, little attention is paid to those with ranks below general. Many good stories are lost in this bit of necessary discrimination but history is the story of the 5 percent. It is also true that the outcome of battles is most often determined by the skill and creativity of those who lead and what follows is intended to provide a glimpse into the lives of some of the men who led the Union forces during the Civil War.

And there were many significant men in this war. For example, the youngest man to be elevated to brigadier general was Goluder Pennypacker who was promoted at the age of 20 years and 8 months. Five of the Northern generals went on to become presidents of the United States; Andrew Johnson, Ulysses S. Grant, James Garfield, Rutherford Hayes and Benjamin Harrison. There was a density of leadership talent generated by the Civil War in both the South and the North that, disputably, has never been seen since.

Abraham Lincoln (February 12, 1809 – April 15, 1865)

Abraham Lincoln was born in Kentucky on February 12, 1809 in a one-room log cabin on his father's 348-acre farm. He

was never close to his father and, with his mother's death, was raised by his affectionate step-mother, Sarah Bush Johnston.

The family moved from Kentucky as a result of errors in land registration and the young Lincoln made a living cutting fence rails, operating a flatboat on the Mississippi River, managing a store and surveying land parcels. All of these experiences would have seminal impacts on his future political career. He served as a militia captain during the Black Hawk Indian war and finally won election to the Illinois State Legislature in 1834.

From an early age Abraham Lincoln demonstrated significant drive and intelligence. He taught himself geometry and worked as a surveyor. With no formal education he became conversant with the classics of the English language and was admitted to the Illinois bar in 1837. He dispensed wisdom with a backwoods accent and in the form of humorous, rural anecdotes. At six feet four inches tall, he was a capable boxer if somewhat ungainly in his deportment.

In 1842 he married Mary Todd who came from a slave-owning Kentucky family and they had four sons, Robert, Eddie, Willie and Thomas. Eddie died at age 3 of diphtheria and

Willie, perhaps the most like his father, died at age 11 during the first year of Lincoln's presidency. Robert, the eldest, was never close to his father but faithfully fulfilled his duty to preserve his father's memory following his assassination. Thomas, named after Lincoln's father, was nicknamed "Tad" at birth due to his unnaturally large head. He lived until he was 19.

Lincoln's political career was stalled due to his vigorous arguments against the war with Mexico and throughout the 1840's he developed his prospering legal practice in Springfield, Illinois. In 1846 he served a single term in the House of Representatives as a Whig but it was in 1854 that Abraham Lincoln began to find his political voice. His opponent was Democratic Senator Stephen A. Douglas and the campaign produced the first of many riveting debates between these two men.

Douglas held to the Popular Sovereignty argument that democracy and subsidiarity demand that people have the right to determine their own path with respect to slavery and that such a decision does not rightfully rest with a legislature. In his Peoria speech of October 16, 1854, Lincoln launched his salvo as perhaps the pre-eminent proponent of the Free Soil position.

"The Act has a declared indifference, but as I must think, covert real zeal for the spread of slavery, I cannot but hate it. I hate it because of the monstrous injustice of slavery itself. I hate it because it deprives our republican example of

its just influence in the world — enables the enemies of free institutions, with plausibility, to taunt us as hypocrites — causes the real friends of freedom to doubt our sincerity, and especially because it forces so many really good men amongst ourselves into an open war with the very fundamental principles of civil liberty — criticizing the Declaration of Independence, and insisting that there is no right principle of action but self-interest."

The mid-term elections of 1858 again pitted Lincoln against Douglas in a series of debates which became the platform of Lincoln's 1860 presidential campaign. Although the fledgling Republican Party of Illinois did not win any seats, it did gain more votes than the Democrats and Lincoln was transformed into a national politician. In what was to become a typical reaction to this "backwoods bumpkin," Lincoln shocked the New York audience at his Cooper Union speech in 1860 by his shabby appearance and heavily accented pronunciation. The elites of yesterday were no different in their social prejudices than they are today. But the erudition and wisdom of Lincoln, coupled with his ability to explain difficult concepts in accessible language identified him as the intellectual leader of the Republican Party and its best speaker.

By the time of his inauguration in March 1861, President Lincoln faced assassination plots and a Union from which 7 states had already seceded. Eventually, eleven states would secede and elect Jefferson Davis as their President. The border states of Missouri, Kentucky, Maryland and Delaware did not secede even though they practiced slavery and Lincoln refused to interfere with their internal politics.

Managing the affairs of state and quelling a civil war was not an easy assignment. Mr. Lincoln was opposed on one side by the Radical Republicans of his own party who wanted immediate abolition of slavery and on the other by anti-war Peace Democrats, known as "Copperheads" who wanted to negotiate a peace with the Confederates. In order to silence those Copperheads who incited insurrection, Lincoln suspended habeas corpus and arrested many, including Ohio Democrat, Clement Vallandigham.

President Lincoln had never hidden his views on slavery and felt strongly that it was morally and economically wrong but nor was he a strong abolitionist. He felt that the best route out of the slavery morass was to respect property rights by purchasing the freedom of the slaves and sending them to their own colony. The British abolitionists maintained contacts with the ex-slave colony of Haiti and established a colony at Free-town in Sierra Leone. The Americans developed their colony in Liberia.

As a result of his personal views and the ambivalence in the North regarding the issue of slavery, Lincoln began the Civil War with the sole purpose of retaining the continental integrity of the Union. How, he argued, could one nation, forged in battle, separate and occupy the land as two distinct peoples? As the war dragged on and the reality of slavery was seen by more

Northern soldiers, the Great Cause of the Union was broadened to include the end of slavery. By the summer of 1862, Lincoln had decided to issue the Emancipation Proclamation but was cautioned by his cabinet to await a military victory which came in September near Sharpesburg, Maryland. It was unclear how the Union army would react to the Proclamation and so it was written as a purely political document and issued on January 1, 1863. Its final objective, the emancipation of all the slaves, was finally achieved in February 1865 with the passage of the Thirteenth Amendment.

President Lincoln's strong attachment to his army was legendary but his relationship with his generals was often less than cordial. He cycled through 6 generals (one of them twice) in the Eastern Theatre before he found Ulysses S. Grant, the man who would bring him the victory he was so desperate to achieve. Perhaps Lincoln's horror at the war and his respect for those who fought in it is best summarized in his Gettysburg Address of November 19, 1863;

> *"Four score and seven years ago our fathers brought forth on this continent a new nation, conceived in Liberty, and dedicated to the proposition that all men are created equal.*
>
> *Now we are engaged in a great civil war, testing whether that nation, or any nation, so conceived and so dedicated, can long endure. We are met on a great battle-field of that war. We have come to dedicate a portion of that field, as a final resting place for those who here gave their lives that*

that nation might live. It is altogether fitting and proper that we should do this.

But, in a larger sense, we can not dedicate—we can not consecrate—we can not hallow—this ground. The brave men, living and dead, who struggled here, have consecrated it, far above our poor power to add or detract. The world will little note, nor long remember what we say here, but it can never forget what they did here. It is for us the living, rather, to be dedicated here to the unfinished work which they who fought here have thus far so nobly advanced. It is rather for us to be here dedicated to the great task remaining before us—that from these honored dead we take increased devotion to that cause for which they gave the last full measure of devotion—that we here highly resolve that these dead shall not have died in vain—that this nation, under God, shall have a new birth of freedom—and that government of the people, by the people, for the people, shall not perish from the earth."

It is altogether typical of the low regard with which President Lincoln was held by many that the invitation for him to speak came as an afterthought. In his address, Lincoln defined 1776 as the birth of the United States and demonstrated that its founding document was a moral declaration rather than a political constitution. The main speaker of the day was the noted orator, Edward Everett, who recognized Lincoln's genius, declaring that the President had more accurately captured the spirit of the day in five minutes than he had in two hours.

By late 1863, over 250,000 Union soldiers were in cemeteries and anti-war sentiment spilled over into anger for the president who had "brought the country to ruin." President Lincoln was re-elected to lead the Republican ticket in the election of 1864 but he had to overcome the conspiracy of his Treasury Secretary, Salmon P. Chase, and the misgivings of many in his party who feared he could not win. Indeed by September 1864, Lincoln himself felt that he would certainly lose and prepared a strategy to win the war prior to the inauguration of a new president in March 1865.

> *"This morning, as for some days past, it seems exceedingly probable that this Administration will not be re-elected. Then it will be my duty to so co-operate with the President elect, as to save the Union between the election and the inauguration; as he will have secured his election on such ground that he cannot possibly save it afterwards."*

And then General Sherman captured Atlanta bringing the end of the war within sight. Lincoln won the election over Democratic candidate, George Brinton McClellan, the former commander of the Army of the Potomac. He gained particular pleasure in capturing almost 80 percent of the votes of the Northern soldiers. Preservation of the Union and freedom of the slaves had become the reasons to fight and no one represented those ideals better than the tall lawyer from Illinois. It is best expressed in the words of his second inaugural address;

> *Fondly do we hope — fervently do we pray — that this mighty scourge of war may speedily pass away. Yet, if God wills that it continue, until all the wealth piled by the bondman's two hundred and fifty years of unrequited toil shall be*

sunk, and until every drop of blood drawn with the lash, shall be paid by another drawn with the sword, as was said three thousand years ago, so still it must be said "the judgments of the Lord, are true and righteous altogether." With malice toward none; with charity for all; with firmness in the right, as God gives us to see the right, let us strive on to finish the work we are in; to bind up the nation's wounds; to care for him who shall have borne the battle, and for his widow, and his orphan — to do all which may achieve and cherish a just and lasting peace, among ourselves, and with all nations.

President Lincoln is correctly recognized as the "War President" who saved the Union but few recognize that nation building continued in the midst of war and that his government was responsible for much more than the guidance of armies. In 1862 he enacted the Homestead Act making millions of acres of government-held land in the West available for purchase at low cost. Also in that year the Morrill Land-Grant Colleges Act provided government grants for agricultural universities in each state. The Pacific Railway Acts of 1862 and 1864 granted federal support for the construction of the First Transcontinental Railroad which was completed in 1869. The National Banking Acts of 1863, 1864, and 1865 created a system of national banks. And the Legal Tender Act established the first paper currency in United States. Also the final Thursday in November was declared to be a day of thanksgiving.

On Good Friday, April 14, 1865 Lincoln and his wife attended the play "Our American Cousin" at Ford's Theatre. It had been a hectic time following the surrender of General Lee's Army of Northern Virginia. The president was working on plans for the reunification and reconstruction of the South anticipating difficult negotiations with Congress. John Wilkes Booth, a failed soldier and mediocre actor who, disheartened by the loss of the Confederacy and wanting to finally do something heroic in his life, slipped into the Lincoln box and fired a 0.44 caliber derringer at point blank range into the back of the president's head. He briefly fought Major Henry Rathbone who was also in the box before jumping onto the stage calling out "Sic semper tyrannus" (So shall it be to tyrants), Thomas Jefferson's motto for the State of Virginia. He escaped the stunned crowd on a broken leg and was captured in a Virginia barn on April 26, 1865 dying within hours of wounds received during his capture.

President Lincoln never regained consciousness and died at 7:22 a.m., April 15, 1865.

Ulysses S. Grant
(Hiram Ulysses Grant, April 27, 1822 – July 23, 1885)

Born in a log cabin at Point Pleasant, Ohio, and the eldest of six children. Grant wrote his name as Ulysses Hiram Grant to avoid being saddled with the acronym "HUG." Boys have not changed much over the years. At age 17 he entered the US Military Academy at West Point, New York with registration papers incorrectly giving his name as Ulysses S. Grant and, for want of a middle name, he was known by his classmates as 'Sam'.

He graduated in 1843 and, though noted for his equestrian capabilities, was assigned to a quartermaster role upon graduation. He served in this capacity in the Mexican-American War and saw limited action. His sudden resignation from the army on July 21, 1854 was the subject of much speculation and some concluded that he resigned for being drunk on duty; an accusation which later damaged his military career. Others suggested that separation from his wife prompted his resignation.

He spent the next 7 years of civilian life scrambling unsuccessfully to make a living. He eventually went to work with his younger brother in Galena, Illinois and when war broke out he re-enlisted and was appointed brigadier general of a militia unit. In August of that year the commander of the Union forces in the Western Theatre, Major General John C. Fremont appointed him to command the forces of southeast Missouri.

His prowess as a commander who could coordinate naval and army attacks was demonstrated three months later with the capture of Fort Henry on the Tennessee River and Fort Donelson on the Cumberland River. It was at Fort Donelson that he first demonstrated his almost inhuman calm in the face of grave danger by counterattacking the surging Confederate units. This quiet determination was to become his most noted quality. It was here as well that he demanded of his former classmate, Confederate Major General Buckner "no terms except unconditional and immediate surrender." Thus was born the mythology of General U.S. "Unconditional Surrender" Grant. With the surrender of 12,000 Confederate troops, Grant was lauded in the northern press. With the laurels came cigars from well wishers – and likely the throat cancer which would take his life.

Success, of course, breeds envy and perhaps it was envy that caused the problems between Grant and his superior, Major General Henry Halleck. Halleck believed the rumours of Grant's drinking and removed him from command only to restore it at the urging of President Lincoln. His Army of West Tennessee became the Army of the Tennessee, units of which eventually pushed across Tennessee into northern Mississippi to Atlanta, Georgia and finally to North Carolina. On April 6, 1862, however, it suffered a significant setback at the Battle of Shiloh when the Confederate army of Albert Sidney Johnston and P.G.T. Beauregard made a surprise attack at Pittsburg Landing, Tennessee. The first day of the battle, which saw the death of the popular Johnston, was a rout of the Federal troops who were pinned on the bank of the river. In response to William Tecumseh Sherman's comment on the difficulties of the day, Grant laconically drew on his cigar and replied,

"Yes. Lick 'em tomorrow, though."

Emboldened with reinforcements from Don Carlos Buell, Grant ordered a charge the next day and drove the Confederates back to Corinth, Mississippi. However, his huge losses were due to poor defensive preparation and General Halleck relegated Grant to an administrative position. His close friend William Tecumseh Sherman convinced him to remain in the army in hopes of finding another opening. In July 1862, the opening presented itself when Halleck was recalled to Washington to take command of all the Union armies leaving Grant to command the Army of the Tennessee once again.

During the winter of 1862/63 Grant pressed the siege of Vicksburg, Mississippi. In one of the most brilliant and original campaigns of the war he avoided the Confederate guns by floating past them during the night and then took his army on an unsupported and fast-moving, destructive campaign to the south and east of Vicksburg before turning back and cutting the rail lines to the city. The speed of Grant's army did not allow Confederate Major General John C. Pemberton to mass his forces for a battle. The Southern army retreated into Vicksburg and suffered a 6 week siege with no outside relief. Grant took the city on July 4, 1863 and split the Confederacy in two – the same day that Union Major General Meade defeated General Robert E. Lee at Gettysburg. In assessing Grant's defeat of Vicksburg and Meade's failure to crush Lee's Army of North Virginia, Lincoln said,

"Grant is my man and I am his, for the rest of the War."

When Grant was given the expanded command of the Military Division of Mississippi he immediately replaced the overly cautious William Rosecrans with Major General George Thomas, the "Rock of Chickamauga" and came to Chattanooga to lead the breakout of the city. The two day battle was to witness an almost leaderless Union success as the Confederate forces were driven back by the sheer enthusiasm of the charging Northerners.

On March 12, 1864, Grant replaced Major General Halleck as general-in-chief of all the Union armies and was promoted to the rank of Lieutenant General, the first such person to hold the rank since George Washington. Recognizing the poisonous atmosphere of an over-politicized Washington, Grant moved his office into a tent and traveled with the Army of the Potomac commanded by General George Meade whose resignation letter was not accepted. Less than two months later Grant crossed the Rapidan and opened the final stages of the Civil War with the Battle of the Wilderness on May 4, 1864. The two day battle, bloody and without a conclusion, left the Union troops demoralized and expecting a pull-back to Washington. To their delight and surprise they were ordered to move forward in what would become a regular "flanking to the left" maneuver which finally brought them to the outskirts of Petersburg, Virginia. The two sides mauled each other at Spotsylvania (May 8-22), Cold Harbour (June 3) and finally fought to a draw at Peters-

burg. In the first three encounters Lee had successfully anticipated Grant's move and was well dug in by the time the Union
soldiers arrived. However, Grant arrived at Petersburg 3 days
before Lee and, were it not for an overcautious campaign,
Petersburg and Richmond would have been taken.

By April 1865, with Sherman moving north and leaving a
path of destruction through Georgia and the Carolinas and no
hope of a breakout battle, General Lee advised the cabinet to
move out of Richmond while he and his army made a dash for
the Blue Ridge Mountains anticipating a prolonged guerrilla
campaign. Grant anticipated the move and captured Lee's
Confederate forces near Appomattox Court House on April 9,
1865.

The exultation of Northern success was soon overwhelmed
by grief over the assassination of President Lincoln only 5 days
later. Grant wept openly at the news and was a pallbearer at the
state funeral. He refused overtures by President Andrew
Johnson to replace Edwin Stanton as Secretary of War choosing
to remain with the military. In 1868 he was able to leverage his
war hero status and defeated Horatio Seymour for the presidency under the slogan, "Let us have peace." He won a second
term, defeating Horace Greely, again leveraging his Civil War
credentials.

Grant took a position of benign neglect with respect to Reconstruction and worked to improve the civil rights of the freed

slaves confronting the apathy of the North and the violence of the Ku Klux Klan. He created the first national park (Yellowstone) and made Christmas a national holiday. In economics he ratified the use of the greenback as the official currency and guaranteed its value in gold. It can only be wistfully remembered that he dealt with the 1874 Wall Street crisis by refusing to print money. His two terms are remembered for their scandals; the first occurring when his administration was convinced to underwrite a scheme that would unwittingly allow Wall Street icons Jay Gould and James Fisk to corner the market on gold. When the details of the scheme were revealed, Grant sold gold onto the market thus destroying the scheme and the men behind it. The Whisky Ring embezzlement scandal of 1875 was mishandled and the theft of $3 million from the treasury did not result in prison time for anyone involved.

In 1881, at the urging of his son, Grant became a partner in a New York investment bank. In a move reminiscent of more current events, Grant was swindled by his partner and saddled with a bankrupt firm. His destitution was compounded when he learned that he suffered from throat cancer. Determined to leave a financial legacy to his family, Grant began to write articles on the Civil War and was offered a contract by Mark Twain to write his memoirs. Grant died on July 23, 1885 days after completing his manuscript and his family received over $450,000 in royalties from the 300,000 books sold.

Perhaps the best summary of Ulysses S. Grant was Lincoln's laconic summation when he was urged to replace Grant following the debacle at Shiloh, *"I can't spare this man. He fights."*

The total war doctrine of Lincoln, Grant and Sherman has been revisited in every major armed confrontation and was implicit in the decisions to bomb civilian centers in England, Germany and Japan during the Second World War. However one judges the prudence of Grant's Civil War strategy, what cannot be in dispute is his ability to evaluate a battlefield and place his divisions to best effect. And when that was not enough he doggedly tried again the next day until he found the combination that would give success to his armies. Ulysses S. Grant liked to win.

Don Carlos Buell (March 23, 1818 – November 19, 1898)

Don Carlos Buell, of Lowell, Ohio, graduated from the US Military Academy in 1841 and was recognized for bravery during the Mexican-American War under the command of Zachary Taylor and Winfield Scott. Prior to the Civil War he served in California.

As a brigadier general he was

given command of the Department of the Ohio with responsibility for eastern Tennessee. While the Confederate army was occupied fighting Brigadier General Ulysses S. Grant at Forts Henry and Donelson, Buell moved west and captured Nashville on February 25, 1862.

Buell arrived at Pittsburgh Landing during the night following the first disastrous day of fighting at the Battle of Shiloh and his reinforcements allowed Grant to carry the field on April 7, 1862. He fought for Major General Halleck at Corinth, Mississippi and then moved slowly north to capture Chattanooga. However, his exposed supply lines were disrupted by the Confederate cavalry commanded by Nathan Bedford Forrest and the advance was halted.

Don Carlos Buell, as a slaveholder, was often under suspicion of being a Confederate sympathizer. This suspicion was not alleviated by his enforced policy of respecting the rights of civilians. When Union soldiers rampaged in the town of Athens, Alabama, Buell disciplined their commander and his subordinates petitioned to have him removed from command. A reluctant President Lincoln ordered that he be replaced by Major General George Thomas who, in an act of solidarity, refused the assignment.

Buell then moved to stop the advance of Confederate forces under Braxton Bragg in Kentucky. The ensuing Battle of Perryville ended the Confederate advance but Buell's lack of pursuit of the retreating Rebels resulted in his being replaced by Major General William Rosecrans. Buell was stationed in Indianapolis hoping for a new command and, when that command never came, he resigned his commission on May 23, 1864.

Following the war Buell became president of an iron foundry in Kentucky and served as a pension agent for the government from 1885 to 1889. He died at his home in Kentucky on November 19, 1898.

Ambrose Everett Burnside
(May 23, 1824 – September 13, 1881)

Burnside, one of 9 children, was raised in Liberty, Indiana, and when his mother died he quit school to take a trade. In 1843 he entered the US Military Academy graduating in 1847. He fought briefly in the Mexican-American War and then served under Captain Braxton Bragg to protect the mail routes between Nevada and California from hostile Indians. In 1852 he took command of Fort Adams at Newport, Rhode Island.

He resigned his commission in 1853 in order to work on the development of the Burnside carbine under contract to the army. Unfortunately, his contract was broken and the business failed. In 1858 he found employment with a railroad company and worked with his future commanding officer, George McClellan.

Burnside re-entered the army as a colonel on May 2, 1861 and took part in the First Battle of Bull Run. He then commanded the North Carolina Expeditionary Force and between September 1861 and July 1862 led a series of successful raids against coastal batteries. His successful battles at Roanoke Island and New Bern led to his promotion to major general.

Burnside was a realist and understood his own limitations and for this reason declined President Lincoln's offer to command the Army of the Potomac as a replacement for George McClellan. He fought in the Second Battle of Bull Run under the command of Major General John Pope and was the star witness in the court martial of Major General Fitz John Porter.

Burnside fought once more under the leadership of George McClellan at the Battle of Antietam and his lack of creativity led him to funnel his soldiers across a stone bridge that was enfiladed by deadly Confederate fire. President Lincoln finally forced a reluctant Burnside to take command of the Army of the Potomac when Major General McClellan was removed for his failure to pursue the retreating Confederate army.

Under pressure to prosecute the war, Burnside hastily prepared a plan for the invasion of Virginia. The plan was viable but its execution was lacking and resulted in the costly loss to Robert E. Lee at the Battle of Fredericksburg on December 15, 1862. Burnside's offer to resign from the army was refused and he launched another offensive in January 1863 known as the Mud March which, due to heavy rains, never achieved its objective.

Open hostility erupted in his general command and Burnside asked that several commanders be relieved of duty. Instead, President Lincoln replaced Burnside with Major General Joseph Hooker who had been the most critical of his former commanders.

Major General Burnside was reassigned to command the Department of Ohio and was instrumental in arresting Clement Vallandigham, leader of the Copperhead peace movement, for seditious opposition to the war. Vallandigham was found guilty by a military tribunal and exiled to the Confederate South. He made his way to Canada and later ran for Governor of Ohio from his northern safe haven.

Burnside saw action in Knoxville, Tennessee and was besieged by Confederate forces led by Lieutenant General James Longstreet who marched north following success at the Battle of Chickamauga. The two commanders had fought each other at The Second Battle of Bull Run and Burnside now kept Longstreet occupied while General Grant drove back the armies of Confederate General Braxton Bragg at the Battle of Chattanooga. Major General William Sherman then marched north from Chattanooga to relieve the siege of Knoxville sending Confederate General Longstreet back to Virginia.

Burnside took his 9th Corps back to Virginia where he voluntarily placed himself under the leadership of the lower ranked Major General George Meade. He fought in the Battles of the Wilderness, Spotsylvania and Cold Harbour as well as the siege of Petersburg. During the siege Burnside earned his greatest notoriety as the commander of the Battle of the Crater. The battle turned out to be a Northern fiasco due mainly to the last minute countermanding of Burnside's order of battle by Meade. When he was relieved of command following this, Burnside contemplated resigning but was asked by both Lincoln and Grant to remain in the army. Finally, on April 15, 1865 having been idle since the previous summer, Burnside resigned his commission.

Following the war, Ambrose Burnside found employment as president and director of a number of railway companies, was elected to three terms as Governor of Rhode Island and was the first president of the National Rifle Association. In 1870 he offered mediation to both sides of the Franco-Prussian War and in 1874 was elected as US Senator from Rhode Island and served in this capacity until his death in 1881.

An accomplished military commander and politician, Ambrose Burnside is most remembered for his unusual facial hair worn in a continuous trace down the sides of his face and joined to a moustache. This style, originally known as "burnsides," is now known to us as "sideburns."

Benjamin Franklin Butler
(November 5, 1818–January 11, 1893)

Benjamin Butler was raised in Deerfield, New Hampshire and lived with his mother in the boarding house she operated after the death of his father. He graduated from Colby College in Maine in 1838 and was called to the Massachusetts bar in 1840.

For political reasons, President Lincoln appointed the untrained Butler as major general of volunteers and he was given command of the Department of Virginia stationed at Fort Monroe. His leadership at the Battle of Big Bethel resulted in a humiliating defeat. By refusing to return runaway slaves in defiance of the Fugitive Slave Law and labeling them "contraband of war" he set a practical standard for all other Union generals.

Following successful campaigns to capture Fort Hatteras and Fort Clark in North Carolina, Butler was given command of

New Orleans after it was captured. The residents of the city uniformly despised him for his firm and, at times, severe rule. In a direct affront to Southern honour, he retaliated against women who showed contempt for Union soldiers by treating them as women "who ply their avocation." Chamber pots that had his image impressed on the bottom of the porcelain bowl became coveted items and he was called "Spoons" for his alleged theft of cutlery.

As a result of the strong feelings against him, Butler was recalled to Washington in November 1863 and in May 1864 was given command of the newly created Army of the James. His battle orders were to draw off some of Robert E. Lee's forces by attacking Richmond from the east while Grant attacked from the north. Unfortunately, with the help of important political patrons, he had long since risen to his level of incompetence and his attack was rendered ineffective by the much smaller forces of Confederate General P.G.T. Beauregard. In some disgust, Grant had him removed from command and he eventually retired his commission on November 30, 1865.

Following the war, Butler left the Democratic Party and sat in the US House of Representatives as a Radical Republican (1867-1875 and 1877-1879) becoming a strong ally of President Ulysses S. Grant. He served one term as Governor of Massachusetts and made an unsuccessful bid for the presidency against Grover Cleveland. Butler was a brilliant lawyer, an erratic administrator and a terrible military leader. He died arguing a case in a Washington, D.C. courtroom on January 11, 1893.

Henry Wager Halleck
(January 16, 1815 – January 9, 1872)

Henry Halleck started life at Westernville, New York as one of 14 children. Rather than farm with his father he ran away to Utica, New York and was raised by an uncle. He graduated from the US Military Academy in 1839 and five years later he was chosen by Winfield Scott to study the organization of the French military and report on European fortifications. The twelve lectures he gave upon his return, published in 1846 under the title, *Elements of Military Art and Science*, became a standard textbook at the US Military College.

He later served in California and was on the committee that wrote the California State Constitution. He also joined a San Francisco law firm and became so busy that he resigned his commission in 1854. His success as a lawyer and land speculator made him wealthy but he returned to the military with the outbreak of war and was given the rank of major general. On

November 9, 1861 he replaced Major General John C. Fremont in the Department of Missouri to reorganize the military infrastructure and deal with the charges of fraud which attended the Fremont administration.

Halleck did not have a close relationship with Brigadier General Ulysses S. Grant believing that Grant was an alcoholic and too aggressive in his battle plans. Under pressure from President Lincoln he relented in his opposition to Grant and in February 1862 both Forts Henry and Donelson were captured with 14,000 Confederate prisoners.

Grant's newfound hero status in the North no doubt bothered the more cautious Halleck and when his request for overall control of the Western Theatre (then shared with Major General Don Carlos Buell) was refused, he relieved Grant of command. Again his decision was overruled by Lincoln and Halleck reinstated Grant making him believe that he was righting a wrong rather than backing down from a bad decision.

Halleck, however, continued to work against Grant. When Grant's Army of the Tennessee was battered in a surprise attack at the Battle of Shiloh on April 6, 1862, Halleck had what he needed to demote his subordinate. He took personal command of Grant's forces and moved very cautiously against the smaller army of Confederate General P.G.T. Beauregard. Events in the Eastern Theatre intervened and a few months later, in July 1862, Halleck was recalled to Washington as General-in-Chief of all Union Armies. It was the president's hope that Halleck would provide leadership in coordinating the actions of the Union armies in a strategy to destroy the Confederate forces.

Halleck remained very cautious prompting Lincoln to christen his chief military strategist "a first rate clerk." Two years later, when Grant was promoted above Halleck to Lieutenant General, the first rate clerk was freed to apply his considerable administrative skills in supplying the advancing Union armies with war materiel and replacement soldiers. It was finally a powerful partnership.

Halleck remained in the army following the war and commanded the Military Division of the James with his offices in Richmond, Virginia but was transferred to the Division of the Pacific in August 1865 following a bitter disagreement over Sherman's lenient treatment of former rebels. He again transferred to the Division of the South in March 1869 and died at his headquarters in Louisville, Kentucky on January 9, 1872.

Joseph Hooker
(November 13, 1814 – October 31, 1879)

Another New Englanders, (Hadley, Massachusetts), Joseph Hooker graduated from the US Military Academy in 1837. He fought in the Florida Seminole Wars and held staff positions in the Mexican-American War. He resigned his commission in

1853 to settle in California as a land developer where he earned a reputation as a hard drinker and spendthrift.

Following the Northern disaster at the First Battle of Bull Run, he re-enlisted as a brigadier general in the defense of Washington. Hooker fought well during the Peninsula Campaign and the ensuing Seven Days Battles and on May 5, 1862 he was promoted to major general. He fought under Major General Pope in the Second Battle of Bull Run and later distinguished himself at South Mountain and Antietam. At Fredericksburg his men suffered staggering losses in the fourteen attacks they mounted against Marye's Heights.

Hooker joined other commanders in complaints against Major General Burnside and President Lincoln, taking a big political risk, replaced Burnside with Hooker. Unlike Burnside, Hooker was given the opportunity to rebuild his army and plan for his campaign against Lee's Army of North Virginia. He did a remarkable job of restoring the spirit of his men by improving their diet and camp sanitation and allowing 10 day leaves on a rotating basis. His request for the re-instatement of the unfairly dishonoured Brigadier General Charles Stone is seen by historian Bruce Catton as an expression of moral courage which provides an insight into Hooker's personality.

In May 1863, Hooker met Confederate forces at the Battle of Chancellorsville. His plan was well thought out but once again the Union army was forced into a costly and ignominious retreat. In the first day of fighting Hooker suffered a concussion from a well-placed cannon ball strike and, rather than turn control over to subordinates, he continued in command. Undoubtedly the subsequent, questionable decisions he made resulted in the agonizing defeat.

When Robert E. Lee began his second invasion of the North, Hooker proposed to invade Richmond. This idea was vetoed by Lincoln and the Army of the Potomac set off to find the Confederates who were making their way up the Shenandoah Valley. Hooker disputed plans for the defense of Harper's Ferry and offered his resignation in an attempt to make his point. Lincoln immediately accepted it and appointed Major General George Meade to lead the Union forces only 3 days before the Battle of Gettysburg.

Following the Union loss at the Battle of Chickamauga, Hooker was sent west with his men to reinforce the Army of the Cumberland at Chattanooga where they distinguished themselves at Missionary Ridge and he continued with William Tecumseh Sherman on the Atlanta Campaign. When he was passed over for promotion he asked to be relieved and was sent to a non-battlefield command in the northwest states.

He retired from the US Army on October 15, 1868 and suffered from poor health throughout his retirement. He died on a visit to Garden City, NY on October 31, 1879.

George Brinton McClellan
(December 3, 1826 – October 29, 1885)

George McClellan was from a prominent family in Philadelphia, Pennsylvania on December 3,1826 to a prominent, local family. He entered the University of Pennsylvania at age 13 with a view to becoming a lawyer but changed his mind and was given clearance to enter the US Military Academy prior to his 16th birthday.

He served in the Mexican-American War as an engineering officer and was promoted for his courage under fire. For the rest of his life he suffered recurring bouts of malaria contracted in Mexico. Following the war he participated in the Pacific Railroad surveys under Secretary of War Jefferson Davis and continued to fulfill assignments for Davis including an assess-

~~799 933~~

455 200   Sat.&Sun   2-4 30
Silver Spring   7611 - 68 Ave NW

469 000   C358/939
258 Arbour Cliff Cl.
        W.O. bungalow

    3817   PT.   McKAY. RD.
    539 900.

$ 650⁰⁰⁰ - 1932   GREEN RIDGE RD SW
bungalow.   MAXWELL - matthew.

669⁰⁰⁰   128 ✓ Wedgewood Dr
                            SW.

$ 739 000 - 2421 - 33 ST. SW
            Killarney - Cheung

        ↗ 923 & 925   35 ST NW
799 500⃠
                PARK DALE

ment of the defenses of Santo Domingo, Dominican Republic and an estimate of the capacity of US railroads. In 1855 he was sent to be a military observer during the Crimean War and, strangely, his report neglected to mention the impact of the newly introduced rifled musket.

Due to his political and military connections, wartime experience and understanding of the railroad system, McClellan was pursued by the governors of Ohio, Pennsylvania and New York to lead their militia units. Due to his lack of abolitionist tendencies, he was approached by some Southern states as well. At age 34, he was promoted to major general in the regular army and was the highest ranking officer apart from Major General Winfield Scott who was the General-in-Chief of the Union armies.

McClellan moved his forces into western Virginia and was successful at the Battle of the Philippi Races and then at Rich Mountain. With a flair for self-promotion, McClellan was lauded in the press and complaints of his over cautious leadership were ignored. After the Union defeat at the First Battle of Bull Run, Lincoln summoned McClellan and on July 26, 1861 appointed him commander of the Military Division of the Potomac. He created the Army of the Potomac, writing to his wife;

"I find myself in a new and strange position here—Presdt, Cabinet, Genl Scott & all deferring to me—by some strange operation of magic I seem to have become the power of the

land. ... I almost think that were I to win some small success now I could become Dictator or anything else that might please me—but nothing of that kind would please me— therefore I won't be Dictator. Admirable self-denial!"

Whatever his faults, McClellan proved himself to be brilliant at training an army, instilling a strong esprit de corps and planning the defenses of Washington. Ever the ardent student of Napoleon, McClellan dismissed Scott's Anaconda Plan and prepared himself and his 273,000 man army for a Napoleonic battle to the end. For reasons unknown to history, McClellan routinely overestimated his enemy's strength by a factor of three. Whether this blindness to the truth was willful or not, it sapped him of initiative and allowed Confederate General Robert E. Lee to understand his moves before he made them.

Upon the retirement of Winfield Scott, McClellan was promoted to General-in-Chief of all Union armies as well as maintaining direct command of the Army of the Potomac. McClellan became increasingly insubordinate to the wishes of Lincoln and regularly referred to the president as 'the baboon' and 'gorilla' in his private correspondence. Finally President Lincoln forced McClellan's hand by ordering offensive operations to begin by February 22, 1862. McClellan rejected Lincoln's strategy of an overland attack at Manassas Junction and successfully argued for his Urbanna Plan. On March 8, 1862 with the Army of the Potomac still snug in Washington, Lincoln called a council of war, assigned corps commanders and polled the senior staff for their assessment of the new battle plans.

When Confederate General Joseph Johnston pulled his army across the Rappahannock River the Urbanna plan was scuttled and McClellan opted instead to sail his army to Fort Monroe, Virginia and march them to Richmond. This was known as the Peninsula Campaign and was a logistical tour de force. Unfortunately the over cautious nature of McClellan ensured that it was less than a military tour de force.

He slowly moved his 121,000 man army up the peninsula and was stopped at Yorktown by the much smaller forces of Confederate General John Magruder who marched his divisions in and out of the woods to give the impression of a large entrenched force. As McClellan completed his siege works, the Confederate forces pulled back to defend Richmond. For McClellan it was a major victory but to all others it was an embarrassment.

Upon reaching Richmond, McClellan positioned his army on both sides of the Chickahominy River allowing General Johnston to attack the southern flank without fear of reinforcements from the northern force. The Battle of Seven Pines was a classic attack in detail and the Union forces were driven back. General Robert E Lee was given command of the Confederate Army of Northern Virginia when General Johnston was wounded and in seven days and several battles including Mechanicsville, Gaines Mill, Glendale and Malvern Hill, he drove McClellan and his army back to the ocean. On notable occasions, McClellan could not bring himself to lead his army on the field instead retiring to Union gunboats and for this reason Lincoln began to search for a replacement. He appointed Henry Halleck as general-in-chief and offered McClellan's command to Ambrose Burnside who refused it.

Anxious to pursue the war, Lincoln created the Army of Virginia commanded by Major General John Pope but after the debacle of the Second Battle of Bull Run he was forced to fall back on McClellan again. The appointment recognized McClellan's unique ability to instill confidence in his soldiers through rigorous training.

McClellan was not to have much time in rebuilding his army as General Lee crossed the Potomac at Harper's Ferry on September 4, 1862. As the Union army slowly closed with the Confederate army the Confederate battle plans were discovered and even with this information McClellan delayed his attack for 18 hours allowing Lee time to reunite his divided armies. It was a lost opportunity that resulted only in a very bloody tactical win for the North. McClellan felt it was a magnificent success. President Lincoln felt otherwise and McClellan was replaced by a reluctant Major General Ambrose Burnside on November 7, 1862.

McClellan was removed from all field command and would never command forces again. In October 1863 he declared himself a candidate for the Democratic ticket and was nominated to run against Abraham Lincoln in the 1864 presidential election. He resigned his commission on election day, November 8, 1864. While he personally supported fighting the war to a successful conclusion, the Democratic party platform which had been written by the Peace Democrats ("Copperheads" or "Butternuts") called for immediate negotiation to end the war. It was a difficult balancing act for McClellan and, in the end, the army which had loved him voted overwhelmingly for Lincoln.

Following the war McClellan traveled for three years in Europe and considered another run at the presidency until the Republicans nominated General Ulysses S. Grant as their candidate. He worked as an engineer for the City of New York and simultaneously served as president of the Atlantic and Great Western Railroad. He returned to Europe for two years in the mid 1870's and served a term as Governor of New Jersey until 1881.

George McClellan wrote of his war experiences and continued to travel. At age 58 he died suddenly in Orange, New Jersey on October 28, 1885 likely of a heart attack.

Irvin McDowell (October 15, 1818 – May 4, 1885)

Although originally from Columbus, Ohio, Irvin McDowell
attended school in France and
entered the US Military Academy
in 1834. He graduated with Pierre
Gustav Toutant Beauregard and
later the two met across the
battlefield at the First Battle of
Bull Run. He was posted to an
artillery unit and instructed tactics
at the Military Academy prior to
the Mexican-American War. He served in the war and was
promoted to major while working in the Adjutant General
department after the war. On May 14, 1861 he was promoted to
brigadier general and given command of the Army of Northern
Virginia (to become Army of the Potomac).

Succumbing to political pressure from Washington to "have
a little skirmish and end the war" McDowell put his raw and
untested volunteers into the field at the First Battle of Bull Run
and followed a battle plan that was decidedly too complex for
his untrained army. The disaster, known as the "Great Skedaddle," was an embarrassing rout and McDowell was given
command of a division under the new commander, Major
General George McLellan. For the next year he was responsible for the defense of Washington and did not see action until

the Second Battle of Bull Run commanding a corps in the Army of Virginia under Major General John Pope. In the confusion of this battle, McDowell was accused of disobeying orders and exculpated himself by testifying at a court martial against Major General Fitz John Porter. While he escaped the ignominy of a court martial, McDowell was removed from leadership in the army.

In July 1864 he was given command of the Department of the Pacific and during Reconstruction was responsible for the military government of Arkansas and Louisiana. In 1879, after dogged pursuit by Fitz John Porter, a Board of Review issued its report on the failures of the Second Battle of Bull Run and McDowell was assessed most of the blame for the loss. His leadership during the battle was described as inept and indecisive and he was accused of being uncommunicative and faulted for not taking initiative when required as the battle progressed.

He served as Park Commissioner in San Francisco following his retirement from the army in 1882 and died on May 4, 1885.

George Gordon Meade
(December 31, 1815 – November 6, 1872)

George Meade was born in Cadiz, Spain, one of eleven children. The family returned from Spain following his father's death in 1828 and in 1835 he graduated from the US Military

Academy. Meade served with distinction during the Mexican-American War and was subsequently involved in the construction of coastal light houses and breakwaters and completed the antebellum years on the Great Lakes Survey mission.

Meade was recalled to Washington at the outbreak of hostilities to plan and execute the defenses of the city. His brigade was then attached to the Army of the Potomac and saw action in the Peninsula Campaign under Major General George McClellan. Meade was severely wounded in the campaign but still fought in the Second Battle of Bull Run where his unit made a heroic stand at Henry House Hill to cover the retreating Union army. Later, he distinguished himself at the Battle of South Mountain under Major General Joseph Hooker and was wounded at the Battle of Antietam.

Meade led the only successful breakthrough at the Battle of Fredericksburg but the action was not reinforced and his losses were high. On June 28, 1863 Meade was elevated to command the Army of the Potomac replacing Major General Hooker. So intense were the politics in the Union command structure that, while opening President Lincoln's communication, he feared he was being put under arrest.

When he was promoted, Meade had no idea where the Confederate army was. Three days later, after a chance encounter, the two armies arranged themselves for battle at the small Pennsylvania town of Gettysburg. The Northern generals managed to take and hold the high ground and in many ways the Battle of Gettysburg was the reverse of Chancellorsville. It was a significant if bloody victory for the Union forces and Meade acquitted himself well in the disposition and coordination of his army. Unfortunately his political skills were not up to his military prowess and his reputation was bruised by commanders loyal to Joseph Hooker. He also suffered the disappointment of President Lincoln who viewed his inaction against the retreating Confederate forces as another lost opportunity to end the war.

For the remainder of the campaigning season, Meade and Lee played cat and mouse and did not fight. From his experiences of Fredericksburg and Chancellorsville, Meade had no stomach for frontal assaults on entrenched positions. In March 1864, Lieutenant General Ulysses S. Grant was appointed General-in-Chief of all Union armies and chose to locate his office in the field with the Army of the Potomac. Meade understood the significance of this move and his offered resignation was refused.

Meade worked with Grant even though he strenuously disagreed with Grant's policy of relative attrition in which matched casualties were a greater impairment to the South than to the North. He was also unhappy with the decision to use Philip Sheridan's cavalry to attack in force rather than in a raiding and intelligence gathering function. Meade's tardiness in reinforcing the initial attack on Petersburg allowed the Confederates to hold off the Union advance long enough for the outflanked army of General Robert E. Lee to recover and reinforce the defensive position thus extending the war for an additional 10 months. Major General Ambrose Burnside's plan to undermine the Confederate trenches and blow a hole in their line was approved by Meade. At the last minute, however, he refused to allow the specially trained soldiers to take part in the ensuing attack. The Battle of the Crater became an uncoordinated attack by untrained soldiers resulting in a total and costly fiasco.

Grant promoted Meade to the rank of major general and he fought until the surrender of the Confederate forces at Appomattox Court House. He continued to serve in the military and, in January 1868, replaced Major General John Pope as the Reconstruction Governor of the Third Military District. He died in Philadelphia on November 6, 1872 of complications arising from his war wounds.

John Pope (March 16, 1822 – September 23, 1892)

From Louisville, Kentucky, John Pope graduated from the US Military Academy in 1842. He served in the Seminole

Battles, surveyed part of the border between Canada and the United States and fought in the Mexican-American War.

When the Civil War broke out he was assigned to the Western Department under Major General John Fremont and actively worked to have his commander replaced. He enjoyed a minor victory which brought him to the attention of Major General Henry Halleck who had replaced Fremont and was sent east to command the newly formed Army of Virginia. As Pope moved into northern Virginia, Robert E. Lee sent Stonewall Jackson to defeat Nathanial Banks at Cedar Mountain and then swing around to capture Pope's main supply base at Manassas Junction. Pope was confused as to the location of the Confederate army and did not believe that Jackson could have returned so quickly to threaten his flank. Thus he walked straight into Lee's trap. On the following day, August 29, 1862 Confederate Major General Longstreet smashed into Pope's army and forced the retreat.

In the aftermath of the battle, Pope blamed his loss on command level politics and, in particular, pointed the blame at Fitz John Porter. This made Pope very unpopular in the North and he was relieved of his command and spent the remainder of the war dealing with the Dakota War in the Department of the Northwest.

During Reconstruction he was named governor of the Third Military District headquartered in Atlanta and promoted the civil rights of the freed slaves. President Andrew Johnson replaced him in this office with George Meade on December 28, 1867 and he returned to the West where he continued to create controversy by criticizing the corruption of the Indian Bureau and calling for more humane treatment of Native Americans.

The 1879 Schofield Board of Inquiry did great damage to Pope's reputation by absolving Fitz John Porter of primary blame in the defeat of the Second Battle of Bull Run assigning the blame to Pope for his reckless disregard for the information he was given and for not apprising himself of battlefield conditions. He resigned his commission in 1886 and died in Sandusky, Ohio in 1892.

William Starke Rosecrans
(September 6, 1819 – March 11, 1898)

William Rosecrans from Ohio, graduated from the US Military Academy in 1842 with James Longstreet and D.H. Hill. He worked as an engineer at Hampton Roads, Virginia and later as an instructor at the academy. Following his resignation in

1854 he took over a profitable mining company in what is now West Virginia.

In the early stages of the Civil War he commanded an Ohio unit which included future presidents Rutherford Hayes and William McKinley. He fought in the western Virginia campaign as a brigadier general and his success launched the military career of his commanding officer, Major General George McClellan. Rosecrans was given command of the Department of West Virginia when McClellan was moved to the Army of the Potomac.

He was subsequently assigned to the Army of the Mississippi and took part in the siege of Corinth. In July 1862 he was given command of the army and took part in the controversial Battle of Iuka. At the Battle of Corinth he defeated Confederate Major General Earl Van Dorn who suffered heavy casualties by attacking Rosecrans' defensive positions. In October he replaced Major General Don Carlos Buell as commander of the renamed Army of the Cumberland and was promoted to major general of volunteers. Rosecrans became as cautious as Buell and was threatened with replacement for not taking to the field at Nashville.

In December 1862 Rosecrans met Braxton Bragg's Confederate forces at the Battle of Stones River near the town of Murfreesboro, Tennessee. In terms of casualty rates it was the bloodiest battle of the war and was considered a Union victory because Bragg left the field first. Although it was tactically unimportant, it gave the Union forces a psychological lift following their terrible defeat at Fredericksburg, Virginia. His army then successfully pursued Bragg in the Tullahoma Campaign but the relatively bloodless affair which ended on July 4, 1863 was unnoticed in the excitement of the fall of Vicksburg and the important victory at Gettysburg. His subsequent loss at the Battle of Chickamauga and retreat to Chattanooga destroyed his career and he was replaced by Major General George Thomas.

Rosecrans was given command of the Department of Missouri but would never command a force in the field again. He resigned his commission in 1867 and served on a diplomatic mission in Mexico. He then returned to mining and served as a California congressman from 1881 to 1885. From 1885 until 1893 he was the Registrar of the Treasury before retiring to his ranch, in what is now a suburb of Los Angeles, where he died in 1898.

Philip Henry Sheridan
(March 6, 1831 – August 5, 1888)

To President Lincoln it was dis-
putable that Sheridan ever "grew
up," gaining a height of less than 5
feet 6 inches. He graduated from
the US Military Academy in 1853
having spent a year on probation for
fighting with a classmate and was
posted to the Pacific Northwest. In
1861 he was sent to Missouri to
work for Major General Halleck in
reorganizing the administration of the transferred Major General John C. Fremont. At the siege of Corinth he came to the
attention of Brigadier General William Tecumseh Sherman and
was appointed colonel of a cavalry unit on May 27, 1862.

He fought in the Tullahoma Campaign and during the Battle
of Chickamauga he and his division withstood a drive by
Confederate Lieutenant General James Longstreet. Overwhelmed by the numbers of retreating Union soldiers Sheridan
and his men left the field but returned upon hearing of the stand
being made by Major General George Thomas thus ensuring
that his career did not suffer for abandoning the field.

At the Battle of Chattanooga, on November 25, 1863, Sheridan was under the command of Major General George Thomas. He told his men to "Remember Chickamauga" and that

became their battle cry as they carried the Confederate army before them on their romp up Missionary Ridge. They pushed the Confederates back from their supply lines and gave up the chase only when it became obvious that they were the only ones in pursuit.

Grant brought Sheridan with him to the Eastern Theatre where he was assigned to a standard cavalry role of screening, reconnaissance and guarding the supply lines. At Sheridan's request, Grant allowed him to undertake raiding missions and his first raid, while not strategically important, resulted in the death of Major General J.E.B. Stuart of the Confederate cavalry at the Battle of Yellow Tavern.

When Lieutenant General Jubal Early of the Confederate cavalry attempted to relieve the siege of Petersburg by raiding Washington, D.C., Grant created the Army of the Shenandoah under Sheridan's command. Sheridan's campaign of destruction in the Shenandoah Valley was called "The Burning" and he met Jubal Early's reinforced army on October 19, 1864. The Battle of Cedar Creek was a well planned surprise attack which drove back the Union forces. Demonstrating their poor physical condition, the Rebel soldiers refused to push their advantage and instead focused on raiding the Union camp of food and clothing. Sheridan rallied his army and destroyed the Confederate forces in a counter-attack. For this action Sheridan was promoted to major general and reveled in the notoriety he gained from Thomas Read's popular poem *Sheridan's Ride.*

With the surrender of Confederate General Joseph Johnston on April 26, 1865, Sheridan was dispatched to Texas as commander of the Military District of the Southwest in order to procure the surrender of the remaining Confederate forces.

During Reconstruction he was appointed military governor of the Fifth Military District of Texas and Louisiana and was confronted with violence from a mob which refused to integrate former slaves into the economy. He was finally removed from his post by President Andrew Johnson over the outrage of Lieutenant General Ulysses S. Grant. Sheridan summed up his experience with one of the funnier quotes from the Civil War,

"If I owned Texas and Hell, I would rent Texas and live in Hell"

In August 1867 Sheridan was sent to pacify the Great Plains which had erupted in violence from Indians upset with their treatment by the US government. He adopted a strategy similar to that used in the Shenandoah Valley by attacking the Indians in their winter camps and destroying their food supplies.

Sheridan was sent as an observer to the Franco-Prussian War and coordinated the military relief efforts during the Great Chicago Fire of 1871. In 1875 he protected Yellowstone National Park and placed its operation under military control.

On November 1, 1883 Sheridan became Commanding General, U.S. Army following the retirement of William Tecumseh Sherman but good living had swollen him to over 200 pounds and at the age of 57 he suffered a series of heart attacks finally dying on August 5, 1888 at his summer home at Nonquitt, Massachusetts.

William Tecumseh Sherman
(February 8, 1820 – February 14, 1891)

Like Sheridan, William Tecumseh Sherman was born in Ohio. He was named after the Shawnee leader, Tecumseh and, at the age of 9, he and his 10 siblings lost their father. As a result, William was raised by family friend Thomas Ewing, a prominent lawyer and politician.

He entered the US Military Academy at age 18 and was a classmate of George Thomas and William Rosecrans. Upon graduation he fought in the Second Seminole War and surveyed much of Georgia and South Carolina – an experience which provided him important local knowledge. He was then assigned to California and was involved in confirming the gold discovery which led to the Rush of 1849.

Having missed the war in Mexico, Sherman resigned his commission in 1853 and accepted the presidency of a San Francisco bank. His return to the Golden State was marred by shipwreck and he made land in the San Francisco harbour clinging to the hull of the overturned schooner which had brought him thus far. When his bank collapsed in the panic of 1857 he turned to law, opening a practice at Leavenworth, Kansas but this also failed. He gladly accepted the position of superintendent of a military academy in Louisiana and acquitted himself well. His response to secessionist friend David Boyd was prescient of what was to come;

"You people of the South don't know what you are doing. This country will be drenched in blood, and God only knows how it will end. It is all folly, madness, a crime against civilization! You people speak so lightly of war; you don't know what you're talking about. War is a terrible thing! You mistake, too, the people of the North. They are a peaceable people but an earnest people, and they will fight, too. They are not going to let this country be destroyed without a mighty effort to save it... Besides, where are your men and appliances of war to contend against them? The North can make a steam engine, locomotive, or railway car; hardly a yard of cloth or pair of shoes can you make. You are rushing into war with one of the most powerful, ingeniously mechanical, and determined people on Earth—right at your doors. You are bound to fail. Only in your spirit and determination are you prepared for war. In all else you are totally unprepared, with a bad cause to start with. At first you will make headway, but as your limited resources begin to fail, shut out from the markets of Europe as you will be,

your cause will begin to wane. If your people will but stop and think, they must see in the end that you will surely fail."

Sherman resigned his position at the academy in January 1861 and was commissioned as a Union army colonel on May 14, 1861. He distinguished himself in the First Battle of Bull Run by running into a hail of bullets which, fortunately, were more harmful to his clothing than to his body. His behaviour caught the eye of President Lincoln who promoted him to brigadier general. He was reassigned to the Department of the Cumberland under Robert Anderson and subsequently replaced him. In the west, Sherman grew increasingly despondent and his morose view of the war led to his being replaced by Don Carlos Buell.

Recovering from a nervous breakdown and with the encouragement of Ulysses S. Grant, he returned to active service in the Department of the Missouri under Major General Henry Halleck. When offered Grant's position, Sherman refused it and on March 1, 1862 he was transferred to the Army of West Tennessee under the command of Grant. His baptism into this command occurred a month later at the Battle of Shiloh. His performance during the counter attack on April 7, 1862 was noted by those with whom he fought and he was promoted to major general on May 1, 1862. When Grant became depressed by his removal from command by Halleck, it was Sherman's turn to encourage him to remain in active service in the hope that future opportunities would soon arise. And those opportunities did arise for both Grant and Sherman.

Sherman was on the battlefield at Chickasaw, Vicksburg and Chattanooga. He was sent to relieve the besieged Ambrose Burnside at Knoxville and made an expedition in force to disrupt Confederate infrastructure at Meridian, Mississippi. Known by his soldiers as "Uncle Billy," Sherman was given command of the Military Division of the Mississippi when Grant was promoted to general-in-chief by President Lincoln. In the laconic style of the two generals, Sherman expressed his strategy to Grant,

"If you can whip Lee and I can march to the Atlantic I think ol' Uncle Abe will give us twenty days leave to see the young folks."

Sherman moved into Georgia headed for Atlanta with George Thomas and the Army of the Cumberland (60,000), James McPherson and the Army of the Tennessee (25,000) and John Schofield and the Army of the Ohio (13,000). All spring and summer the Union troops drove back the army of Confederate General Joseph Johnston who retreated to the outskirts of Atlanta. The cautious style of Johnston did not support the need of President Davis for an aggressive, offensive win and so he was replaced by the young firebrand, John Bell Hood. Hood met Sherman in a set piece battle which Sherman won and Atlanta fell on September 2, 1864.

The total war tactics of the Union army were now demonstrated by Sherman's destruction of the military infrastructure of the South and not a few elegant civilian homes as well.

When Hood moved his army north to recover Tennessee, Sherman sent Thomas to intercept him and then set off to *"make Georgia howl."* His unsupported 'March to the Sea' put him out of contact with Grant and Lincoln and the North was jubilant when Sherman and his army emerged at Savannah having left a path of destruction across Georgia.

With Grant bogged down at Petersburg, a movement arose to have him replaced by Sherman. Aghast, Sherman quickly put down any consideration of the plan and famously declared,

> *"General Grant is a great general. I know him well. He stood by me when I was crazy, and I stood by him when he was drunk; and now, sir, we stand by each other always."*

The Civil War began to roll quickly to a conclusion. Sherman defeated Johnston at the Battle of Bentonville on March 19-21, Grant accepted Lee's surrender at Appomattox on April 9 and Lincoln was assassinated on April 14, 1865. The world had changed. On April 26, 1865 Sherman accepted the surrender of Confederate Joseph Johnston.

Sherman stayed in the army following the war and was promoted to Commanding General of the United States Army with the election of Ulysses S. Grant to the presidency in 1869. To escape the controversies of the Grant administration he moved his command to St. Louis, Missouri and finally retired from the military in February 1884.

In retirement, Sherman was much in demand as a dinner guest and speaker. Sherman has been immortalized as a military general in the rank of Scipio Africanus and Napoleon and his strategy of total war has been much debated. In response to the city council of Atlanta who appealed to him to spare their city he summarized his view of such a strategy and why he pursued it,

> *"You cannot qualify war in harsher terms than I will. War is cruelty, and you cannot refine it; and those who brought war into our country deserve all the curses and maledictions a people can pour out. I know I had no hand in making this war, and I know I will make more sacrifices to-day than any of you to secure peace. But you cannot have peace and a division of our country... I will ever conduct war with a view to perfect and early success. But, my dear sirs, when peace does come, you may call on me for anything. Then will I share with you the last cracker, and watch with you to shield your homes and families against danger from every quarter."*

William Tecumseh Sherman died in New York City on February 14, 1891. His former antagonist, General Joseph E. Johnston served as a pallbearer and, refusing to put on his hat in the rain, contracted pneumonia and died a month later.

George Henry Thomas (July 31, 1816 – March 28, 1870)

George Thomas was born in the South (Virginia) and, following his graduation from the US Military Academy in 1840, he served in the Seminole Wars and the Mexican-American War. From 1851 to 1854 he taught at the academy.

Thomas' decision to remain faithful to the United States in deference to the wishes of his Northern-born wife caused an irreparable rupture with his family. When he offered financial aid to his sisters after the war the money was returned with the explanation that they had no brother. Thomas was never free of the suspicion that he might be a spy. He fought in the Shenandoah Valley during 1861 and then transferred to the Western Theatre where he won an important Union victory at the Battle of Mill Springs pushing the Confederates out of eastern Kentucky.

He arrived too late for the Battle of Shiloh but was present at the siege of Corinth and fought under Don Carlos Buell to push Bragg's Confederate army out of Tennessee. When Buell was chastised for not pursuing the retreating Confederate army his command was offered to Thomas who refused to accept it. Buell was eventually replaced by Major General William

Rosecrans and Thomas fought the Battle of Chickamauga on September 19, 1862 under his command. As the Union forces were retreating in disarray, Thomas reformed those that he could and made a stand on Horseshoe Ridge to cover the retreat. Future president James Garfield was sent to tell Thomas to retreat. He later told Rosecrans that when he left the field, Thomas was "standing like a rock" and thus he became known as the "Rock of Chickamauga."

For leaving the field at the Battle of Chickamauga, Rosecrans was replaced as commander of the Army of the Cumberland by Thomas. At the Battle of Chattanooga his men stormed Missionary Ridge and swept over the Confederate defenders. Thomas and the Army of the Cumberland took part in the advance against Atlanta and provided all the logistical and engineering support for Sherman's forces. His army was a key to the success at the Battle of Peachtree Creek on July 20, 1864 and when John Bell Hood broke away from Sherman's advance, Thomas was sent to intercept his move back into Tennessee. The two forces were involved in a mauling action at the Battle of Franklin on November 30, 1864 and Hood's Army of the Tennessee was finally destroyed by Thomas at the Battle of Nashville.

Following the war Thomas remained in active service and commanded the Department of the Cumberland during Reconstruction. To avoid partisan politics he refused an appointment to General-in-Chief as a replacement to Lieutenant General

Ulysses S. Grant and instead accepted an assignment to command the Division of the Pacific at San Francisco where he died on March 28, 1870 of a stroke.

7: 1863 - Emancipation and the Turning Point

The year 1863 opened with mixed results for the Union armies and the debacle of Fredericksburg burned in the collective memories of Northern residents. They were not impressed with the lengthy casualty lists that were starting to show up in local newspapers and emancipation seemed a very expensive dream. President Lincoln again changed the commander of the Army of the Potomac. Major General Ambrose Burnside was replaced with the man who most condemned Burnside's performance and was most immodestly cocksure of his own. In January, Major General Joseph E. Hooker was placed in command of the Union army in the Eastern Theatre.

Hooker started by revamping the military intelligence gathering system that had provided consistently incorrect information to previous commanders. Finally, reliable information about Confederate activities was being compiled, indicating where enemy forces were concentrated and how they were deployed. While the methods of accumulating this information were unchanged, Hooker developed a system of triangulating to ensure its validity prior to incorporating it into military decision-making.

President Lincoln wanted Hooker to move quickly against Lee but Hooker wisely took time to retrain his army and build their morale by rotating them through short leaves of absence. Hooker recognized that Lincoln had gambled on his leadership and he wanted to reward that risk with a stunning victory. He planned to move half of his force northwest and cross the Rappahannock and Rapidan Rivers well to the rear of the Confederates and then march east to engage them from behind as the rest of the army attacked at Fredericksburg. Major General George Stoneman would simultaneously raid deep into Virginia with his cavalry to put the Confederates off balance. That was the plan.

The Battle of Chancellorsville

By the time the Army of the Potomac crossed the Rappahannock River on April 27–28, Hooker commanded a numerically larger and more prepared fighting machine than did General Robert E. Lee. The Confederate army had spent the months since the Fredericksburg disaster in active duty all over Virginia and, to meet the advancing Union armies, the Confederates had to be marshaled together.

The two Union forces began to advance as planned and the encircling divisions crossed the Rappahannock near its confluence with the Rapidan at the hamlet of Chancellorsville. With good information coming to him from the cavalry forces of Major General J.E.B. Stuart, Lee confounded Hooker's plan by splitting his already outnumbered forces. He left fewer than 15,000 men to resist the advance at Fredericksburg and marched 40,000 men under Stonewall Jackson to meet the Union troops crossing at Chancellorsville. Jackson's men were vulnerable as they emerged from the relative safety of the Wilderness of Spotsylvania and moved east towards the Union army.

When, on May 1, fighting broke out on the Union flank at Spotsylvania, Hooker stopped the offensive and retired his men from the field. Fearing a repeat of Fredericksburg, he was determined to force Lee to attack his larger forces. Lee was happy to accommodate and on the morning of May 2 he divided his army yet again to send Jackson with 12,000 men on a 12 mile flanking maneuver. The decision was breathtakingly risky as it relied on Jackson remaining undetected, Hooker staying on the defensive and no breakout occurred at Fredericksburg. If any of these three conditions had changed, the Civil War might have been a two year engagement. But, as always, Lee understood his opponent.

Once again a Union general failed to receive timely battlefield information and it was not a good day for Major General Hooker. The divisions at Fredericksburg did not go on the offensive and Hooker's right flank at Chancellorsville was overwhelmed by Jackson as his men burst out of the wilderness while the Union soldiers were cooking their dinner. Perhaps if Northern commanders had provided meals to their Southern opponents, they might have had fewer of their own meals interrupted. Union Brigadier General Dan Sickles was ordered to retreat from the salient that had been formed by the forward progress of the Confederate attack but, in doing so, gave up the high ground from which Confederate artillery subsequently pounded the Union lines. Of those who didn't run, 4,000 were taken prisoner. During the late afternoon fighting Hooker suffered a concussion when struck by wooden debris from an errant cannon ball. Whether the concussion confused Hooker is open to question but without doubt, he should have relinquished command as the quality of his subsequent decisions was very suspect.

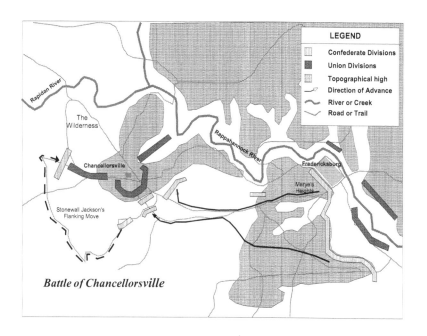

Battle of Chancellorsville

It was not a good day for Major General Jackson either. In the evening, while scouting his next move, he was struck by friendly fire and lost his arm to amputation. Worse, he contracted pneumonia and died 8 days later dealing a terrible blow to the Confederate army. On May 3, Jackson's replacement, Major General A.P. Hill, was also hauled off the battlefield and command passed to cavalry commander J.E.B. Stuart who immediately launched two massive assaults which drove Hooker back onto his interior lines which were his only avenue of retreat.

Hooker maintained his defensive position awaiting the flanking maneuver of Major General Sedgwick as he broke through the Confederate lines at Fredericksburg. Unfortunately, Sedgwick neglected to consolidate his position and, as he moved towards Chancellorsville, the Confederates under Jubal Early moved into the vacuum behind his troops. With Confederates now in front and back Sedgwick decided to retreat across the Rappahannock and Hooker, seeing no viable option to continue the fight did likewise. Had Hooker's men at Fredericksburg made their assault earlier on May 3 it is possible that they might have been able to flank Lee at Chancellorsville. As it was, the successful attack came too late to be pressed. With the setting sun, a total of 18,000 men lay killed or injured in the furious action. President Lincoln's bet on Hooker had not paid a dividend and he began to look for a replacement.

***

The Enrollment Act of 1863 made all Northern men between the ages of 20 and 45 eligible for army service. Volunteers were paid $300, almost a year's wages, but by July 1 insufficient men had volunteered and Lincoln was forced to use a draft. The draft law was hated everywhere because it allowed people with money to commute their responsibility or pay to have a substitute take their place.

President Lincoln had available to him vast reserves of blacks to serve in the Northern armies. However, many believed that they could not fight and that white men would not fight alongside them. Lincoln was also afraid of the reaction of Northern voters if they saw armed, black men marching through the country. But due to the shortage of soldiers he quietly allowed his commanders in South Carolina to enroll up to 5,000 ex-slaves into their armies. By the spring of 1863 the Union armies began to fill up with blacks who were eager to defend their honor. The Confederacy was outraged by this action and threatened to kill white officers who were captured while leading ex-slaves in battle. Commanders, therefore, tended to keep black recruits in support roles. On July 18, 1863 a black infantry unit attacked Fort Wagoner and put to rest any fears that black men could not fight. It was during this action that surgeon William Carney became the first black man to be awarded the Congressional Medal of Honor. President Lincoln summarized his views about black soldiers;

"You say you will not fight to free Negroes although some of them seem willing to fight for you; but no matter. .... Peace does not appear so distant as it did and there are some Black men who can remember that with silent tongue, and with clenched teeth, and steady eye, and well poised bayonet, they have helped mankind onto this great consummation; while I fear, there will be some White ones, unable to forget that, with malignant heart, and deceitful speech, they strove to hinder it."

As the Union armies bogged down at Vicksburg and with the Army of the Potomac reeling from its loss at Chancellorsville, the Northern peace movement began to gain momentum. The Peace Democrats, referred to as "Copperheads" because of their poisonous influence, used the failures of the Union Army, emancipation, inflation, and the draft to create protests and riots across the North. Clement Vallendigham of Ohio, the most vocal of the Copperheads, was eventually convicted of treason and exiled to the Confederacy from where he traveled to Canada.

The most notorious riots occurred in New York City in mid-July and these remain the deadliest riots in American history. Recent immigrants, fearing wage competition from the newly freed blacks, expressed their fears in a rampage that lasted several days, resulted in an enormous destruction of private property and in the deaths of more than a dozen blacks. At its height more than 50,000 people rioted and Union troops, fresh from the battlefield of Gettysburg, confronted the rioters and killed more than a hundred in confrontations throughout the city. The New York City riots hurt the peace movement and undermined the legitimacy of the Democratic Party.

***

By the spring of 1863 it was becoming apparent that Confederate forces had fewer resources to reinforce themselves than did the Union Army. Jefferson Davis needed a bold move to either force Lincoln to the negotiating table or to bring European powers into the war on his side. General Grant was tied down in Vicksburg and his supply lines were being constantly harassed by the cavalry of Nathan Bedford Forrest.

The Battle of Stones River which had both closed 1862 and opened 1863 was an inconclusive affair for the Confederates but viewed as a tactical win for the Union forces in the Western Theatre. It marked the end of Confederate attempts to recapture lost ground in Kentucky and Tennessee. President Lincoln was concerned that Bragg might become emboldened to send some of his units to the relief of Vicksburg then under siege by Ulysses Grant and entreated Rosecrans to go on the offensive. Rosecrans demurred fearing the muddy and slippery conditions. While Rosecrans suffered the frustration of his president, Bragg and his army suffered privation due to a lack of food and forage. Ironically, much of the food that was grown in the area was sent to sustain General Lee's army in the Eastern Theatre. The disrepute in which some of Bragg's commanders held him deepened during the long months of waiting.

It was during this period that one of the more memorable cavalry raids was undertaken – that of Union Colonel Abel Streight. It must have been one of those "it seemed like a good idea at the time" moments that resulted in this head-scratching event. If running around burning things with trained riders on horses was a good idea, how much better for untrained riders to run around on mules and burn things. The novelty of the idea wore off after the first week and it became a losing struggle as the hapless Union forces tried to outrun the Confederate cavalry forces of Nathan Bedford Forrest. Exhausted and fearing they were outnumbered, the Streight raid ended in the ignominy of surrender.

Bragg had retired his army to Tullahoma and picketed his position against incursions by the Union army led by William Rosecrans. All of the passes through the mountains that separated the two armies were protected by Bragg. At Hoover's Gap, a steep, narrow pass almost 4 miles long, entrenchments were constructed but only lightly manned.

The Tullahoma campaign in Tennessee opened in heavy rain which continued unabated for 17 days. Popular belief in the Union army was that the compound word "Tullahoma" was comprised of the Greek words tulla, meaning "mud" and homa meaning "more mud." Greek or not, the mud was not to spoil a brilliant Union victory. According to Union Cavalry commander David Stanley;

"If any student of the military art desires to make a study of a model campaign, let him take his maps and General Rosecrans's orders for the daily movements of his campaign. No better example of successful strategy was carried out during the war than in the Tullahoma campaign."

The Tullahoma Campaign

On June 24, Rosecrans satisfied Lincoln's request and made a feinting attack against Bragg's left flank. His intention was to prove that after six months of training, his men were capable of a complex wheeling maneuver which would rout Bragg and his army. Outfitted with the new 7 shot Spencer repeating rifles, his 1,500 man cavalry unit was sent with haste to control the narrow Hoover's Gap. Not only did they successfully take control of the passage but they prevented the displaced Confederates from escaping to report the presence of the Union advance forces. Six miles away another mountain pass was also opened up and day one of Rosecrans' strategy uncharacteristically unfolded according to plan.

By June 26, the Union divisions feinting to the Confederate left were moving and it was not until later in that day the Bragg realized that it was his right flank that was most endangered. Rosecrans' successful strategy was reinforced when Bragg's own subordinates, having little confidence in his leadership, began to operate on their own initiative without reference to his commands. Following the days fighting, Bragg consulted his subordinates and concluded that a retreat was warranted to save the army. As the Confederates continued to pull back under the relentless forward drive of Rosecrans, they gave up position after position and Bragg finally ordered a retreat to Chattanooga, Tennessee. Unfortunately Rosecrans did not pursue his victory and finally vanquish Bragg. Had he done so the ignominy of the Battle of Chickamauga would not have cast such a long shadow on his military record.

Perhaps recognition of Rosecrans' victory was muted due to his apparent indifference to President Lincoln's earlier appeals to go on the offensive; or perhaps it was because his victory came on the same day as the Union victory at Gettysburg; perhaps it was overshadowed by the fall of Vicksburg; or perhaps, as Rosecrans himself suggested, his victory was diminished by not being smeared with the blood of thousands. Whatever the reason, the Tullahoma campaign has never been widely recognized as the brilliant campaign it most certainly was.

***

Vicksburg, Mississippi, the "Gibraltar of the Confederacy" was located near a swamp in a bend of the Mississippi River and represented the last hope of maintaining the connected integrity of the Confederacy. In the words of President Jefferson Davis,

"Vicksburg is the nail head that holds the South's two halves together."

President Lincoln echoed Davis' views and pushed Grant to take the city,

"Vicksburg is the key. The war can never be brought to a close until the key is in our pocket."

The natural defenses of the city had already withstood the naval attacks of Admiral David Farragut during July 1862. Heat prostration and tropical disease ended his attempt to dig a canal across the de Soto Peninsula on which the city sat.

Ulysses S. Grant was given the order to push overland and capture the city which had been re-fortified following the naval attacks. Ordering it to be conquered and conquering it were two disparate issues. Commanding the fortifications of the city manned with 12,000 soldiers was Lieutenant General John Pemberton of the Confederate army. Pemberton, from Pennsylvania, was married to a Southern girl and he followed his heart out of the Union. However, his concern for being a Northern officer in a Southern army coloured his decisions and made him a cautious leader.

In the first 3 months of the year Grant attempted to construct waterways that would bring his troops close to the city. His first effort was to expand the 6 foot wide canal started by Farragut to a width of sixty feet and a depth of seven feet. Bad hydraulic design resulted in a wasted effort as the rising Mississippi overflowed and washed out the canal. Efforts were abandoned in March.

A canal to by-pass Vicksburg and connect the Mississippi north and south of the city was then attempted but there were insufficient shallow-draft boats to move his army. A total of seven attempts to bypass Vicksburg were undertaken and all ended in failure. Swamp fevers and hard work were taking a toll on the Union forces and filling their Confederate counterparts with increasing confidence. The South was winning its share of the gun boat battles on the Mississippi River as well and emboldening dreams of a Confederate reconquest of New Orleans. While not significant to the course of the war, these gun boat battles were an aggravation to the North and made depressing newspaper headlines.

The last, and successful, attempt to move his troops past the city was made with corduroy roads and bridges over the swamps. His gunboats and transport ships also successfully moved down river by passing close to the artillery emplacements whose cannons could not depress enough to fire on the ships. By April 22 his army and boats were located south of the city and ready to cross the Mississippi to the eastern shore. In order to contain the Confederate forces during the river crossing, Grant created two successful diversions to draw the city garrison to the north.

Grant then turned his attention to attacking Vicksburg from its relatively unprotected eastern bank. He planned to join with Major General Banks downriver so that a united assault could be made. However, Banks was not ready to march north to Vicksburg and Grant decided to move alone abandoning his supply lines and traveling east to Jackson, Mississippi before swinging back to attack Vicksburg. It was a lightening fast and successful campaign.

The Battle of Vicksburg

On May 12 Union forces advancing eastward encountered Confederate units at Raymond, Mississippi and, in heavy fighting, the larger Union forces drove back the Confederate defenders, cutting off the rail link to Vicksburg. Vicksburg was under siege. Grant feared that Generals Joseph Johnston and P.G.T. Beauregarde were within days of reinforcing the garrison at Jackson. This would dangerously compromise his army by placing the Union forces between two Confederate armies. So it was off to Jackson.

General Johnston decided on an orderly retreat from the city rather than fight Grant and by noon on May 14, the Confederate army was safely away. Jackson, however, was the capital of Mississippi and by not stopping Grant, Johnston dealt a psychological blow to the Confederacy. Grant marched into the town and toasted his men at local hotels then destroyed factories and rail connections.

The Union army then wheeled to the west and turned its attention on Vicksburg. At Champion Hill, on May 16, Grant caught up with Confederate general Pemberton and by 1:00 p.m. drove the Confederates off the hill. Union troops were, in turn, driven back by a counter offensive but a second Union attack with fresh troops took and held the hill.

The final battle leading to the siege of Vicksburg took place the following day at Big Black Bear River Bridge. The Confederates had built emplacements on the eastern bank of the river and began to shell the approaching Union forces. With the main army pinned down by cannon fire, a brigade of soldiers approached the Confederate breastworks via a sunken river meander and, crossing in front of the embankments, routed the inexperienced Southerners. In the ensuing confusion 1,800 Confederate prisoners were taken and the soldiers returning to Vicksburg were depressed and disorganized.

Pemberton's forces were now depleted and he could count on only 18,000 soldiers to defend against Grant's forces of 35,000. General Johnston urged Pemberton to save his army and abandon the city. However, Pemberton, conscious of being a Northerner, would not offer such easy bait to those who were suspicious of him. Instead he deployed his forces to take advantage of the terrain and fortifications that formed the perimeter of the city.

On May 19, Grant mounted an artillery barrage and made two unsuccessful attempts to over-run the hills around the city. On May 21 and 22 Union gunboats and artillery bombarded the city for several hours before an assault along a 3 mile front was ordered. The rough terrain and enfilading fire did not permit any advance. By May 25 Grant decided that Vicksburg would only be won by a siege and both sides dug in. Pemberton's only hope was that Johnston would be able to bring some relief.

By June 14, Grant had 77,000 troops encircling Vicksburg. Pemberton attempted to disrupt Grant's supply lines on the west

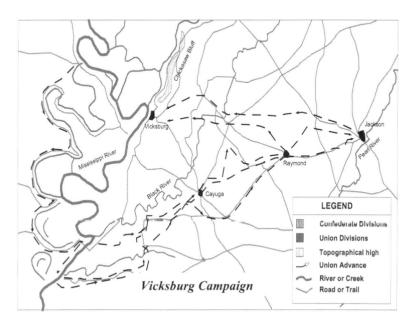

Vicksburg Campaign

side of the Mississippi River by attacking at Milliken's Bend against mostly black troops who, with high casualties, successfully drove off the attack. By the end of June the siege was having a telling effect and Confederate soldiers became sick from a variety of fevers, citizens were starving and pet animals began to disappear in the night. To avoid the constant artillery bombardment the citizens left their houses and dug homes in the soft, yellow clay river banks earning Vicksburg the nickname "Prairie Dog Village."

On June 25th Union troops packed a forty foot tunnel with explosives and detonated it leaving a large crater which penetrated the Confederate line. The soldiers who ran into the crater in an effort to overwhelm the Confederate line were soon trapped and shot down by Confederate gunners from the crater's rim. Perhaps emblematic of the economic power to be found at the junction of freedom with creativity, historian Shelby Foote recounts the flight of Abraham, a black slave in the Confederate army. While preparing a meal for his master, Abraham was blown by the explosion from his position near the campfire only to find himself upright behind Union lines, unhurt and suddenly free. His journey was converted to cash by an enterprising Union sergeant who put him in a tent and charged 5 cents to have a look.

Pemberton sued for peace on July 3rd and Grant at first asked for an unconditional surrender. Upon considering the logistics of transporting so many sick soldiers to prisons in the

North, Grant reconsidered and granted parole to all. The oak tree under which the surrender took place was immediately torn apart by trophy hunters from both sides of the battle line. With the declaration of surrender, brothers and cousins who had been firing at each other, now poured across the no man's land to embrace each other in relief and, no doubt, mild remonstrance.

The South had been sundered. Those citizens who had been hoarding food waiting for better prices saw a sudden drop in their net worth and Northern soldiers shared their rations with the starving Confederate troops. President Lincoln commemorated the fall of Vicksburg as that day in which *"The Father of Waters again goes unvexed to the sea."*

The Vicksburg campaign cost the lives of 10,000 Union and 9,000 Confederate dead and injured in addition to the surrender of 29,500 men, 172 cannons and 50,000 rifles. The capture of the city was the second major Union victory of that day and the citizens of Vicksburg did not celebrate July 4th again until World War II.

***

Following their brilliant victory at Chancellorsville on May 6, 1863, the Southern leadership in the Eastern Theatre decided to invade Pennsylvania to relieve the siege of Vicksburg, feed the Southern troops on Northern food, animate the Northern peace movement and to demonstrate to European leaders that the South was a viable nation.

General Lee split his 72,000 man army into three corps and started north on June 3. The first test came at the Battle of Brandy Station near Culpeper, Virginia where J.E.B. Stuart's cavalry, with difficulty, won both the day and a new respect for the Northern cavalry. The first Southern troops crossed the Potomac on June 15 and by June 25, Lee's entire Confederate army was on Union soil. Joseph Hooker watched and maintained his army between the Confederates and Washington. The Southern army was given instructions to treat the Northern civilians with respect and to pay for all services, food and equipment taken. Northerners could be forgiven for thinking that payment in worthless Southern scrip was less than respectful. And the forty black freedmen who were captured and sold back into slavery in the South might also have wondered about Southern respect. But the impact of the Southern invasion of the North was considerably less than the Northern invasions of the South.

Major General Jubal Early passed through Gettysburg on June 26 and departed the next day for York County where he collected tribute from the local citizenry. His was the deepest penetration into the Pennsylvania countryside. J.E.B. Stuart led part of his cavalry around the Union flank but left no instructions for the disposition of the remaining cavalry units. For several days he and his mounts struggled to reconnect with the main Confederate army while evading capture. With the temporary loss of his cavalry, Lee was unaware of the movement of his enemy.

In a fateful act of brinksmanship, Hooker offered his resignation over a jurisdictional dispute. President Lincoln, who had taken an unsuccessful political risk in promoting Hooker, replaced him with the more popular Major General George Gordon Meade. On June 28 the Army of the Potomac had their penultimate commander. Meade, thrust into a role he had not sought, was a cautious man by nature and intended to draw the Confederate army into battle at his carefully prepared battlements at Pipe Creek. He had no desire nor expectation of a fight at the small town of Gettysburg.

Northern troops were supplied with comfortable, fitted boots and the mere rumor of a supply of these boots at Gettysburg was motivation enough for a division of Southern troops to investigate. Approaching Gettysburg they observed the arrival of the Union cavalry under Brigadier General John Buford and hurried back to inform their commanders. On the following morning, July 1, a large reconnaissance force was sent to verify the reports.

The Battle of Gettysburg

In response to the Confederate reconnaissance, Buford occupied the high ground approaches to the town in order to provide a defensive cover for the arriving infantry. As the Confederate units approached from the west they were confronted by Buford's now dismounted cavalry on Herr, McPherson and Seminary Ridges.

Confederate forces pushed the Union line off one ridge and onto the next until the thinly garrisoned Union troops formed a semi-circle from the west to the northern boundaries of Gettysburg. Jubal Early's division, returning from York County outflanked the Union line to the north forcing them to retreat through Gettysburg to Cemetery Hill where infantry Major General Winfield Hancock took command of the Union troops. With Union forces holding the high ground, Gettysburg became the reverse of Fredericksburg. Recognizing his ill-favoured position, Lee told Ewell to make every effort to capture Cemetery Hill. Ewell demurred and the die was cast. This first day of battle at Gettysburg involved 50,000 men and should not be viewed as a skirmishing prelude to larger battles. It was a bloody brawl in its own right.

The next day Lee and Meade rushed the remainder of their armies to Gettysburg and, by the afternoon of July 2, both sides were at full strength with the Union army continuing to occupy the high ground from Culp's Hill on the northeast boundary of Gettysburg and hooking into the two mile north-south trending stretch of Cemetery Ridge then anchoring at the Big and Little Round Tops. The Confederate troops were located on Seminary Ridge facing east towards the Union forces on Cemetery

Ridge. Lee planned to outflank the Union forces on the southern extreme of Cemetery Ridge and roll them toward the center where

they would be met with forces advancing from Seminary Ridge. Unfortunately, the absence of J.E.B. Stuart meant that Lee had incorrect information, and he was not aware of the Union forces in the Devil's Den at the base of the Round Tops or of the men holding the Union line on the Little Round Top.

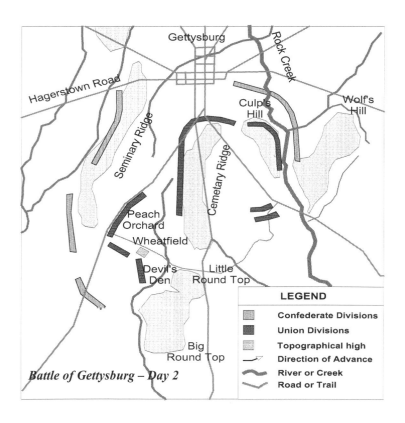

Battle of Gettysburg – Day 2

Confederate Major General Longstreet delayed making his flanking move until late in the afternoon and then his troops slammed into the Union forces pushing them back from the Wheatfield and Peach Orchard. A final desperate counter attack from the Northern troops finally pushed the Confederates back from the base of the Little Round Top and ended their attempts to flank the Union army from the south. Coincidentally with the furious action at the Devil's Den, a Confederate brigade made its way up the slopes of the Little Round Top expecting to break out on the Union troops positioned on Cemetery Ridge. The Union line, however, had extended in front of the Confederate advance and held off a series of uphill charges by the Southerners. The Union defenders who suffered 50 percent casualties were reduced to throwing rocks when their ammunition was exhausted. Their leader, Colonel Joshua Lawrence Chamberlain, was awarded the Congressional Medal of Honor for his role in maintaining the Union line.

In the waning light of evening the Union troops on Culp's Hill on the northern flank were attacked. Union commander Meade had been forced to shift his troops from the north and center of his line to the south in order to defend against the Confederate attacks in the Devil's Den and the two Round Tops. Fortunately, the remaining troops had spent the day entrenching and erecting their defenses and were able to repel the attacks when they came. The Confederates suffered heavy losses in the intense fighting. This second day of battle produced slaughters in locations poetically known as the Peach Orchard, the Wheatfield, the Devils Den, and the Slaughter Pen.

Lee originally planned for the third day of fighting to mimic the second day with flanking attacks and a drive into the center. However, the plan was upset when Union positions on Culp's Hill began an artillery barrage to drive the Confederate troops further back. The Confederates countered with a charge up the hill and after 7 hours of fighting retreated at 11:00 am. This led Lee to make his historic decision to advance a massed attack on the Union center at Cemetery Ridge. With memories of Fredericksburg and the awful slaughter of Union soldiers, Longstreet and others attempted to dissuade him from this plan of attack. Lee, however, had his blood up and was convinced that his soldiers were capable of anything. He wanted to destroy Meade and he wanted to do it on that day.

The 150 Confederate field guns opened up at 1 p.m. with a frightening barrage on the Union positions atop Cemetery Ridge. In order to conserve their ammunition and draw out the Confederate battalions, the Union guns responded with less than half of their weaponry. Their tactics were successful on both counts and Confederate gunnery commander Alexander, convinced that his shots were telling, indicated that the battle could begin. Pickett's Charge, which involved two other divisions in addition to Pickett's, started off at 3 p.m. when the artillery halted. Pickett loved the pomp and circumstance of the military life but he never forgot the sixty percent casualties his men suffered that afternoon in which two brigadier generals and all of his colonels were killed or wounded. His 12,500 soldiers emerged from the treeline of Seminary Ridge and advanced a mile and a half across open fields to Cemetery Ridge where they were greeted with fire from field guns and rifled muskets that ripped through the Confederate ranks. The only advance made was at a jog in a stone wall called the "Angle" which was

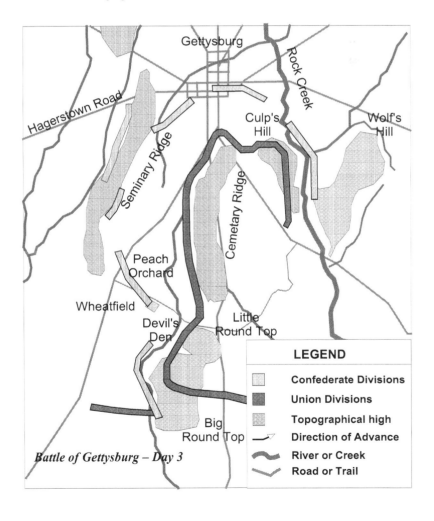

Battle of Gettysburg – Day 3

LEGEND

- Confederate Divisions
- Union Divisions
- Topographical high
- Direction of Advance
- River or Creek
- Road or Trail

quickly retaken by Union reinforcements.

The third day of battle ended the Southern dream of dealing a punishing blow to the Union. There would be no support from Europe and the Northern peace movement would have to await other events to generate support. On July 4 the Confederate forces reorganized into a defensive position hoping that the Union forces could be drawn into an offensive battle. However, apart from small skirmishes and probing actions little was done other than to bury the dead, treat the injured and plan for a better day. The Union forces had earned their third major success for that day. The result of three days of battle dramatically reduced the Confederate army strength and morale. As a result many believe Gettysburg to have been the turning point in the war.

In the pouring rain of July 5 Lee decamped his Confederate army, under their protests, and began the long walk home. Despite the frantic efforts of both President Lincoln and General-in-Chief Halleck, Meade refused to make any but the most peremptory of attempts to intercept Lee and finally destroy the Rebel Cause. This lassitude following a major military action was a hallmark of the Civil War and it occurred on both sides of the battlefield. After viewing such death and destruction no general, to paraphrase Northern Secretary of the Navy Gideon Welles, could take hold of the war that was placed in his hands and close his fingers on it.

Gettysburg was a tactical success for the North and North-erners were delighted with their army but Lincoln was furious for the lost opportunity. In the three days of battle 7,000 men died on the battlefield and another 5,000 died of their injuries soon after. Each side lost 23,000 men from death, wounds or capture but for once the Union forces made fewer mistakes than the Confederates and, by holding the high ground, were able to carry the day.

***

On August 16, under pressure from Washington, William Rosecrans began his move towards Chattanooga and by Sep-tember 4 the Union armies crossed the Tennessee River. In order to buttress Bragg's position, General Johnston sent him 9,000 men and a further 5,000 were sent with Lieutenant General Longstreet from Lee's Army of Northern Virginia.

As Rosecrans advanced, Bragg slipped into Georgia and the Union army was able to occupy Chattanooga without firing a shot. Bragg set a trap for Rosecrans by sending "deserters" from his army north to the Union army with tales of confusion and demoralization. Against the advice of his subordinates, Rosecrans set off in pursuit certain that Bragg could be easily defeated. One of his scattered divisions narrowly escaped annihilation and Rosecrans, recognizing his peril, stopped to regroup his army.

The Battle of Chickamauga

The two armies jockeyed for position south of Chattanooga and on September 17, Bragg decided to move against Rosecrans and either push him north or provoke him to fight. On September 18, as he awaited the arrival of Longstreet, there were minor skirmishes to gain control of the fords and bridges across the West Chattanooga Creek and by nightfall both armies faced each other on the same side of the water.

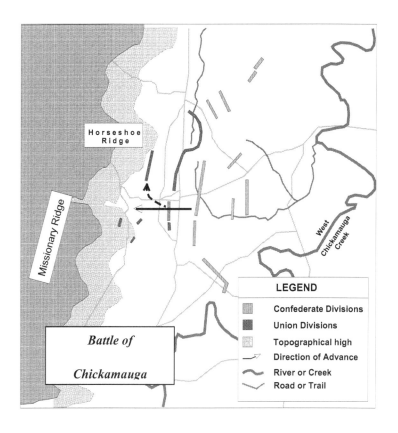

Battle of

Chickamauga

LEGEND

Confederate Divisions
Union Divisions
Topographical high
Direction of Advance
River or Creek
Road or Trail

As dawn broke on September 19, the Confederates opened the battle on several fronts and drove the Union line back almost 2 miles. Several Union counter attacks failed and as darkness was falling a concerted Confederate attempt to turn the Union lines towards the south almost met with success but by the time the shooting stopped the Union line had reconsolidated into a defensive position. The heavy losses of the day reduced opportunities for a major victory in subsequent fighting but the Confederate forces could smell success.

Both commanding generals reformulated their battle plans for September 20 and Rosecrans determined to make a defensive stand. Bragg wanted to attack at first light but no one thought to inform the commander of the division which was to lead the attack of his role. When the attack came against the center of the Union line it was poorly executed and conflicting orders prevented the Confederates from driving through the Union position. An ambiguous order from Rosecrans resulted in one division leaving the line creating a breach and, in one of those strangely fateful events that shape history, Longstreet's attack hit the Union line precisely when it was weakest and where the breach had been created. As his men crashed through the line they over-ran the Union artillery positions and captured 15 of 26 cannons. The Union troops who had erroneously vacated the line then wheeled and counter-attacked driving the Confederates back. Brigadier General John Bell Hood, who had led the Confederate attack, was shot in the left leg during the retreat and it was subsequently amputated. He had previously lost the use of his right arm while fighting in the Devil's Den at Gettysburg and for the remainder of the war had to be tied onto his horse each morning.

Fighting on the southern end of the battle line intensified and the Confederate advantage became a Union rout. Soldiers left the line to flee towards Missionary Ridge and when attempts to rally his men failed, Rosecrans also left the field with several of his senior commanders. The center of the Union line, under the command of Major General George Thomas, was able to slow the Confederate attack so that the fleeing army was not pursued. When Thomas finally withdrew under orders from Rosecrans, he left a sacrificial unit behind who protected the withdrawal and then surrendered to the Confederates.

For his courageous stand, George Thomas earned the nickname "Rock of Chickamauga" and his star continued to rise as that of his commander fell. Rosecrans ignored his subordinates appeal to avenge their loss and remained in Chattanooga, happy to accept President Lincoln's advice to protect his army until Burnside could arrive with reinforcements.

Bragg likewise was finished fighting and did not pursue Rosecrans and destroy his fleeing army. He did manage to capture Union supplies but the value of his success was muted by its cost – 18,500 Confederate casualties to 16,000 Union casualties. These were the highest of any battle in the Western Theatre and second only to Gettysburg for the Civil War.

According to Lieutenant General D.H. Hill of the Confederate army, Chickamauga was the final battle in which Southern soldiers fought with their usual verve and inspiration,

It seems to me that the elan of the Southern soldier was never seen after Chickamauga. ... He fought stoutly to the last, but, after Chickamauga, with the sullenness of despair and without the enthusiasm of hope. That 'barren victory' sealed the fate of the Confederacy.

With Rosecrans and his army behind barricades at Chattanooga, Bragg moved his army onto the heights overlooking the town. Both commanders then settled in to face the personal consequences of Chickamauga. In October Rosecrans and two of his subordinates were replaced as a result of leaving the battlefield and George Thomas was given command of the Army of the Cumberland.

Braxton Bragg disciplined those of his subordinates who most loudly decried his leadership and the response was a near mutiny of his senior commanders. When President Davis visited the army to assess the situation he endorsed Bragg and subsequently "re-assigned" the leaders of the mutiny.

The city of Chattanooga, located along the banks of the navigable Tennessee River, was a transportation and manufacturing center in the South. Rail lines linked it with Nashville and Knoxville in the northwest and Atlanta to the southeast. It was protected by the river on all but the east side which was well protected by embankments thrown up by Bragg himself. Bragg decided to fortify himself on Lookout Mountain and Missionary Ridge overlooking the city with its supply lines on the far bank.

By the end of October, raids on the Union supply lines and the siege of the city were beginning to have an effect. Joseph Hooker and 15,000 men from the Army of the Potomac were sent to assist in lifting the siege. Joining him was William Tecumseh Sherman and 20,000 men from Grant's Army of the Mississippi. At the end of September, a reorganization of the Western Theatre brought all of the Union armies under the command of Major General Ulysses Grant and Thomas was ordered to hold the city at all costs. On October 27 the Union army moved out of Chattanooga and attacked the Confederate forces at a crossing known as Brown's ferry. Bragg ordered James Longstreet to retake Brown's Ferry but Hooker's men were able to hold on opening a permanent access to Chattanooga and relieving the siege.

The Battle of Chattanooga

Grant ordered the breakout of Chattanooga to begin in earnest on November 23. Between the defenses of Chattanooga and the high hills of Missionary Ridge was a small knoll called Orchard Knob. A reconnaissance-in-force was sent out to determine the strength of the Confederate lines and the 14,000 Union soldiers overwhelmed the 600 Southern defenders. The

Northern soldiers fortified their new position and it became their headquarters for the remainder of the battle.

Bragg, recognizing the importance of the coming battle combined his forces at positions of strength on the crests of Lookout Mountain and Missionary Ridge. Rifle pits were dug at the base of the hills and defensive positions added reinforcement higher up the slopes. The following day, November 24, Hooker, with 10,000 men was given the task of driving the Confederates off Lookout Mountain and removing their clear line of fire into Union positions. He moved his men across Lookout Mountain Creek to begin his advance against the 7,000 Confederate soldiers. At 3:00 p.m. a thick fog enshrouded the mountain obscuring the Union advance from the Confederate soldiers waiting above, giving the battle its poetic name of "The Battle Above the Clouds." The only evidence of a battle being fought was the crackle of sporadic rifle fire as ghostly apparitions shot blindly and to little effect. The Union soldiers were making steady progress up the mountain and captured it during the night when Bragg recalled all his troops to Missionary Ridge. The Federal army now was anchored on the south end of the Confederate line.

While Hooker consolidated in the south, Sherman brought three divisions of men across the Tennessee River onto the right flank of the Confederate line. Attacking what he thought was the northern extent of Missionary Ridge, Sherman was dis-

mayed to find that he was about to win control of the entirely
separate Goat Hill. Separated from Missionary Ridge by a deep

and well protected ravine, Sherman told his men to fortify their
position and proceed no further. The Federal army was now
anchored on the north end of the Confederate line.

The battle plan for November 25 called for Hooker on the
south and Sherman on the north to move towards each other in
a double envelopment which would hopefully squeeze the
Confederate position and force a retreat to the east. On the
north, the Union attack was repelled by a bayonet charge. Both
attacks quickly bogged down under stiff Confederate resistance

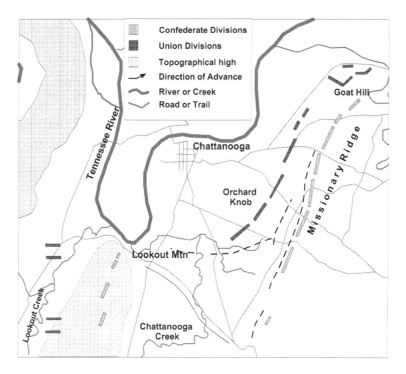

so George Thomas was ordered to attack the center, control the lower rifle pits and await further orders.

In a remarkable nexus of raw courage and poor command, the Union troops surged into the Confederate rifle pits under steady and deadly fire from the Southern soldiers on the crest above. However, the defense of the crest had been poorly organized and allowed a firing "shadow" to develop upslope from the newly acquired rifle pits. Rather than retreat to avoid the fusillade from above, the Union soldiers moved uphill to stay safe. Once out of range of the enemy fire, remembering their retreat at Chickamauga, and in the absence of clear orders, they decided to keep climbing.

As the Union soldiers struggled towards the top of the hill they overran the retreating Confederate soldiers and the upper defenders were loathe to fire on the approaching blue mass for fear of hitting their own men. The Union soldiers moved so quickly that the defenders on the ridge had no time to prepare themselves and almost as many surrendered as retreated. At one point Braxton Bragg himself was almost captured by the surging Union forces. As Grant and Thomas watched the unfolding scene from below, the senior commander became furious that his orders had not been obeyed. Thomas, still stinging from Chickamauga was sure his career was over and only relaxed when it became obvious that the Confederate line had been breeched. Chickamauga was redeemed and now the Confederates retreated in panic. On November 26, Bragg reformed his army and ordered a retreat to Dalton, Georgia. Grant did not make any effective effort to pursue but instead set about to relieve Ambrose Burnside at Knoxville.

Confederate casualties in the fighting were 12,000 and when asked whether the dead soldiers should be buried by state Thomas rendered his opinion on the politics of the war;

"Mix 'em up. I'm tired of State's rights!"

Chattanooga was the beginning of the end for the Confederate effort in the Western Theatre. Bragg was in full retreat and by the beginning of December had resigned his command to Joseph Johnston. With the approach of Sherman, Longstreet abandoned the siege of Knoxville, went into winter quarters and then returned to Virginia in the spring of 1864. The jubilation of Chickamauga was replaced with an air of impending doom throughout the South.

***

The year 1863 closed poorly for the Confederate government. It could not replace the men lost in the many battles and General Lee's foray into Pennsylvania had been a fiasco. The high cost of the war closed in on both the North and the South but the vastly superior resources of the North allowed it to face 1864 with increased optimism and hopes for success. On November 17 at the consecration of a 17 acre cemetery in the battered town of Gettysburg, President Lincoln produced the most succinct and beautiful prose in American history; the Gettysburg Address. Immediately following his 2 minute address Lincoln told an aide, "That speech won't scour."

The Union success in Chattanooga opened an important new supply terminal which fed Sherman on his subsequent march through Georgia and President Lincoln was sure he had now found his general. Ulysses S. Grant was called to Washington in March 1864 to assume command of all the Union armies.

8: Confederate Leaders of the Civil War

The Confederate Army commissioned approximately 400 generals during the Civil War. The youngest Confederate general was William Paul Roberts who was 23 years and seven months old when he was promoted in February 1865. There were also four generals older than age 70. Interestingly there were 6 generals with the name "Jackson" and three had nicknames, eight with the name "Johnston" and six with the name "Lee"; two being closely related. One general had the appropriate name of "Slaughter" and there was even a Brigadier General States Rights Gist. Some parents took their politics untinctured. It is unknown by which name their son was called.

What follows are brief descriptions of Confederate generals who achieved some degree of fame and notoriety during the Civil War. While not an exhaustive list these men provide a good sampling of the remarkable men who managed the war from the Confederate perspective.

Jefferson Finis Davis (June 3, 1808 - December 6, 1889)

Jefferson Davis was the youngest of 10 children and he spent most of his youth near the town of Woodville, Mississippi attending a log cabin school near his home. His later education was at a Dominican Catholic school in Kentucky and he graduated from Transylvania University in Lexington, Kentucky in

1824. Following his graduation from the US Military Academy in 1828 his military career started at Fort Crawford, Wisconsin and later transferred to Galena, Illinois.

In 1835 he resigned his commission to marry the daughter of his commanding officer but the newlyweds contracted malaria and his bride died three months after the wedding. Davis returned to health and in 1844 was elected to the US Congress. In 1845 he married Varina Howell of Natchez, Mississippi.

When the Mexican-American war broke out he re-enlisted and raised a volunteer regiment, serving as its colonel. Following the war he refused a commission from President James Polk on the basis that only state governments had the right to appoint militia officers. State rights was in his blood.

After the war Davis restarted his political career, serving as a Senator from Mississippi, and then left to become Regent of the Smithsonian Institute. He campaigned for Franklin Pierce and became his Secretary of War, losing his cabinet post when James Buchanan was elected president in 1856. He was re-elected to the Senate on March 4, 1857.

Although he was committed to the constitutional right of states to secede Davis had become a reformed secessionist because he knew such a course would lead to hostilities against the stronger US army. Nevertheless he accepted the result of the Mississippi decision to leave the Union and resigned his Senate seat on January 10, 1861.

Upon his return to Mississippi he was commissioned a major general of the state militia until being named provisional president of the Confederate States of America on February 9, 1861. On November 6, 1861 he was duly elected to a 6 year term as president and was inaugurated on February 22, 1862.

There is debate as to whether Davis' military career aided his military decisions during the Civil War. There is, however, no ambiguity about his decision to appoint Robert E. Lee to command of the Army of Northern Virginia, replacing the wounded Joseph E. Johnston. At the time of his appointment the decision created great controversy.

General Lee provided Davis with the support and superior leadership he required in the Eastern Theatre but the situation was much different in the West. Controversy over the leadership of Braxton Bragg was a constant problem and Davis sent Joseph Johnston to resolve the issue before visiting the troops himself to understand the issues and come to a resolution. His replacement of Joseph Johnston with the more aggressive John

Bell Hood prior to the fall of Atlanta was a decision that would haunt his legacy.

Davis certainly faced more daunting economic and social challenges than his Northern counterpart. Unable to recruit black soldiers and with most of white males in uniform, the Southern economy was put in the hands of those who would gain most from a Northern victory. The blockade of Southern ports was so effective that imports into and exports from the South were reduced to a trickle and the economy was almost entirely dedicated to the war effort. As a result, those who were not in the army suffered from shortages of just about everything and available items were inflated in cost beyond the means of all but the very rich.

Proportionately the South lost more men in the war than did the North and the death toll was felt at every hearth. Support for the war flagged much earlier in the South than in the North and most soldiers received a steady supply of letters urging desertion especially as economic conditions reduced families to beggary. As the Northern armies invaded and laid waste to the Southern countryside, pressure to end the war mounted. President Davis undoubtedly was a strong contender with President Lincoln for the "tiredest man alive."

Davis had to balance the economic exigencies of the war and find a way to raise money without impoverishing the struggling new state. He also had to embolden his armies to find victory while navigating complex political mine fields. That he was able to sustain the war speaks to his skill in that balancing act.

In April 1865, with Union troops at the entrance to Richmond and at the urging of General Lee, the Confederate cabinet decamped to Greensboro, North Carolina. He officially dissolved the government on May 5, 1865 and five days later was captured at Irwinville, Georgia. Davis spent the next two years in a military prison in Fort Monroe, Virginia. While in prison he sold his Mississippi estate to a former slave who, a precocious thinker and businessman, became wealthy. Prominent citizens of both the North and South including publisher Horace Greeley and tycoon Cornelius Vanderbilt financed Davis' bail and he was allowed to travel widely outside the US until the case against him was dropped in February 1869.

Davis then became president of a life insurance company based in Memphis, Tennessee and was re-elected to the US Senate in 1875 although, under the terms of the 14th Amendment, he was ineligible to take his seat.

Davis again traveled abroad returning to spend three years in Biloxi, Mississippi in order to write his memoirs, *The Rise and Fall of the Confederate Government*. In October 1889 he completed *A Short History of the Confederate States of America* and died three months later on December 6, 1889. His funeral was the largest ever held in the South and his cortege moved from New Orleans, Louisiana to Richmond, Virginia where his remains are interred.

Robert Edward Lee (January 19, 1807 - October 12, 1870)

Robert E Lee was born into a wealthy and privileged Virginia family. His father, "Light Horse Harry" Lee participated in the War of Independence and died when Robert was 11 years old. Unfortunately he left his family with little but debt. Nevertheless his son was able to receive a classical education and spiritual development from his deeply religious mother.

In 1825 he entered the US Military Academy and excelled in each of his four years, graduating as a brevet second lieutenant in the Army Corps of Engineers. He worked with the Army Corps of Engineers at Fort Monroe where he finalized completion of the battlements, in Ohio where he surveyed the state line with Michigan and at St. Louis where he supervised the dredging of the Mississippi and Missouri Rivers. In 1831, the young army engineer married Mary Anna Randolph Custis and they had four daughters and three sons – all of whom served in the Civil War with him.

During the Mexican-American War he was an aide to General Winfield Scott and won notoriety for his reconnaissance of innovative routes of attack. As a fighting officer he was given battlefield promotions to the level of Colonel but with the peace he returned to being a captain in the Corps of Engineers. From 1852 – 1855 he served as the Superintendent of West Point and left to take a commission as Lieutenant Colonel in the cavalry under Colonel Albert Sydney Johnston.

When John Brown and his fellow rebels attempted to lead a slave revolt at Harper's Ferry, Lee was sent to capture them. In a three minute fusillade, the twenty two insurrectionists were either killed or captured, and the first fatal step towards war was initiated. During the politically unstable days of 1860, Lee was not supportive of secession and considered it to be a betrayal of the wishes of the Founders. As the nation drifted toward war, Abraham Lincoln offered him the position of Major General of the U.S. Army. Lee, however, felt honour-bound to follow his state and on April 18, 1861 he turned down Lincoln's offer;

Lee also turned down an offer to become Major General of the Confederate forces and became the senior officer of the Virginia militia instead. His first field assignment was commanding Confederate forces in western Virginia, where he was defeated at the Battle of Cheat Mountain and was widely blamed for Confederate setbacks.

His less than stellar performance in western Virginia earned him the sobriquet of "Granny Lee" and he was reassigned as a special military advisor to President Davis. After the Battle of Seven Pines on June 1, 1862 he replaced the wounded Joseph E. Johnston as Commander of the Army of North Virginia and quickly dispelled any notion that he was an inferior leader.

Lee displayed his genius in creatively altering the accepted dogmas of warfare and often split his smaller forces and divided them again to obtain the element of surprise or gain the most advantageous position in pending battles. He had an uncanny ability to predict the moves of his opponents and developed a very high regard for both his generals and his soldiers, believing them capable of almost any maneuver required. His men returned the compliment by believing in his invincibility.

In the Seven Days Battles he out-generaled George McClellan of the Northern Army of the Potomac and drove Union forces off the Peninsula. At the Second Battle of Bull Run he split the division of Stonewall Jackson from the main army and sent them on a rapid flanking maneuver that caught Union Major General John Pope by surprise crushing his army between those of Longstreet and Jackson. He again split his army for the march into Maryland and was almost destroyed when a set of field orders fell into the hands of Union Major General McClellan. But he recovered quickly, reformed his army and met the much larger Union army from well entrenched positions at Antietam Creek. At both Fredericksburg and Chancellorsville his army was well anchored and entrenched. The Union attacks on Marye's Hill had no real chance of success against his concealed and enfilading positions.

The famous Pickett's Charge on the third day of the Battle of Gettysburg was perhaps Lee's only significant tactical error. Against the better judgment of his subordinates, he ordered a frontal assault on the well protected Union high ground resulting in the annihilation of Pickett's division. Humbly, Lee apologized to his troops, accepting the blame for the bloodshed and offering his resignation to President Davis who wisely refused to accept it.

With each battle that Lee and his army fought, their numbers were reduced. By the final battle at the Appomattox Court House, many of Lee's soldiers were barefoot, clothed with rags and had little to eat. In fact, General Grant's first order following the surrender of the Confederate forces was to feed Lee's impoverished army.

Following the cessation of hostilities, Lee moved to a friend's plantation, as his home at Arlington had been confiscated by the Union. It was returned to his son in 1882 and then purchased for $150,000 in March 1883. Within months of the end of the war General Lee was offered the position of president of Washington College in Lexington, Virginia and he remained there until his death in 1870. During his tenure Lee upgraded the curriculum of the college and made efforts to attract students from the North as well as the South.

The fight over reconstruction in the South led Lee to recant his decision to surrender and he once stated;

> *"Governor, if I had foreseen the use those people [Yankees] designed to make of their victory, there would have been no surrender at Appomattox Courthouse; no sir, not by me. Had I foreseen these results of subjugation, I would have preferred to die at Appomattox with my brave men, my sword in my right hand."*

On September 28, 1870, Lee suffered a stroke that left him without the ability to speak and he died two weeks later from the effects of pneumonia.

Pierre Gustav Toutant Beauregard
(May 28, 1818 – Feb. 20, 1893)

P.G.T. Beauregard, from New Orleans, was one of 7 brothers and sisters and did not learn to speak English until he attended school in New York City at age 12. In 1838 he graduated from the US Military Academy. It was at West Point that he changed "Toutant" from a surname to a middle name and from where he took artillery training from Robert Anderson, his opponent at Fort Sumter.

Beauregard served under Winfield Scott during the Mexican-American War and then worked as an army engineer in Louisiana for the next twelve years. He was appointed Superintendent of the military academy in 1861 but served only five days in that capacity. His engineering experience made him the logical choice to  command the Confederate forces in Charleston and he ordered the cannonade of Fort Sumter on April 12, 1861 – the opening shot of the Civil War. For 34 hours Beauregard shelled Anderson who finally surrendered with his Union forces on April 14 making Beauregard a bona fide Southern hero.

He was then given responsibility to prepare for the expected offensive from his classmate Major General Irvin McDowell at Manassas Junction. His strategy was too complex for the untrained soldiers under his command and fortunately his opponent suffered from the same defect in strategy. McDowell's attack on the Confederate left flank on June 21, 1861 was not in Beauregard's battle plans and the Union forces almost overran the Southern flank at Henry House Hill being stopped by the "stonewall" of Thomas Jackson.

On March 14, 1862, Beauregard, who had political ambi-
tions, was transferred to "safety" in the Western Theatre serving
under Albert Sidney Johnston. He was instrumental in the
planning and execution of the Battle of Shiloh on April 6, 1862.
With the death of General Johnston, Beauregard assumed
command and called off the attack assuming that mop-up
operations would be best completed the next day. Unfortunately for the Confederate side, the Army of the Ohio commanded
by General Don Carlos Buell arrived to reinforce Grant during
the night and the "mop-up" became a general retreat of the
Southern forces back to Corinth, Mississippi.

In order to keep the Union forces under Major General Henry Halleck from attacking Corinth, Beauregard resorted to
subterfuge by running the trains and cheering the troops to
suggest the arrival of reinforcements. When he finally pulled
his troops out of Corinth it was to protect his army in the face
of a larger opponent and because the Corinth water supply was
killing more of his men then had died at Shiloh. It was not a
decision shared by his president however. Beauregard himself
became sick at Corinth and went on leave without asking
permission, prompting the less than sympathetic President
Davis to replace him with General Braxton Bragg. No amount
of coaxing could change Davis' mind and Beauregard was reassigned back to the Eastern Theatre.

Davis sent Beauregard to Charleston, South Carolina to defend the coastal defenses which he did with singular success.

While not happy in a non-combat role he was nevertheless instrumental in commissioning the use of submersibles and floating mines.

In 1864, he fought in the Battle of Petersburg and held off the larger Union force allowing General Lee to arrive and garrison the besieged town. In a remarkable display of chutzpah, Beauregard then suggested that he lead an invasion across the Potomac but was instead re-assigned to the Western Theatre where he would be less of a problem to General Lee. He fought alongside General Joseph Johnston to stall the advance of William Tecumseh Sherman but, with most of his forces tied up in the west, there were insufficient men to accomplish this goal. Finally he and General Joseph Johnston capitulated to Sherman on April 26, 1865.

Following the war he managed railway companies in the South and invented a system of cable operated street cars. Beauregard died February 20, 1893.

Braxton Bragg (March 22, 1817 – September 20, 1876)

Braxton Bragg, from North Carolina, graduated from the US Military Academy in 1837 and served as an artillery officer in the Second Seminole War, the occupation of Texas and the Mexican-American War where he was given a promotion to brevet lieutenant colonel. He was not popular with his troops and on one occasion his bed was destroyed by an artillery shell

placed beneath it. To everyone's surprise the worst injury he suffered was the disruption of his sleep.

On March 7, 1861 he transferred his allegiance to the Confederate army and was commissioned a brigadier general. By September 1861 he was promoted to major general and commanded all the Confederate forces in Florida and Alabama. His troops were known for their discipline and he was ordered to bring that discipline to the troops at Corinth, Mississippi. He fought under Albert Sidney Johnston at the Battle of Shiloh and was the commanding officer responsible for dislodging the Union forces at the Hornet's Nest. On that day, April 6, 1862 Bragg was promoted to general and given the responsibility to stop the advance of Major General Don Carlos Buell in Tennessee. He invaded Kentucky and won several strategic victories but retreated from his gains for fear of having his supply lines cut, because his men had no winter clothing or tents and because he doubted the strategic value of the land he had captured.

Bragg was roundly criticized for his lapse in judgment and President Davis gave Joseph Johnston the task of replacing Bragg. Johnston evaluated the situation and decided there was no need of a replacement and kept Bragg in his position. Union Major General William Rosecrans kept up a relentless pursuit of Bragg during the Tullahoma campaign and drove him into

Georgia. On September 19 and 20, 1863, Bragg, with reinforcements from other Confederate armies, attacked Rosecrans, defeated him at the Battle of Chickamauga and besieged him at Chattanooga. Bragg then took advantage of his again-rising star to transfer those generals who most vociferously spoke against him.

When Grant and Sherman broke out of Chattanooga on November 24/25, 1863, Bragg was pushed again into Georgia and subsequently replaced by General Joseph Johnston. In February 1864, Bragg moved to Richmond and was given General Robert E. Lee's old position as military advisor to President Jefferson. The two escaped together after the surrender at Appomattox.

Following the war, Bragg took civilian positions as the superintendent of the New Orleans water system, chief engineer for Alabama and a railroad inspector in Texas. On September 20, 1876 while walking down a Galveston street with a friend he dropped dead of unknown causes.

Jubal Anderson Early
(November 3, 1816 – March 2, 1894)

Jubal Early was a Virginian and the third of ten children. He graduated from the US Military Academy in 1837 and fought in the Seminole Wars in Florida before resigning his

commission in 1838 in order to practice law as a prosecutor. He re-enlisted at the outbreak of the Mexican-American War.

Beginning the Civil War as a brigadier general, Early saw action in most of the battles of the Eastern Theatre including both Battles of Bull Run, the Seven Days Battles, Antietam, Fredericksburg, Chancellorsville and Gettysburg. While Early earned the affection of his men and his commander, General Robert E. Lee, he was known amongst his peers for his bad temper and inability to accept differing opinions.

During the Gettysburg Campaign, Early's division passed through the small town of Gettysburg, captured the town of York, Pennsylvania and reached the Susquehanna River before being recalled to Gettysburg where his division saw action during the three day battle. During the winter of 1863-64, Early served in the Shenandoah Valley before being recalled to support the Confederate forces blocking Ulysses S. Grant's inexorable drive into Virginia. He fought in the Battle of the Wilderness, Spotsylvania and Cold Harbor before embarking on the wartime adventure that was to make him a remarkable Civil War commander.

In an attempt to divert Union forces from the siege of Petersburg, General Lee sent Early into the Shenandoah Valley and from there to cross the Potomac to threaten Washington, D.C. His soldiers reached the outskirts of Washington on July 11 giving a scare to the residents of the city but they were quickly driven back by Union forces which reinforced those guarding the city.

Fearing more attacks on Washington, Grant dispatched Major General Philip Sheridan to defeat Early and lay waste to the Shenandoah Valley so that it could not be used as a staging ground for subsequent Confederate attacks. In a surprise attack on October 19, 1864, Sheridan's larger forces were overwhelmed by Early at the Battle of Cedar Creek. The starving Confederate soldiers broke off their attack in order to loot the Union camp of food and clothing and, when the Union army regrouped for a counter-attack, Early was soundly defeated and routed.

Early escaped to Texas following the Confederate surrender at Appomattox on April 9, 1865 and when the forces there capitulated he proceeded south into Mexico, sailed to Cuba and then moved to Canada. Living in Toronto, he published his memoirs in 1867 and returned to Virginia in 1869 to resume his law practice. On March 2, 1894 he fell down a flight of stairs and died – an unrepentant and proud Rebel.

Richard Stoddert Ewell
(February 8, 1817 – January 25, 1872)

Richard Ewell was born in Washington, D.C. and raised in Virginia. In 1840 he graduated from the US Military Academy and served as an escort along the Santa Fe and Oregon Trails. During the Mexican-American war he was promoted for battlefield courage and conducted reconnaissance patrols with Captain Robert E. Lee. In 1859 he was wounded in a skirmish with Apache Indians and in 1860 the wounds required him to take leave from the army.

Ewell resigned his commission when his state seceded and in January 1862 he was promoted to major general and fought with Stonewall Jackson in the Shenandoah. He was as profane and lively as Jackson was pious and reserved. When Jackson was recalled to assist in the defense of Richmond, Ewell returned with him and fought well in the Seven Days Battles. He fought at the Second Bull Run but shortly afterward was injured and lost his left leg below the knee.

After a recovery period, during which he married his nurse, Ewell returned to fight at Chancellorsville. When Jackson was injured, Ewell took command of the Second Corps from the temporary commander J.E.B. Stuart.

In the opening campaigns of Lee's invasion into Pennsylvania, Ewell was in the lead and captured a Union garrison of 4,000 at Winchester. For the second time in the war he was hit by a spent bullet and suffered only bruising. Returning from the north to join the Confederate forces he smashed his way through the Union forces which retreated to Cemetery Hill. Lee suggested that he push them off the hill "if practicable" and most would have interpreted this to mean "push them off the hill." Ewell, however, accepted the option and declined to engage the Union forces. It was a turning point in the battle but this is not to say that Ewell was wrong. His men had endured a punishing march, there was no hope of reinforcements and he knew that the Union line was being reinforced. But battles are won by action and not caution so the reputation of Ewell was injured by his decision. He was immediately compared to Stonewall Jackson and the inevitable, "If Jackson had been here he would have taken Cemetery Hill." And perhaps he would have or perhaps he would have just lost a lot of men in the attempt. On the final day of the battle Ewell lost his wooden leg to a bullet but he was able to lead his men on an orderly retreat back to Virginia.

During the Overland Campaign, Ewell led his men to a victory in the Battle of the Wilderness and controlled the defenses of the Mule Shoe during the Battle of Spotsylvania. In the heat

of the engagement he was observed by Lee to be acting errati-
cally and was upbraided for having lost control of himself.
Ewell was then reassigned to the defense of Richmond and was
eventually captured at the Battle of Sayler's Creek just days
before Lee's surrender at Appomattox Court House.

Ewell retired to the life of a gentleman farmer with property
in both Tennessee and Mississippi. He and his wife died
together of pneumonia in 1872.

Nathan Bedford Forrest
(July 13, 1821 - October 29, 1877)

Nathan Bedford Forrest was born
to a poor blacksmith in Tennessee
and never received any military
training. At age seventeen, on the
death of his father, he became head
of the family and was burdened with
the responsibilities of their care. He
went into business with his uncle in
Hernando, Mississippi and, during a
dispute with some "clients" his uncle
was killed. Forrest, however, managed to kill two and wound
the others during the altercation. He eventually made a fortune
as a land speculator and slave trader in Memphis, Tennessee

and had a net worth of over $1,500,000 by the outbreak of hostilities in 1861.

Answering the call to enlist, Forrest signed on as a private in the army, was immediately upgraded to colonel and authorized to raise his own regiment. Some have described him as the most complete officer and leader of the Civil War even though he had no formal military training. He lived by the dictum, *"git thar fust with the most men"* and his use of the cavalry was a precursor to the deployment of tank regiments in later wars. He was also unique in the Confederate army in that he encouraged the use of black troopers, 65 of whom surrendered with him in 1865.

Forrest oversaw the dismantling of the industrial capacity of Nashville before it fell to Union forces and fought in the Battle of Shiloh providing rearguard protection to the retreating Confederate army. During this action he was caught alone having broken through a line of Union skirmishers. With blue uniforms all about, he fought his way free and suffered only a wound in the hip making him the last casualty of the battle.

In July 1862 he was promoted to brigadier general and given an expanded command. His tactics generally involved using the speed of the cavalry to outflank his opponent and then, as dismounted troops, to turn the enemy and prevent their resupply and reinforcement. His success worked against him and his troopers were reassigned to the army of General Braxton

Bragg. After forming a new brigade, he took the raw recruits deep into Union territory in an attempt to cut off General Grant's lines which supplied his siege of Vicksburg. Through brilliant leadership and constant motion Forrest was able to keep the Union army off balance and frustrated in their inability to find and destroy him. When he returned to Mississippi he led more men than he started with and they were all supplied with the best Union equipment.

When Colonel Abel Streight and his mule brigade cut the supply lines of General Bragg, Forrest was sent to intercept them. By a simple subterfuge, Forrest was able to convince Streight that he had the superior force prompting the 1,700 exhausted Union soldiers to surrender on May 3, 1863. He expressed his frustration at Bragg's unwillingness to pursue the Union army of William Rosecrans after the Battle of Chicka-mauga in the form of death threats and was subsequently reassigned to Mississippi.

On December 4, 1863 he was promoted to major general and on April 12, 1864 his reputation was darkened at the Battle of Fort Pillow on the Mississippi River. The controversy over the killing of black Union soldiers centers on whether the soldiers were surrendering or still fighting. The official Confederate account is that the soldiers continued to fight even though Forrest beseeched them to surrender. However, letters written by Confederate soldiers who took part in the battle paint a much darker picture.

Forrest fought with the Army of Tennessee under John Bell Hood and vigorously promoted a strategy of crossing the Tennessee River to cut off the retreat of Union Major General John Schofield. When permission was finally granted the effort was repulsed and the battle proved to have been fought in vain. With the collapse of the Confederate armies in the west at the Battle of Nashville, Forrest successfully protected the retreating remnants of the army and was promoted to lieutenant general.

Following the war, Nathan Bedford Forrest was impoverished by the burst of the railway bubble in the early 1870's and he lived the remaining years of his life in a small log cabin while managing a prison work farm on the Mississippi River. He died on October 29, 1877 from complications of diabetes.

Ambrose Powell Hill (November 9, 1825 – April 2, 1865)

Ambrose Hill, another Virginian, graduated from the US Military Academy in 1847. As an artillery officer he served in the Mexican-American and Seminole wars and resigned his commission in the US Army when Virginia seceded from the Union. He was appointed colonel in a Virginia regiment and was promoted to brigadier general in the Army of North Virginia on the strength of his performance at the First Battle of Bull Run.

He fought with distinction as a part of Jackson's army corps in the Seven Days Battles, the Second Bull Run, Sharpesburg, Fredericksburg and Chancellorsville. He briefly took command of the corps when General Jackson was shot but was then wounded himself. Promoted to lieutenant general he led the Third Corps of the Army of Northern Virginia through the Battle of Gettysburg to the siege of Petersburg. On April 2, 1865, seven days prior to Lee's surrender, Hill was killed while riding the front lines at Petersburg.

Like many other generals, A. P. Hill was idiosyncratic and always entered battle wearing a red wool shirt which was the signal to his men that they would be fighting that day. He earned the respect of his soldiers by his unfailing courtesy but has subsequently been criticized for lapses of judgment. His decision to take to the field against the Union cavalry of Brigadier General John Buford on July 1, 1863 at Gettysburg without gaining the favourable ground or first allowing the Confederate forces to concentrate was a tactical error. Error or not, A. P. Hill is entered into history as one of the most highly regarded generals of either flag.

Daniel Harvey Hill (July 12, 1821 – September 24, 1889)

Following graduation from the US Military Academy in 1842, Daniel Hill fought in the artillery during the Mexican-American War. He resigned his commission in 1849 to teach mathematics at Washington College in Lexington, Virginia, which, after the Civil War, would be headed by General Robert E. Lee. He also taught at Davidson  College and was superintendent of the North Carolina Military Institute.

He successfully drove back the Union attack from Benjamin Butler at the Battle of Big Bethel on June 10, 1861 and fought with distinction with his brother-in-law, Thomas Jackson, at the Battle of Seven Pines and other Seven Days Battles. In 1862 his division was prominent at both South Mountain and the Battle of Antietam seeing fierce action in the Bloody Lane. His men were held in reserve at Fredericksburg and were charged with the protection of Richmond when Robert E. Lee took his army to Gettysburg. In the fall of 1863 he was assigned to the Army of Tennessee, promoted to lieutenant general and fought in a bloody action at the Battle of Chickamauga. With other unhappy generals Hill openly criticized his commander, Braxton Bragg, for not pursuing the retreating Union army and President Davis ruled in favour of Bragg effectively ending

Hill's career. He saw limited action for the remainder of the war and participated in the Battle of Bentonville under the command of General Joseph Johnston.

Following the war he lived at Charlotte, North Carolina and edited an historical magazine. From 1877 until 1884 he was the first president of the University of Arkansas and then moved to an agricultural college in Georgia. He resigned his position due to failing health and died a month later on September 24, 1889.

John Bell Hood (June 29, 1831 – August 30, 1879)

Against his Kentucky father's wishes, John Bell Hood studied at and graduated from the US Military Academy in 1853 having narrowly escaped expulsion for too many demerit points. In one of life's ironies, seven years later the academy offered him a post instructing the cavalry. He declined the offer preferring to remain with an active regiment as hostilities approached.

Hood served as an infantryman in California and later transferred to the cavalry in Texas where he was commanded by Albert Sidney Johnston and Robert E. Lee and sustained the first of many war injuries. With the fall of Fort Sumter, Hood resigned his commission, joined the Confederate army as a cavalry captain and was quickly promoted to colonel of the 4th Texas Infantry. He became brigadier general of "Hood's Texas Brigade" on March 3, 1862 and earned a reputation as an aggressive and bold battlefield commander. It was his charge at the Battle of Gaine's Mill which broke the Union line greatly aiding the expulsion of the Union forces from Virginia during the Seven Days Battles. His units were responsible for the massive assault on the Union flank during the Battle of the Second Bull Run and he supported Stonewall Jackson at the Battle of Antietam. At Jackson's recommendation he was promoted to major general on October 10, 1862. His units were in reserve during Fredericksburg and Chancellorsville but were called to action during the Battle of Gettysburg.

On the second day of the battle Hood was assigned the task of attacking the Union forces through the Devil's Den – a rugged boulder strewn approach on rising ground. His protests over the assignment and request for a flanking maneuver around the Big Round Top were refused and at 4 p.m. on July 2, Hood led his men into battle. Almost immediately Hood was wounded by a bursting shell and lost the use of his left arm. His troops were deflected from the Devil's Den and saw action trying to take the Little Round Top.

Following his recovery, Hood was reassigned to the Western Theatre where he saw immediate action at the Battle of Chickamauga on September 18, 1863. He led the breakthrough

which gave the victory to General Longstreet over Major
General William Rosecrans. A second wound during this battle
resulted in the amputation of his right leg. General Jackson's
arm was given a respectable burial but General Hood's leg was
sent with him in the mistaken view that it would soon be buried
with the rest of his body. Instead he survived and was promoted to lieutenant general on September 20, 1863. For the
remainder of the war he had to be tied onto his horse at the
beginning of each day.

Hood did not mask his unhappiness with the manner in
which General Joseph Johnston was fighting the army of Union
Major General William Tecumseh Sherman and his complaints
and President Davis' frustration resulted in the replacement of
Johnston by Hood. At age 33, he was the youngest man on
either side to lead an army. Perhaps his youth prevented him
from tempering his aggressive nature and at the Battle of
Peachtree Creek he mounted four unsuccessful assaults taking
high casualties. Atlanta fell on September 2, 1864 and the
wisdom of replacing Johnston with Hood has been debated ever
since.

Hood's reputation suffered most for his careless attack on
the Union army of Major General John Schofield at the Battle
of Franklin on November 30, 1864. Schofield marched past the
sleeping Confederate forces and was able to prepare for the
battle in which he successfully held off Hood and joined forces
with Major General Thomas at Nashville. When Hood realized

that Schofield had marched past him in the night, he destroyed the morale of his generals by publicly calling their courage into question and then destroyed his army by sacrificing most of those commanders on the field at Franklin. When he reached Nashville he committed his final fatal error by sending the cavalry under Nathan Bedford Forrest to cut the Union lines into Nashville. Recognizing Hood's weakened situation, Thomas marched out of Nashville on December 15, 1864 and defeated Hood's army such that it would never fight again.

Hood surrendered at Natchez, Mississippi and after the war became a cotton and insurance broker in Louisiana. He married and fathered eleven children including three sets of twins – all in the space of ten years making a post bellum hero of his wife. During the yellow fever epidemic of 1878-79, Hood lost his eldest child, his wife, his business and finally succumbed to it himself. His ten orphaned children were adopted by families in Louisiana, Mississippi, Georgia, Kentucky and New York.

Thomas Jonathan "Stonewall" Jackson (Jan. 21, 1824 -May 10, 1863)

Virginia born Thomas Jackson lost his lawyer father and older sister to typhoid fever when he was two years old. His mother sold the family belongings to pay debts and remain independent of her parents. She supported herself and three children for four years until remarrying in 1830 to another lawyer who did not like his stepchildren. Within a year his

mother died in childbirth and Jackson was sent to live with an uncle in what became West Virginia.

He was accepted into the US Military Academy at West Point, NY in 1842 and had difficulty with his course work owing to a less than adequate preparatory education. With dogged persistence he tutored himself and moved from the bottom of his class to within the top twenty by graduation in 1846.

From 1846 to 1848 the young artillery lieutenant fought in the Mexican-American War where he met Robert E. Lee. He became a Professor at the Virginia Military Institute in 1851 and was noted as a stern disciplinarian and inadequate teacher. At one point he was forced to put down a student movement to have him removed. As unpopular as he was with his pupils he was revered by the local black population for organizing and teaching Sunday school at their Presbyterian church. In the words of the church pastor, Dr. William White,

"In their religious instruction he succeeded wonderfully. His discipline was systematic and firm, but very kind. ... His servants reverenced and loved him, as they would have done a brother or father. ... He was emphatically the black man's friend."

Jackson owned six slaves but in every case his purchase was made at the behest of the slaves themselves. He was silent on the issue of slavery but accepted that it was allowed by Providential will and, therefore, could not be challenged.

Jackson earned his nickname of "Stonewall" during the First Battle of Bull Run when he held his troops on the field against several Union assaults thus saving the Confederate line until reinforcements arrived. Brigadier General Bernard Elliott Bee, Jr. was overheard to remark, "Look at Jackson; standing there like a stone wall." Bee himself subsequently died in the battle. Jackson was a rigid disciplinarian and insisted on both drill and rapid marches. The training he gave his troops paid dividends as he was successful in keeping the Union army off balance in the Shenandoah Valley for the first two years of the war by rapid marches which gave the appearance of him being everywhere. His success in driving off the Union forces during the Battle of Chancellorsville was to cost him his life. Returning to camp in the dusk he was fired on by Confederate soldiers who mistook his party for Union soldiers. He was hit by three bullets and several of his aides were killed. His shattered arm was amputated and buried at the nearby Lacy graveyard causing General Lee to remark, *"He has lost his left arm but I have lost my right arm."* Unfortunately, Jackson contracted pneumonia and died eight days later on May 10, 1863 before reaching the hospital in Richmond.

General Jackson is remembered as one of the most idiosyncratic individuals who fought in the Civil War. He had a preference for eating lemons and believed that one arm was longer than the other and held up the longer of the two to "equalize" his circulation. His hearing was diminished as a result of his artillery duty, he easily got lost and his ability to sleep under any condition was legendary. Most importantly he understood the wishes of General Lee without them being communicated to him in any but the most rudimentary terms. He lived by maxims such as;

"Always mystify, mislead, and surprise the enemy, if possible; and when you strike and overcome him, never let up in the pursuit so long as your men have strength to follow; for an army routed, if hotly pursued, becomes panic-stricken, and can then be destroyed by half their number. The other rule is, never fight against heavy odds, if by any possible maneuvering you can hurl your own force on only a part, and that the weakest part, of your enemy and crush it. Such tactics will win every time, and a small army may thus destroy a large one in detail, and repeated victory will make it invincible."

"War means fighting. The business of the soldier is to fight. Armies are not called out to dig trenches, to live in camps, but to find the enemy and strike him; to invade his country, and do him all possible damage in the shortest possible time. This will involve great destruction of life and property while it lasts; but such a war will of necessity be of brief continuance, and so would be an economy of life and property in the end."

He was a deeply religious man who felt that he was called by God to fight, fight hard and kill as many Yankees as he could.

Albert Sydney Johnston
(February 2, 1803 – April 7, 1862)

Although born in Kentucky, Albert Johnston lived most of his life in Texas which he considered home. He first met Jefferson Davis at Transylvania University in Lexington, Kentucky and studied with him at the US Military Academy. He served eight years in the military and left in 1834 to care for his wife who was dying of tuberculosis. Their one son also served in the Confederate army.

Johnston rejoined the military following his wife's death and, in a practice since discontinued, fought a duel for command of the army in Texas. Refusing to fire on his opponent, he was wounded in the pelvis and lost the promotion. In December 1838 he was named the Secretary of War for the Republic of Texas and fought both Mexicans and Indians. In 1840 he returned to Kentucky and remarried in 1843. He fought in the relatively bloodless Utah War in 1857 and took command of the army in California in December 1860. With the secession of Texas in April 1861, he resigned his commission and, in September 1861, was appointed a full general in the Confederate army by his friend President Jefferson Davis.

Johnston was given command of the western forces of the Confederate army charged with defending the Mississippi River. Unfortunately he was given little more than the command as resources in men and material were scarce. For almost a year he was able to bluff the Union army into believing that he was strong on the ground. General P.G. T. Beauregard was finally sent to reinforce his command after the embarrassing fall of Nashville to Union General Don Carlos Buell. The two generals combined their forces at Corinth, Mississippi and prepared to defeat Grant. Their opportunity came as the Union forces rested at Pittsburg Landing on the Tennessee River.

The ensuing Battle of Shiloh was the deadliest conflict of the war up to that time. The Confederate forces marched north to the Union forces on May 6, 1862 and made a frontal assault on the unprepared Union army. During the fighting, Johnston irresponsibly led an attack in which he was wounded in the knee. The bullet, entering from behind, was likely shot from a Confederate gun and it severed an artery. Within minutes Johnston fainted from his horse and was helped to safety in a nearby ravine where he died of blood loss. It is speculated that his previous pelvic wound resulted in nerve damage which numbed the pain making him unaware of his injury. He had also dismissed his personal surgeon to attend the more seriously wounded but none of this explains the lack of simple medical attention that would have saved his life.

The loss of General Albert Sydney Johnston was a blow to the morale of the Confederate army and President Jefferson took the loss of his friend particularly hard.

Joseph Eggleston Johnston (February 3, 1807 – March 21, 1891)

With his fellow Virginian, Robert E. Lee, Joseph Johnston graduated from the US Military Academy in 1829. He served in the artillery and retired from the army in 1837. While working as a surveyor in Florida he became embroiled in the Seminole War and the excitement of battle convinced him to re-enlist.

Following service in the Mexican-American War he transferred to California and in 1860 was promoted to Quartermaster General of the US Army. When Virginia seceded from the Union, he became the highest ranking officer to resign his commission and on May 14, 1861 he was appointed a brigadier general of the Confederate Army charged with organizing the Army of the Shenandoah.

During the First Battle of Bull Run he brought his Army of the Shenandoah to reinforce the Army of Northern Virginia under the direction of the hero of Fort Sumter, General P.G. T. Beauregard.   In August he was promoted to full general but was unhappy that he was not the highest ranking officer and his relationship with President Davis declined from this point. When Major General George McClellan entered the Virginia peninsula, Johnston allowed his army to be pushed back relentlessly to the outskirts of Richmond before counter-attacking at the Battle of Seven Pines on May 31, 1862. On the second day of the battle General Johnston was struck on the arm and chest by shrapnel and was replaced by General Robert E. Lee.   To his great credit he acknowledged Lee as more capable of commanding the army while managing the ever present politics.

Upon recovering from his wounds General Johnston was given titular command of the Western Theatre. He urged Lt. General John Pemberton to abandon Vicksburg so that the two armies could combine and defeat Grant but this plan was not approved by Davis who, for political reasons, needed a stout defense of the city. Vicksburg fell to Union forces on July 4, 1863; the same day as the Northern victory at Gettysburg. When General Braxton Bragg was later defeated by Grant at the Battle of Chattanooga, Davis reluctantly ended the political intrigue within the Confederate high command by replacing Bragg with Johnston.

When campaigning recommenced in the spring of 1864, Johnston was pushed back to Atlanta by the relentlessly bull-dozing army of General William Tecumseh Sherman. Johnston's tactic of slowing the bulldozer while taking fewer losses than Sherman saved his army but eventually lost Atlanta. On July 17, 1864, prior to the Battle of Peachtree Creek, Johnston was replaced by the young and aggressive John Bell Hood. In September, Atlanta fell to Sherman. The political consequences of the fall of Atlanta allowed Lincoln to be re-elected and the South was further demoralized.

When Hood made his attempt to regain Tennessee by at-tacking the Union forces at Franklin and Nashville, Johnston continued to slow the advance of Sherman as he moved north from Savannah to join Grant at Richmond. He fought Sherman at the Battle of Bentonville and was relentlessly pushed further north. When General Schofield joined Sherman on March 24, 1865 the Union army had 80,000 troops to Johnston's 30,000 and it was clear that the end was near.

On April 12, following news of the capitulation of General Lee's army at Appomattox, Johnston met with the escaping Confederate President Davis at Greensboro, North Carolina to obtain permission to seek terms of peace. On April 17/18 Johnston and Sherman concluded an agreement which was subsequently rejected by Washington because it encroached into political issues. A military agreement was reached on

April 26 and on May 3, 1865, Johnston and all 89,000 Confederate soldiers east of the Mississippi River lay down their arms.

Following the war, Johnston became president of a railroad company and dabbled in insurance sales. In 1877 he moved to Richmond, Virginia and served as a Democratic congressman from 1879 to 1881. Not surprisingly his 1874 recollection of the war, *Narrative of Military Operations*, was highly critical of the handling of the war by President Davis.

In one of the odd twists of the Civil War, Johnston grew close to his opponent, William Tecumseh Sherman and served as a pall bearer at his funeral on February 19, 1891. He followed Sherman to the grave a few weeks later on March 21, 1891, dying of pneumonia caught while standing bare-headed in the rain during Sherman's funeral.

James Longstreet (January 8, 1821 – January 2, 1904)

James Longstreet, from South Carolina, earned the name "Pete" from his father who was impressed with his rock-like character. He entered the US Military Academy in 1838 and disciplinary issues almost resulted in his removal. As happens with such students, he was very popular and became close with many who would become famous generals including his best friend, Ulysses S. Grant. In fact, Longstreet introduced Grant to his cousin Julia Dent, who soon became Mrs. Grant. Longstreet fought in the Mexican-American War and was promoted to major.

He resigned his commission in June 1861 and was appointed to brigadier general of Confederate forces on June 25. His units did not see much action in the First Battle of Bull Run and he was unhappy at not pursuing the Union forces during the "big skedaddle." In October he was promoted to Major General and in January 1862 he lost three children to a scarlet fever plague. His distraction over the loss of his children may be one of the reasons for his lackluster performance during the first battle of the Peninsula Campaign, the Battle of Seven Pines. When General Lee replaced the injured General Johnston, Longstreet was given command of fifteen brigades and was prominent in the ensuing rout of Union Major General McClellan's forces.

Some criticize Longstreet for his late arrival on the battlefield at the Second Battle of Bull Run and for being slow to engage the enemy but it was the hammer blow of Longstreet on the second day of battle that destroyed the momentum of the Union advance and pushed Major General Pope's army off the field. Building on General Lee's "defensive" offensives, Longstreet developed a reputation for utilizing strong defensive positions to worry his foe and finally overwhelm him. Following the Battle of Antietam, Longstreet was promoted to lieutenant general.

Longstreet's view of defensive strategy was brilliantly displayed at the Battle of Fredericksburg where he built strong
defenses and positioned enfilading artillery batteries. His use of
the stone wall at Marye's Hill as a defensive barrier repelled 14
assaults inflicting 10,000 Union casualties. In the spring of
1863, Longstreet was detached from Lee's army to support
actions in southern Virginia and he did not see action at the
Battle of Chancellorsville. Again he was criticized for not
marching north to the battlefield but, in fact, this demonstrated
that Lee could hold Virginia with fewer troops than formerly
believed and he proposed to Lee that he be dispatched to the
Western Theatre to provide relief to the embattled Braxton
Bragg. Instead, Lee reorganized his army following the injury
and death of Stonewall Jackson and Longstreet moved his
division through the Shenandoah Valley into Pennsylvania in
June 1863.

When the two armies caught up to each other at Gettysburg,
Lee was anxious for an offensive battle but Longstreet argued
for a flanking movement to draw the Union forces out of their
defensive positions back towards Washington where they
would have to fight an entrenched Confederate army. Lee
decided against Longstreet's advice and ordered an attack on
July 2. For the delay in getting his corps into position Longstreet has suffered much criticism. He ordered his attack at
4:00 p.m. instead of at 11:00 a.m. as dictated by Lee and this
allowed Union Major General Meade to reorganize and
strengthen in his defenses on Cemetery Hill. When the attack

was launched it was done so with vigour and in strength but the day was given to the Union troops who successfully repelled attacks on the Little Round Top and in the Devil's Den.

On the following day Longstreet was ordered to send the Virginia division of George Pickett against a reinforced Union line. Having prepared such a defensive line himself at Fredericksburg, Longstreet knew the outcome and reluctantly ordered the advance with nothing more than a sad nod of his head.

Longstreet was finally transferred to the Western Theatre, arriving at the end of September in time to participate in the Battle of Chickamauga. His troops took advantage of a Northern communications error and drove through the line sending the Union army off the field in disorder. Even Union Major General William Rosecrans left the field and it was only the stout defense of Major General George Thomas which avoided a complete rout. Unhappy at the failure of Braxton Bragg to pursue the defeated Union army, Longstreet joined a long list of unhappy subordinates in complaining about their leader. The complaints were taken seriously in Richmond and President Davis arrived to resolve the leadership crisis. His response after hearing the complaints was to do nothing and the issue continued to simmer.

Longstreet was detached from Bragg's army and sent to contain the forces of Union Major General Ambrose Burnside in Knoxville, Tennessee. When Union forces under William

Tecumseh Sherman were dispatched from Chattanooga to reinforce Burnside, Longstreet left Knoxville and went into winter quarters.

When his plan for a spring campaign in eastern Tennessee was rejected by President Davis and his new advisor, Braxton Bragg, Longstreet rejoined General Lee and prepared for war against his good friend Lieutenant General Ulysses S. Grant. Understanding the temperament of his friend benefited Longstreet and he played a critical role in the Confederate victory at the Battle of the Wilderness. Unfortunately he was injured by friendly fire and his removal from the field reduced a rout to a win.

Following the war, Longstreet became a businessman in New Orleans and his application for a pardon did not come until his friend, Ulysses Grant, was elected to the presidency. His friendship with the new president resulted in employment but Longstreet was scorned as a turncoat and scalawag. General Robert E. Lee's "old war horse" accepted the results of the war better than many Southerners and was victimized for his willingness to embrace equal rights for blacks. Those who held to the "Lost Cause" interpretation of the war reviled him and attacked his war record. His public disapprobation caused him to move to Gainsville, Georgia where he bought a small farm. In 1880 he was appointed as US ambassador to the Ottoman Empire and later as US Commissioner of Railroads. At the age of 76 he remarried to a 34 year old woman, estranging those of his children still alive and lived another 6 years, dying in 1903.

John Clifford Pemberton (August 10, 1814 – July 13, 1881)

John Pemberton, a Northerner from Philadelphia, Pennsylvania, followed his heart into the South. He and graduated from the US Military Academy in 1837 and fought in the Seminole Wars in Florida before serving as a peace keeper along the US-Canada border. In 1845 he was part of the Texas occupation force and was wounded in battle during the Mexican-American War.

He returned to Florida after the war and fought the Seminoles again in 1849 and 1856. Later he was assigned to frontier duty in Kansas, New Mexico and Minnesota. Due to his marriage to a Virginia woman and his years spent in the South, Pemberton decided to resign his commission at the outbreak of the Civil War and enlisted into the Confederate Army in March 1861. By June 15 he was promoted to brigadier general serving in Norfolk, Virginia.

In January 1862 he was promoted to major general and given command of the Department of South Carolina and Georgia.

He was not a man to make friends and his northern birth did not ensure suspicion-free acceptance. The governors of both North Carolina and Georgia petitioned to have him removed and in September he was reassigned to the Department of Mississippi and replaced by General P.G.T. Beauregard. On October 10, 1862 he was assigned to the defense of Vicksburg and promoted to lieutenant general.

In the spring of 1863 he led his army east to join forces with General Joseph Johnston at Jackson, Mississippi in an effort to divide and conquer the larger army of Union Major General Ulysses S. Grant. In a classical miscommunication, Pemberton and Johnston did not join forces and when Pemberton began to head back to Vicksburg he ran into the Union forces and was defeated at the Battle of Champion Hill. On May 18, 1863 he and his men struggled into Vicksburg and, conscious of his northern birth, resolved to defend it until the end. For six weeks his army and the people of Vicksburg withstood Grant's siege but were finally forced to capitulate on July 4, 1863.

After being released in a prisoner exchange, Pemberton returned to Richmond and, when it became obvious that no one wanted the discredited general, resigned his commission on May 9, 1864. Three days later he re-enlisted as a lieutenant colonel and commanded the artillery in the defense of Richmond. He was captured in North Carolina on April 12, 1865 and retired to his farm near Warrenton, Virginia after being freed from prison. In 1876 he moved back to Pennsylvania and died there in 1881.

George Edward Pickett
(January 28, 1825 – July 30, 1875)

George Pickett studied law in Illinois before accepting a position at the US Military Academy under the sponsorship of a friend of Abraham Lincoln. Following his graduation in 1846 he was rushed to the Mexican-American War where he won recognition for taking the flag from fallen comrade James Longstreet and waving it from the parapet of a captured fortress.

In 1851 he married and his new wife died in childbirth ten months later. He was assigned to Washington Territory and lived in what is now Bellingham. His marriage to a native woman, with the poetic name of Morning Mist, resulted in a new son with the less poetic name of James. Within a few years he lost his second wife. In 1859 Pickett stood against Great Britain in the "Pig War" of San Juan Island and was resolved to fight until Major General Winfield Scott was sent to extricate him, and the country, from the embarrassing incident. In June 1861 he resigned his commission and returned home to

Virginia to take his place as a colonel and then brigadier general in the Confederate army.

Pickett fought in the Peninsula Campaign and was wounded in the shoulder. When he returned to the army in September 1862 he was promoted to major general and served under James Longstreet. His brigade did not see active service at Fredericksburg and were in southern Virginia for the Battle of Chancellorsville. He did, however, see action at the Battle of Gettysburg in July 1863.

Pickett's division arrived at Gettysburg late on July 2 and missed the first day of hostilities. They would not be so lucky the next day. At 4:00 p.m. on July 3 the order was given by a reluctant Lieutenant General Longstreet for three divisions including Pickett's to attack the Union center on Cemetery Ridge. The situation was the reverse of the Battle of Fredericksburg and Longstreet had very good reasons for his reservations. The battle, which followed 2 hours of heavy artillery bombardment was decidedly unsuccessful and Confederate losses were high. The men under Brigadier General Lewis Armistead were the only ones to engage the Union troops and, unsupported, were killed or captured. Armistead and thirteen other regimental commanders were killed or wounded in the fighting. Fifty percent of those who set off across the wheatfield that hot, summer day became casualties.

General Lee immediately took responsibility for the heavy losses and attempted to rally the troops for an expected Union counter-attack which, fortunately for Lee, never came. There is controversy regarding the view that Pickett had of Lee following this event but when asked, after the war, why his charge was unsuccessful Pickett humorously pointed out the obvious,

> *"I have always thought that the Yankees had something to do with it."*

Pickett continued to see action following Gettysburg including the Battle of Cold Harbor and the siege of Petersburg but in a pivotal loss suffered by his troops at the Battle of Five Forks, he was enjoying a meal with other officers and missed the action. Following this defeat, Lee retreated from Richmond and finally surrendered at Appomattox Court House. There continues to be controversy over whether Pickett was relieved of duty in the dying days of the Civil War but it is known that, with his shattered division, he surrendered with Lee on April 9, 1865. Pickett was paroled in late April and eventually returned to Virginia in 1866 where he worked as an insurance agent until his death in 1874.

Leonidas Polk (April 10, 1806 – June 14, 1864)

Leonidas Polk from Raleigh, North Carolina attended the local university before enrolling at the US Military Academy, graduating in 1827. Within 6 months he resigned his commis-

sion and entered the Virginia
Theological Seminary and became
a priest of the Episcopal Church.

In 1832 Polk moved his family
to Tennessee and was elected
Bishop of Louisiana in 1841. With
secession, Polk pulled his convention out of the Episcopal Church of
the United States and accepted a
commission in the Confederate Army at the insistence of his
former roommate President Jefferson Davis. He was commissioned a major general and given authority over the land
between the Mississippi and Tennessee Rivers. In September
1861 he occupied Columbus, Kentucky betraying that State's
declaration of neutrality and delivering it to the Union.

Polk served under the command of Lieutenant General Albert Sydney Johnston in the Battle of Shiloh and was himself
promoted to lieutenant general shortly thereafter. He was
moved from the Army of Mississippi due to disagreements with
Lieutenant General Braxton Bragg and recalled by Joseph
Johnston to the Army of Tennessee during the Atlanta Campaign.

Near Marietta, Georgia, while scouting with General Johnston and staff officers, the group attracted artillery shelling and
Polk was torn apart by a shell which passed through him. As a

field commander Polk was likely a better Bishop but as a leader his death was deeply mourned.

James Ewell Brown "J.E.B." Stuart (Feb. 6, 1833 - May 12, 1864)

James Stuart was born into a Virginia military family as both his father and grandfather had fought for their country. He was a student at the US Military Academy during the superintendency of Robert E. Lee and became friendly with the Lee family.

He graduated in 1854 and fought in the Indian wars. In 1859 he read the ultimatum to John Brown at Harper's Ferry prior to the final fusillade. He resigned his commission when Virginia voted to secede but his father-in-law remained in the Union army. Another family split by the war.

Stuart made his reputation as a daring cavalry commander who was skilled at masking the movements of his troopers while acquiring valuable information on enemy movements. On July 25, 1862 he was promoted to major general and during the lead up to the Battle of the Second Bull Run, he raided Union General John Pope's headquarters and stole his parade uniform and plans for the upcoming battle. He fought with distinction in that battle as well as at Fredericksburg and Chancellorsville, taking control of the Second Corps when General Stonewall Jackson was injured.

On the Confederate march into Pennsylvania, General Lee required Stuart to provide a screen and to maintain contact with the lead divisions of Lieutenant General Richard Ewell. For reasons known only to himself, Stuart attempted to circle the Union forces, lost contact with Ewell and was absent for the opening phases of the Battle of Gettysburg. Lacking much needed scouting information, General Lee was blind to the movements of the Union army and so was not well prepared for the three day battle. Stuart's arrival with Union contraband was coldly received and the expected praise was likewise late in arriving.

Stuart was shot during a confrontation with Philip Sheridan's Union cavalry at Yellow Tavern, and died on May 12, 1864. He was 31 years old and was survived by a wife and two children.

Earl Van Dorn (September 17, 1820 – May 7, 1863)

Following graduation from the US Military Academy in 1842, Van Dorn was posted in the South before moving to Texas during the early stages of the Mexican-American War. He earned several battlefield promotions for his bravery and subsequently fought against the Seminole Indians in Florida. In one noteworthy incident he was shot in the side by an arrow and, in the absence of a surgeon, pushed it out the other side of his body, injuring his stomach and a lung in the process.

With the secession of Mississippi, Van Dorn resigned his commission and replaced Jefferson Davis as major general of the Mississippi state militia when Davis left to accept the presidency of the Confederate States. On March 16, 1861 he accepted a commission into the Confederate Army and saw immediate action in Galveston, Texas. In September 1861, Van Dorn was promoted to major general of Virginia forces and was transferred to command the Confederate forces in the West in January 1862.

Van Dorn's orders were to consolidate the Confederate position in Missouri and protect Arkansas. In the spring of 1862 with an army of 17,000, he overtook the smaller Union army commanded by Brigadier General Samuel Curtis in Arkansas and forced them into a defensive position. His plan was to divide his army and outflank the Union redoubt then reconnect his forces and attack from the rear. Unfortunately he made the decision to leave his supply train behind so that his forces could move lighter and faster. Due to a series of factors, his separated units did not reconnect and the two forces engaged the Union position separately. Two of his subordinates were killed and the Confederate forces were finally reunited having pushed back the Union lines. They were also separated from their supply wagons by the Union forces, however.

During the night of March 8 Curtis moved his men back to a stronger defensive line on Pea Ridge Mountain. In the ensuing artillery battle most of the Confederate batteries and guns were destroyed and the counter attacking Union army routed the Confederates from their position and they retreated south. The Union army now controlled Missouri and could threaten Arkansas at will.

In October 1-5, Van Dorn attacked a strong Union position at the Battle of Corinth and was repulsed with heavy casualties. The Union army commanded by William Rosecrans did not follow up on the Confederate defeat and Van Dorn was able to fight his way back south to safety. His loss in Arkansas earned him the approbation of the Confederate congress while at Corinth it earned him a performance at a military court of enquiry. Although absolved of any blame he was stripped of command.

Perhaps Van Dorn was made for the horse because his performance as a cavalry commander was a significant improvement over his infantry experience. His raids were a significant irritant to Major General Ulysses S. Grant during the Vicksburg campaign and in one raid he captured 1,500 prisoners and destroyed almost two million dollars worth of supplies. He fought other successful battles under the command of General Braxton Bragg and on March 15, 1863 he accepted the surrender of Union Colonel John Coburn at the Battle of Thompson's Station.

Having escaped so many Union bullets, it is ironic that Van Dorn was felled by a Confederate bullet fired in intense fury. Dr. James Peters approached Van Dorn from behind while he was writing at his desk in May 1863 and fired a bullet into the back of his head. Van Dorn had carried on an affair with Peters' wife and for this he was punished. Peters was never brought to trial.

9: War is Hell

The term "mudsill" refers to the foundation upon which sat the first structural members of a house. In the Civil War context it referred to the foundation of the upper levels of a civilized society and was used by Southern cheerleaders of slavery to rationalize their justification for the institution. When applied to "Yankees" of course, it lost its philosophical nuances and was simply an insult. The new combat season of 1864 opened with high hopes in the North for a quick end to the war and renewed determination in the South that they would hold on for as long as it took to defeat the Yankee "mudsills."

By the beginning of 1864, eighty percent of adult, white Southerners were dead or in the army and this created a huge strain on the South economy. Women had to do the work or try to get their slaves to do the work and, as a result, the Confederate economy continued to falter. A principal Confederate strategy had been to create a shortage of cotton in order to force England into the war in a desperate measure to obtain supplies for its mills. This strategy misfired for one basic reason; England had a large empire and therefore had access to cotton from different suppliers in Egypt and India. The strategy also did not take account of the fact that England could not take the side of a rebel "colony" when it had problems in many of its own colonies. Any movement toward the Confederacy, after the publication of the Emancipation Proclamation, would put

England in the position of supporting the re-enslavement of those people freed by Lincoln and this was an untenable political position for the English parliament.

In the economically powerful North, Lincoln financed the war largely through an income tax on the wealthy and the sale of "5 and 20" bonds - so-called because the interest was paid in gold within a period of not less than five but not more than 20 years. These bonds, which were marketed by investor Jay Cooke, eventually raised almost $500 million. Lincoln also created the first uniform currency called the "greenback" and even with such financial success inflation for the period 1861 to 1865 was almost 80%.

By the spring of 1864, the war was taking a terrible economic toll in the South. Inflation had reduced the soldier's pay to the value of the paper on which it was printed and its low nutritional value did not make it worth sending to their families. The women left behind feared the sidelong glances of their slaves and were often incapable of getting them to work. Farms were neglected and many still persisted in growing cotton rather than foodstuffs. The long lists of the dead and wounded demoralized the population and President Davis would soon find himself fighting angry Southern women as well as Yankees. The impact of the war was more muted in the North and its industrial strength led to the making of fortunes and an expansion in the labour market. Farms which had never known slave labour continued to be productive and cost inflation was partially met with rising wages.

The advent of daguerreotype photography made the Civil War the first to be exhaustively chronicled and the thousands of pictures taken by Matthew Brady and his assistants were to be found in newspapers and public exhibitions. For reasons of profit the ugliness of the war was not hidden. Lists of dead and wounded soldiers also brought the war home to every community and the grieving in the North was no less heartrending than that in the South.

Black soldiers had proven their valor at the Battle of Fort Wagner in July 1863 and this fight prompted both a sharp rebuttal by Abraham Lincoln to those who doubted their value and led to a recruiting bonanza for the North. One of the first battles of 1864 also involved black soldiers in a minor battle that has been debated ever since.

Fort Pillow, built on a high bluff of the Mississippi River approximately 40 miles north of Memphis, Tennessee, was located along the route chosen by Confederate Nathan Bedford Forrest who, on March 16, led his cavalry on a raid into Tennessee and Kentucky.

Forrest's first major action in the raid was the Battle of Paducah on March 25 in which a good part of the town was destroyed. By early April he and his men needed more supplies and Forrest decided to send 2,000 men to attack Fort Pillow to take what was needed. About half of the six hundred soldiers guarding the fort were former slaves and under no illusions as to how they would be treated by victorious Confederates. Their commander, Major William Bradford, knew he would have to fight.

The Battle of Fort Pillow

The Confederate cavalry arrived at Fort Pillow on April 12 and by 11 a.m. had positioned sharpshooters to fire into the fort from surrounding hills. In mid afternoon Forrest invited his adversaries to surrender but Bradford declined the invitation and was summarily attacked. Union soldiers were pinned down by sharp shooters allowing other Confederate soldiers to scale the parapet where they a clear line of fire into the Union troops massed below. The Federals were forced to retreat to the river where a Union gun boat lay at anchor but was unable to cover the retreat for fear of killing its own soldiers. The fleeing Union soldiers were easily picked off by the Confederates above them.

At this point, the controversy begins. According to some Confederate and Union documents and witnesses, the Union soldiers, seeing no escape, surrendered but were shot and bayoneted where they stood. However, other Union and Confederate witnesses suggested that the fort was never surrendered, the flag was not lowered and many Union soldiers continued to shoot as they retreated. What is less unclear was the predominance of black soldiers among the dead and it seems likely that the Southerners, angered at being fired on by ex-slaves, gave no quarter even to those who had thrown down their arms.

The Confederate's success at Fort Pillow was a damaging and pyrrhic victory as it became a rallying cry in the North and black soldiers were elevated in stature in the eyes of the doubting white soldiers of the Union army. They could and would fight – that was now obvious. It is ironic that Forrest was famous for having black soldiers in his cavalry and under his command although there is no evidence that they fought at Fort Pillow.

***

In March 1864, Ulysses S. Grant was promoted to Lieutenant General and appointed general-in-chief of all Northern armies. He, like Lincoln, believed that the war would be won by wearing down the Army of Northern Virginia. Grant kept Meade as commander of the Army of the Potomac with 115,000 men and, to escape the toxic and sterile atmosphere of Washington politics, made his headquarters with the army. The strategy was to move towards Richmond from the north while the smaller Army of the James, under Benjamin Butler, comprising 30,000 soldiers, would move towards Richmond from the southeast. General Sherman was to take his 100,000 man army on to Atlanta and destroy the 50,000 man Confederate army of Joseph Johnston. Nathaniel Banks would bring his 25,000 man army from New Orleans and move east until he joined up with William Tecumseh Sherman in Georgia.

Grant's Overland Campaign involved flanking Lee to the left and pushing the Army of Northern Virginia back into Richmond. The battles were ferocious and the casualty rates high. In three months of fighting Grant lost over 100,000 men and Lee proportionately more. For the first time, Lincoln had a general who did not know the meaning of "retreat" and, as badly as his army was mauled one day, it was ready for battle on the morrow. The best that Lee could do was to delay Grant and make his army suffer. The slaughter started at the Battle of the Wilderness.

The Wilderness of Spotsylvania had seen plenty of fighting the previous year during the Battle of Chancellorsville and once again the thick tangle of underbrush and scoured terrain would be ripped apart by dense rifle fire. The Battle of the Wilderness shared only a narrow strip of land that was common to the Battle of Chancellorsville but the difficulty of the terrain was well understood to those who had fought in the previous battle.

Grant crossed the Rapidan River with over 100,000 men and Lee was forced to stop him with a force of 60,000. For Lee the Wilderness would make a good battlefield.

The Battle of the Wilderness

As Grant attempted to skirt south on May 5 he was engaged by two Corps of the Army of Northern Virginia which were driven back and brought to the point of collapse. The Union drive was reversed the next day when Longstreet's two fresh divisions entered the battle and forced the Union line to retreat back to where it started. The confusion of the battle and the difficulty of maneuvering in the brush did not allow the Confederates to advance, however. While directing his men in a location close to where Stonewall Jackson had been shot a year earlier, Longstreet was also hit with friendly fire and spent the next several months convalescing. Darkness ended the fighting but a fire in the dense brush, started by hot wadding expelled from the rifles, burned during the night killing many of the hundreds of soldiers wounded during the day. Both sides sat helplessly as they listened to the screams of their immolated comrades.

Once again Union troops had suffered a humiliating defeat in Northern Virginia after an optimistic start. Once again they would be retreating to Washington, defeated and depressed. Little wonder then, that on May 8, when Grant ordered his army to advance, he was given a rousing ovation. The Northern army had come to Virginia to fight and he was going to let them do just that. In a few days they grappled again and Grant planned to continue grappling until one side ran out of soldiers or had had enough. The Overland Campaign had begun and the casualty lists promised to be long. In the Battle of the Wilderness, the Union army lost 17,000 and the Confederate army lost 11,000; which was a larger percentage of their available troops.

Major General Philip Sheridan, having risen through the Union leadership ranks, was now under the command of Major General George Meade. Meade wanted to use Sheridan's cavalry in a standard role of screening and reconnaissance and Sheridan wanted to burnish his reputation by raiding deep into the Confederate supply lines. Grant and Sheridan had fought together in the Western Theatre and Sheridan's appeal to the General-in-Chief found a sympathetic ear.

Grant felt that a strike-in-force at the rear of the Confederate line would weaken his enemy and perhaps open a more direct route to Richmond. Therefore, on May 9, Sheridan set off behind the enemy lines with 10,000 mounted troopers and 32 field guns to threaten Richmond and engage and defeat the cavalry of J.E.B. Stuart. On the first day they arrived at the smoldering ruins of Beaver Dam Station and freed 400 Union prisoners of war who had been captured during the recent Battle of the Wilderness.

The Battle of Yellow Tavern

On May 11, Sheridan met the 4,500 strong cavalry under Stuart at Yellow Tavern located 6 miles from Richmond. The much larger Union force, equipped with Spencer repeating carbines, was held off for 3 hours by the Confederates. In one of the counter charges, Stuart was shot by a dismounted Union soldier and died the next day in Richmond. The battle continued for another hour before Sheridan broke it off and rode south of Richmond to link up with the Union forces under Major General Benjamin Butler on the James River. While the primary goal of deflecting the attention of Confederate General Robert E. Lee had not been achieved, Sheridan did manage to capture 300 prisoners and recover 400 Union soldiers. But most importantly one of the heroes of the South was lost to General Lee.

In a movement which would typify the Overland Campaign, Grant flanked to the left and headed south towards Richmond. Lee anticipated the move and hurried his forces to intercept Grant at Spotsylvania Court House. On May 9 the two forces peered down their gunsights at each other once again.

The Battle of Spotsylvania Court House

Lee had taken the high ground and his forces were entrenched along a 4 mile front which dog-legged in the middle leaving an exposed salient known as the "Mule Shoe." At one point during the fighting on May 10 the Union lines broke through at the Mule Shoe and were driven back only with difficulty. Sporadic attacks at other points along the Confederate line were unsuccessful.

The next day Grant attacked the salient at corps strength and overran the Confederate line. Lee was able to rush his forces to the breach faster than Grant and the Union attack stalled but not before taking 4,000 Confederate prisoners. During this crisis in the Confederate line, Southern soldiers refused to fight until General Lee removed himself to safety at the rear of the line. The fighting at the Mule Shoe became known as the "Bloody Angle" and was perhaps the most intense of the war. It was hand-to-hand at many points as the Confederates slowly regained their trenches. Bodies of dead and wounded men piled so high that the wounded on the bottom were pressed into the sodden ground and drowned. When a more secure line had been established behind the Mule Shoe, Lee retreated giving the ground back to the Union army. By the early morning of May 13, 10,000 men had fallen and it was obvious that the new line would not be taken. Grant pulled back and again flanked to the left. Again Lee anticipated Grant's move but his army was beginning to hemorrhage.

Union losses at Spotsylvania were over 18,000 and another 20,000 men left when their enlistments ran out. The Army of the Potomac had dropped to 65,000 men. Lee lost a further 12,000 men at Spotsylvania but, unlike Grant, he had no ability to replace them. Grant and Lee hurried to the next battlefield and established themselves on the old battleground of Gaine's Mill fought between Lee and McClellan in the spring of 1862. Digging their trenches, the soldiers dug into the shallow graves of their dead comrades.

Cold Harbor was named for a local hotel which provided "harbor" and was located about 10 miles from Richmond. Like many major engagements during the Civil War, Cold Harbor started with minor battles that tested opposition strength. As the armies concentrated their forces reinforcements were rushed in to balance their lines. The Confederate reinforcements were seasoned troops and the Union had to rely on untested units who had spent the war defending Washington and had seen no action.

The Battle of Cold Harbor

The fighting began on June 1 and was delayed until evening as soldiers who had been marching all day rested before beginning their attack. The strength of the Confederate position had not been reconnoitered and the attack was ferociously repulsed. Union soldiers spoke of the barrage as though a sheet of lightening erupted directly in front of them when the Confederate guns opened up on the unsuspecting soldiers. In the short period of dusk 2,200 Union soldiers fell and no ground was captured. One breach in the Confederate line had been opened and 750 Southern soldiers were taken prisoner but the salient created could not be defended and the Union soldiers retreated.

The battle plan for the following day called for an attack in strength on Lee's right flank but the attack was postponed due to the time and effort required to position the divisions. The Union generals were not given coordinated plans nor were they

told when and in which order to attack. To Grant's subordinates it appeared that there was no plan other than "attack!"
Once again no reconnaissance was undertaken to assess the
strength of the opposition. Lee was fully apprised of the Union
movements and stretched his defensive line until it was anchored on the Chickahominy River thus preventing the flanking
maneuver that Grant wanted to achieve. The Confederate
engineering corps erected elaborate defenses and installed
yardage stakes to allow the enfilading field guns to sight their
shots.

No one on the Union side of the battle line was confused
about what awaited them. Many sewed their names onto their
clothes in hopes of a burial marker and made their final diary
entries in anticipation of the worst outcome. And for too many,
their predictions were deadly accurate. The recovered and
blood-stained diary of one Union soldier summed up the day
simply,

"June 3, 1864. Cold Harbor. I was killed."

As the Union soldiers left their lines at 4:30 a.m., the well
entrenched Confederates opened up with canister and enfilading
fire that resulted in an awful blood bath. In previous wars the
"Forlorn Hope" soldiers were volunteers looking for death or
rapid promotion. At Cold Harbor the entire Union line was a
forlorn hope. In only one location did the Union troops succeed
in overrunning a Confederate trench and their successful hand-

to-hand combat bought them certain death as Confederate field guns opened up at short range.   One Union officer described the carnage,

> *"The men bent down as they pushed forward, as if trying, as they were, to breast a tempest, and the files of men went down like rows of blocks or bricks pushed over by striking against one another."*

When a renewed attack was ordered at 7 a.m. the Union field commanders refused to obey and by noon Grant decided that enough was enough. The blame for the Union debacle at Cold Harbor is widely shared but ultimately it rested with Grant and Meade who did not ensure that their orders were obeyed. In what was to have been a massive assault, less than half of the divisions moved forward which resulted in the awful Confederate firepower massed on a much smaller than anticipated advancing force. In less than ten minutes, 7,000 men paid for the lack of coordination and poor planning of the Union attack.

For the next nine days the two lines bombarded and shot at each other across a muddy no-mans-land that only increased the casualties. As difficult as life was on the trench line, it was inconceivably worse for the injured, who, for five days, remained trapped between the lines without food, water or medical aid. Grant and Lee attempted to negotiate a cease fire so that the Union wounded could be recovered but could not come to terms. Grant did not want to allow any suggestion that he had lost. When a two hour truce was called on June 8 it was

too late for many of the wounded soldiers. Cold Harbor was
the final battle victory for General Robert E. Lee and it came at
a truly horrendous cost to both sides. Grant lost almost 13,000
men and Lee lost close to 5,000.

By June 9 Grant realized that he was in a stalemate that
could not be broken by further assaults. As a result he made
two feinting moves towards the Shenandoah Valley to draw off
some of Lee's men while slowly withdrawing the rest of his
men from the line in order to make a dash across the James
River. His plan worked and Lee was uncharacteristically
caught off guard. By June 14, Grant had crossed the James and
was in a position to threaten Petersburg to the south of Richmond.

Battle and Siege of Petersburg

Petersburg was the commercial hub of northern Virginia at
which 5 railways converged. Its position on the Appomattox
River allowed it navigable shipping to the James River and its
18,000 inhabitants enjoyed commercial prosperity. All this was
about to change. Grant realized that success in Petersburg
would open a lane into Richmond that would effectively end the
war. When Lee realized what Grant was doing, he was late in
deploying his own forces to defend against the attack. For a
week, the fate of the Confederacy rested in the arms of the only
men left in Richmond and Petersburg. For this reason the

ensuing battle is sometimes known as the Battle of Old Men and Young Boys.

The first attack came from Major General Benjamin Butler who dispatched 4,500 soldiers to storm the southern approaches to the city. The Confederate Home Guard repulsed the attack which would not be renewed until Grant and his army arrived from Cold Harbor.

Had Grant's advance units attacked immediately they likely would have over-run the defenses of the city. However, the attack was delayed and Lee was able to get some of his units in place alongside the Home Guard to repel the Union attacks which came on June 17 and 18. It was during these attacks that the hero of the Little Round Top, Joshua Lawrence Chamberlain was wounded again and so severely that his name was somewhat prematurely placed in the obituaries.

The next 10 months were a prelude to the trench warfare of the First World War. Both sides settled into defensive positions, sharpshooters attempted to pick off any hapless opponent who exposed himself and disease caused more deaths than bullets. Grant made several attempts to create openings in the Confederate line and all were ultimately unsuccessful. The most famous of the attempts was the Battle of the Crater which was a re-enactment of the tunneling strategy that had failed at the siege of Vicksburg. Many of the lessons of that debacle had remained unlearned.

The Crater

Lt. Colonel Henry Pleasants had been a mining engineer before the war and enlisted as a way to end his unhappy life – an unsuccessful strategy as it turned out. He suggested to Major General Burnside that a sapper's tunnel be constructed below the Southern trenches, loaded with explosives and exploded to create a breech. The idea was cheered by the Pennsylvania miners but had limited acceptance from either Grant or George Gordon Meade. Nevertheless work commenced on June 25 and by July 23 a single drift with two laterals and four galleries to each lateral was constructed. The drift was 510 feet long and the laterals were each forty feet long. A total of 18,000 cubic feet of earth was extracted and the galleries were filled with four tons of gunpowder in 320 pound kegs. The drift was backfilled to contain the blast which was planned to take place on July 30.

Burnside's plan to use the black troops under General Edward Ferrero was denied at the last moment by Grant and the inexperienced James Ledlie was told to lead the attack with the vague instruction to "...*occupy Cemetery Hill.*" A diversionary movement of Northern troops was planned to draw Confederate attention away from the planned blast.

After a false start when the fuse burned out, the blast ripped through the ground at 4:44 am on July 30. Of the 330 South Carolina troops in the trenches overlying the blast, 278 were casualties. In order to maintain secrecy, the Northern commanders did not warn their men of the blast and the effect was as devastating to them as it was to the Southern soldiers. Bedlam reigned following the explosion and troops who were supposed to attack rushed to the rear. Those who did attack rushed into the crater pulling Southern soldiers out of the ground instead of moving to their objective and no Northern commanders went forward to lead the troops.

Lee reinforced his line and a stout resistance met the Union attackers. The confusion turned into a bloodbath as Southern shooters on the crest of the crater opened fire on the Union troops trapped below them. Northern reinforcements were unable to offer support due to the stalled offensive and the numbers of retreating wounded. The trained black troops were finally sent into the battle and were brutalized by Southern troops incensed at their presence. By 5 p.m. the fighting was over and no ground had been gained by either side. In the ensuing truce both sides recovered their fallen comrades as bands from both sides played "light airs."

Once again poor planning and coordination turned a successful innovation into a brutal killing field. Over 5,200 casualties were recorded of which two thirds were Northern soldiers. Burnside was relieved of command; Ledlie who refused to lead his men was sent home; and Pleasants never forgave himself or his commanders for the horrific result of his innovation.

***

The Northern navy during the Civil War successfully contained the movement of ships into and out of Southern ports. In an attempt to deflect the barricading Union ships, the Confederate government took delivery of a few warships which attacked Northern shipping. The most famous of these was the CSS *Alabama*. The *Alabama* was secretly built in England in 1862 and upon commissioning, sailed with a civilian crew to the Azores where title and control passed to Captain Raphael Semmes of the Confederate States of America. It was then retrofitted with armaments, a coal boiler and manned with a crew of 120 mercenaries.

Following its commissioning, the *Alabama* commenced a career of privateering to disrupt the shipments of Union material. Captain Semmes sank 62 vessels, including the USS *Hatteras,* in seven expeditionary trips. Crew and passengers that were captured were sent home on neutral ships or landed in a neutral port and what could be salvaged was sent to the Confederacy. The rest was sent to the bottom of the ocean.

In June 1864, the *Alabama* arrived at Cherbourg, France for refitting and reprovisioning. Captain John Winslow of the USS *Kearsarge* discovered the location of Semmes and began to patrol outside the harbour. Rather than remain bottled up, Semmes decided to make a break, and, on June 19, sailed out to meet the *Kearsarge*. But for an unexploded cannon shell, the *Kearsarge* might have been sent to the bottom. As it was, the shell only jammed the steering mechanism and within an hour, the hull of the *Alabama* was opened and Semmes was forced to strike his colours and surrender his boat. The *Kearsarge* took on all the *Alabama*'s survivors except for Semmes and his officers who were picked up by a private yacht which spirited them to England and safety. Winslow got his boat but not his prize.

***

When Ulysses S. Grant left for Washington in March, his command was taken by Major General William Tecumseh Sherman. Following the railway link between Chattanooga, Tennessee and Atlanta, Georgia, Sherman pushed relentlessly and when Confederate Joseph Johnston established a defensive position, Sherman would ignore the challenge and continue to Atlanta in a flanking maneuver. Finally at Kennesaw Mountain, muddy, near impassable roads made a flanking manoeuver impossible so Sherman decided to attack Johnston's thin lines.

On the morning of June 27 Sherman opened up on the entrenched Confederates with a pounding artillery barrage and then attacked in force. Johnston was well dug in and repeated assaults did not budge the Confederate line. On July 1, when the roads had dried out, Sherman outflanked the Confederates and continued to Atlanta.

Battles of Kennesaw Mountain and Peachtree Creek

Sherman reached the outskirts of Atlanta on July 20 and President Davis of the Confederate States ran out of patience with General Johnston's strategy of retreat before the advancing Union army. In a controversial move, he elevated the young Lieutenant General John Bell Hood to command the Army of Tennessee.

Sherman had divided his armies as he approached Atlanta and Hood felt that he could defeat or drive off the army of George Thomas as it crossed Peachtree Creek and thus pull Sherman away from Atlanta. Thomas crossed the creek and established a beach head before Hood arrived and so the Confederate advantage was eliminated. Nevertheless, Hood attacked but to no effect other than to take 13,000 casualties. Hood now retreated into Atlanta and another siege began. The long Union supply lines, which stretched back to Chattanooga, were constantly attacked by the Southern cavalry of Nathan Bedford Forrest but this had no effect on Sherman's determination.

With two sieges underway and a presidential election soon to be fought, Lincoln was frantic for some good news to buoy the North and assist in his re-election. His armies had lost over 100,000 men since May and now they were bogged down in expensive sieges while the Confederates controlled Texas and most of Arkansas. His call for more troops resulted in over 65,000 no-shows and almost 30,000 men hired substitutes. The Peace Democrats were jubilant and there were active plans to have Lincoln replaced as the Republican nominee. George McClellan was nominated as the Democratic candidate and favored winning the war and then negotiating a peace. His party, however, called for peace with no preconditions. By late August, Lincoln was so convinced of his defeat that he made plans for the orderly transfer of power and his wife began packing for their move back to Illinois.

On September 3, General Sherman marched into Atlanta following the retreat of Hood's Confederate Army. As a result, Lincoln won an electoral college landslide and captured almost eighty percent of the Union army votes. With another four years of a Lincoln presidency, Confederate hopes for a negotiated settlement were dashed.

***

To relieve the pressure on Petersburg and to make another attempt to demonstrate Southern strength, General Lee sent Jubal Early into the North to attack Washington, D.C. On his march north he stopped for a week to make a futile attack of no strategic value on a small force at Maryland Heights. Alerted to Early's intentions, Grant sent two divisions to reinforce Washington, effectively removing the opportunity to mount an attack on an undefended capital.

On July 11 and 12, the Confederate forces were close enough to shell portions of Washington and fire into the city but without significant effect. President Lincoln watched the Confederate forces from the top of the Fort Stevens wall and, being in range, has the distinction of being the only sitting US president to come under enemy fire. On July 13 the Confederates returned to Virginia having frightened the citizens of Washington without having done any real damage. It was an embarrassment and distraction for Grant and he was determined that it not happen again.

As the Army of the Potomac and the Army of Northern Virginia stared at each other over defensive parapets and from labyrinthine trenches, Philip Sheridan was sent to destroy the cavalry of Jubal Early and render the Shenandoah Valley unfit for agriculture and human habitation. After a month of skirmishes, Sheridan massed his forces at Cedar Creek anticipating a blow from Early and Longstreet. Anticipating the blow is one thing; predicting how it will come is another and the encamped Union armies relied on the physical features of their camp to prevent a surprise attack. Jubal Early did not view those features as restrictive of his movements as did Sheridan and planned to attack in detail at dawn on October 19 after an all night march.

The Battle of Cedar Creek

The Union soldiers were once again caught at breakfast and the surprise attack quickly achieved all of Early's initial objectives. With the capture of more than one thousand prisoners and almost 20 field guns, Early ended his attack assuming the victory was complete. His decision was likely influenced by observing that the starving Confederate victors were busily wolfing down the Union breakfast and had no intention of continuing the fight.

Sheridan, returning to camp, rallied his retreating forces, established a defensive line and began preparations for a counter attack. Following a desultory attack from the Confederates at 3:00 p.m., his counter-attack drove the Confederate forces back to the river and Sheridan recovered not only his guns but also an additional 25 Confederate field guns.

The Cedar Creek Battle was not significant in terms of ground gained or casualties inflicted. But it was one of prodigious timing and assisted in the re-election of President Lincoln. To the victor go the spoils of war and this fight consolidated the reputation of Philip Sheridan while it destroyed the career of Jubal Early.

***

Prior to 1864, men who were captured by the opposing forces were held only for so long as it took to parole them which was to arrange a prisoner exchange on a one-to-one basis. This humane treatment of prisoners of war gave an advantage to the Confederate Army but, with the Emancipation Proclamation and the use of black troops, the prisoner exchange system broke down. President Lincoln wanted to wear down the Southern armies and not replenish them and so when the South refused to exchange black prisoners the practice was ended for all prisoners-of-war. This created the need for large prisoner-of-war camps which neither side had built. Between the North and the South there were eventually 150 such camps which were poorly equipped and disease ridden. Perhaps the worst camp was in Andersonville, Georgia in which tens of thousands of prisoners died from disease and starvation. It is estimated that over 60,000 men died in prisoner-of-war camps.

Andersonville

Camp Sumter, the official name of Andersonville, was the largest Confederate prisoner-of-war camp occupying 16.5 acres of ground. By the time it was captured by the Union armies of William Tecumseh Sherman, it had been enlarged to 26.5 acres. It is best described in the words of a Union prisoner who spent time there;

>   *"As we entered the place, a spectacle met our eyes that almost froze our blood with horror, and made our hearts fail within us. Before us were forms that had once been ac-*

tive and erect;—stalwart men, now nothing but mere walking skeletons, covered with filth and vermin. Many of our men, in the heat and intensity of their feeling, exclaimed with earnestness. "Can this be hell?" "God protect us!" and all thought that He alone could bring them out alive from so terrible a place. In the center of the whole was a swamp, occupying about three or four acres of the narrowed limits, and a part of this marshy place had been used by the prisoners as a sink, and excrement covered the ground, the scent arising from which was suffocating. The ground allotted to our ninety was near the edge of this plague-spot, and how we were to live through the warm summer weather in the midst of such fearful surroundings, was more than we cared to think of just then."

The conditions at Andersonville were deplorable but there is much controversy over whether these conditions were a function of the deteriorating conditions throughout the Confederacy or whether there was a conscious effort to render the Union soldiers unfit for any kind of fighting. Almost 13,000 men died of starvation, exposure and disease from a total population of 45,000 prisoners. Like most overcrowded conditions, the depravations within the boundaries of the prison were Gulag-like and prison gangs brutalized other prisoners until held to account by a self-organized justice system.

The commandant of the prison, Henry Wirz, was court-martialed after the war and became the only Confederate official to be tried, convicted and put to death for his activities during the war. In his defense, Wirz maintained that all his

pleas for additional food and material to clean up the camp
were ignored.

**

In his insightful book, *The Soul of Battle: From Ancient
Times to the Present Day, How Three Great Liberators Van-
quished Tyranny*, Victor Davis Hanson presents a case for
elevating William Tecumseh Sherman to a higher level of
generalship – one in which a well educated commanding
officer, tired of carnage and angry at wrong doing, takes his
citizen army on a spree of property destruction which collapses
the center of a rotten culture while keeping the human cost to a
minimum. Hanson points out that Sherman destroyed the slave
society of the Southern Confederacy, not by destroying its
armies but by destroying the artifacts of that society – its
magnificent plantations. He states that it was Sherman, and not
Grant, who was reviled in the American South even though his
army killed very few while Grant's army killed tens of thousands. The Southern elites were willing to lose other men's
sons but not their great estates. It is an interesting observation.

After conquering Atlanta, Major General Sherman rested
his troops and then did the unthinkable – he moved his army to
the Atlantic without anchoring his supply line. The Union army
disappeared into the Georgia countryside on November 15 and,
for three weeks, no one heard from it. Sherman's objectives
were to destroy the war-making ability of Georgia and to divert

the forces of General Robert E. Lee from the siege of Petersburg.

Sherman's March to the Sea

Sherman's men, marching in two columns, confused the
Confederates as to their final destination. Their chevauchee
was as brazen and successful as anything undertaken by the
English as they ravaged the French countryside during the
Hundred Years War - with the notable exception that it was
characterized by fire rather than rape and murder. The Union
soldiers lived off the land when their rations were exhausted
and everything along their path was destroyed. By December
10 they were at the outskirts of Savannah, Georgia which was
defended with 10,000 men. Finding a weakness in the Confederate line, Sherman attacked and within 15 minutes routed the
defenders and linked up with the Union navy. He then turned
his artillery upon Savannah calling for an immediate surrender.
On December 20 the Confederate forces left Savannah and the
next day the city surrendered to Sherman.

Operating with no interior lines, Sherman was successful in
achieving his goals of destroying Southern morale and making
Jefferson Davis even more unpopular. He estimated that his
army caused over 100 million dollars of damage, mostly to the
magnificent plantations, making good his pledge to "make
Georgia howl." In response to those who protested his destruction he responded;

"war is cruelty, and you cannot refine it; and those who brought war into our country deserve all the curses and maledictions people can pour out."

It was his belief that until Southerners understood what war meant, they would continue to pursue it. Following his march through Georgia, Southerners petitioned their government to end the war.

***

When the Army of Tennessee under Lieutenant General John Bell Hood moved north away from Georgia, Sherman was ordered to intercept and destroy him. Major General George Thomas was assigned the task of following Hood and engaging him before any damage could be done in Tennessee. John Bell Hood was an ambitious Southern commander who rose through the ranks to divisional commander on the basis of raw courage. President Davis favoured Hood and any criticism was dealt with by transferring the critic.

Unfortunately for Hood, Davis made several speeches to rally the Confederacy in which he outlined Hood's new strategy to rid the South of the Northern menace. Reprinted in local newspapers, the strategy was quickly read by the Northern generals. While Sherman continued on his March to the Sea, George Thomas and 27,000 Union troops pursued Hood. The race to Nashville started in the cold, autumn weather of November.

The Army of the Ohio commanded by Major General John Schofield caught up with John Bell Hood on November 29 south of Nashville, Tennessee. Hood, recognizing that the Union forces were divided, determined to attack them individually and in strength before they could unite and destroy him. When the Union cavalry was engaged by Nathan Bedford Forrest, word was sent to Schofield of the approaching Confederate forces. When the Confederate attack came at 4:00 p.m., Schofield was ready and the placement of his artillery allowed him to repel the Southern forces. Hood had left his artillery in the rear and could not retaliate with his own bombardment. Due to a missed communication the final Confederate assault did not occur. Instead the Confederate soldiers ate supper and went to bed while Schofield's men marched past them to Franklin. Hood was furious that Schofield had escaped. Perhaps it was the opiates taken by Hood to ease the pain of his wounds or perhaps it was the drunkenness of his subordinates that was to blame for the ease with which Schofield avoided the well-set but unsprung trap.

Battle of Franklin

On November 30 Hood double marched his 38,000 man army to intercept Schofield's smaller army. Rather than run, Schofield determined to fight at Franklin where he built defenses and hurried his supply train across a local ford. His plan was to withdraw all of his troops across the repaired bridges by 6:00 p.m. if the attack had not started before then.

Hood decided on a single frontal assault to smash the Northern army and by 4:00 p.m. he was ready. The Union army skirmishers held the attackers until they were pushed back into the breastworks. Fearful of shooting their own soldiers, the Union cannons waited until they could decimate the Confederate army with grapeshot at near point blank range and stall the attack. A number of Confederate troops broke the Union line which was recaptured only after a desperate hand-to-hand counter attack. The toughest fighting of the battle was centered on the Carter house which sheltered the six cannons which were tearing the Confederate line apart. Bodies piled up and so many Southern prisoners were taken to the rear that Northern commanders thought that their line had been breached. At nightfall the Union line remained intact.

The Confederate attack at Franklin became known as the "Pickett's Charge of the West." In fact it was a larger engagement in which 19,000 men marched into the guns over a larger field and fought for over 5 hours. By 9:00 p.m. the fighting was over and by 11:00 p.m. Schofield was moving his men over the river and out of Franklin. Hood's battle plans for the morning were superceded by Schofield's retreat and the town was instead converted into a hospital. Eleven of twenty four generals were killed or injured and fifty four regimental commanders were killed, injured or captured. For all intents and purposes, the Army of Tennessee no longer existed. Perhaps Hood could not have hoped for a Southern victory in Tennessee but the Battle of Franklin gained nothing but notoriety. By the end of the next day, December 1, Schofield had united with the Army of the Cumberland at Nashville, Tennessee.

The defensive line formed by the Union army at Nashville was very similar to that at Franklin. A semicircle of breastworks was anchored by a bend of the Cumberland River. When John Bell Hood arrived on December 2 he formed his own defensive line and a waiting game ensued. Both hoped that the other would attack first and be worn out on a futile attack. For two weeks Thomas prepared his army in spite of the increasing pressure being brought to bear by both General-in-Chief Grant and President Lincoln. Grant even sent a replacement for Thomas so concerned was he that Hood would be allowed to escape and march on a punishing expedition into the Northern states.

Battle of Nashville

On December 15, as his replacement arrived at Louisville, Kentucky, Thomas attacked the Confederate position. He had waited for Hood to make a mistake which came when the Confederate general sent Nathan Bedford Forrest to raid the Union supply depot at Murfreesboro. With his adversary further weakened, Thomas put into effect a two-fronted attack.

At dawn his forces moved out of Nashville and by noon had pushed Hood's line back creating a Confederate salient in the center of the Union line. As night approached the Confederates dug in and the Union drive stopped.

The next day Thomas repeatedly attacked and then brought overwhelming force to bear on the weaknesses which developed. The Confederate lines slowly fell back and by nightfall the retreat had turned into a rout. In the darkness and drizzly rain, Hood regrouped and led his men south to Franklin. It was the last time the Army of Tennessee would fight and many men, having lost the will to continue, returned to their homes. The 10,000 soldiers who remained in the army retreated to Tupelo, Mississippi where Hood, still blaming the defeat on his subordinates, resigned his command and was not reassigned.

Lincoln remained in the presidency, the Union controlled most of the South and Sherman was making his way to join Grant at Richmond. The end of the war was in sight and people everywhere looked forward to an end to the killing. With its economy in shambles and its people starving, the South fought for dignity and honor. They didn't know it but President Lincoln, their best ally, was to become the greatest casualty of the war.

10: 1865 - The War is Over: Mr. Lincoln Can Rest

In January, Congress passed the 13th Amendment emancipating all slaves. Shortly after this, in an unrelated event, the Confederate states approved the use of black soldiers making a mockery of the position that slaves were inferior human beings. Robert E. Lee argued strenuously for the use of such soldiers and equally strenuously for their emancipation. The measure, which was approved by the Confederate Congress on March 13, did not allow for emancipation.

Throughout the final months of the war, President Lincoln offered hope for a negotiated peace. At the Hampton Roads Peace Conference of early February, Lincoln offered generous terms of peace to Southern Vice President Andrew Stevens. The terms involved only reunification and emancipation but Davis rejected the offer because Lincoln would not offer a prior cease-fire.

***

As Sherman marched north into the Carolinas, his army continued to cut a swath of destruction. On March 8, he moved into North Carolina and his army divided into two wings which operated independently of one another. Confederate General Johnston decided there was an opportunity to attack in detail and defeat Sherman. His attack commenced on March 19 on the Goldsboro Road south of Bentonville, North Carolina.

The Battle of Bentonville

Thinking that he was facing a small cavalry attack, Union Major General Slocum did not immediately request aid from Sherman. However, when Johnston's attack drove back the Union left flank, Slocum petitioned for support which arrived by mid afternoon. The Confederate assault was stopped and Johnston began pulling his army off the field while a small force covered their retreat. Fighting during March 20 involved only light skirmishing and on March 21 a Union attack drove back the Confederate line almost capturing Johnston's army. Johnston withdrew and burned the bridges across which he had retreated. Sherman's business, however, was to the north and he made no attempt to pursue the Confederate army. The Battle of Bentonville was the last Confederate attempt to engage and destroy Sherman's army.

***

At Petersburg, Grant steadily lengthened his siege lines in order to thin out the Confederate ranks. As Sherman's army approached from the South and Sheridan's cavalry approached from the West, General Lee decided that he would have to break out of Richmond in order to save his army. In order to do so he needed to take a large risk and chose for this service a 33 year old general, John B. Gordon. Gordon identified a weakness in the Union line at the Fort Stedman battery south of the Appomattox River.

The Battle of Fort Stedman

The plan called for small teams of 50 to 100 men to open up the barricades in the no-man's-land between the two lines and then send a large attacking force into Fort Stedman. Because the trench systems were so complex, local guides had to be found and hired to lead the attacking force forward to avoid getting lost in the maze. The attack began in the early hours of March 25. When a Union sentry issued a challenge, the moment was saved by a Confederate private who assured him that they were only collecting corn to augment their rations. At the moment of attack the same private called out a warning perhaps out of guilt for his previous subterfuge. The Fort was quickly overrun as were the supporting batteries around it. The Union commander of Fort Stedman, riding into the fort and exasperated that no one would respond to his orders, soon discovered that he was giving orders to soldiers under a different flag.

Expanding the breach in the Northern line was delayed as Confederate soldiers became lost in the Union trenches and did not achieve their forward targets. Union gunners then began shelling the trenches forcing the Southern troops to pull back.

Northern reinforcements hastened the Southern retreat and many Confederates were taken prisoner. President Lincoln, who was inspecting troops nearby, was informed that there had been a little "rumpus up the line" and was able to see firsthand the many captured Confederate troops as they were marched to the Union rear.

The succession of Union victories and the apparent inability of the Confederacy to stop Grant and Sherman from marching across the South coupled with letters from home describing the hunger and poverty of their loved ones created a tension in Southern soldiers that was not easily resolved. Many decided that the outcome was all but certain. They had done their best for the new country but now it was time to attend to the very real physical needs of their families. Wives who had suffered alone for too long were now being joined by husbands who simply walked away from the Confederate army. In this way General Lee's army at Richmond gradually shrank for reasons other than injuries and disease. When the Union army registered a decisive victory at the Battle of Five Forks, Lee informed President Davis that he could no longer guarantee the safety of the Confederate government and it was moved on April 2 from Richmond to Danville, Virginia. Lee then planned his escape from Richmond and dashed to the safety of the Blue Range Mountains.

On April 8 the Confederate army moved four supply trains to Appomattox Station to await the arrival of General Lee and the Army of Northern Virginia. Twenty five year old, Major General George Custer heard of the supplies and, correctly surmising the implications, set off to capture them before they could be used to support Lee's retreat. The small Confederate garrison at Appomattox Station surrendered to Custer just as the advance units of Lee's retreating army approached and began to shell the Union soldiers.

The Battle of Appomattox Station

Neither the Union nor the Confederate soldiers had a clear picture of what was happening and neither made effective efforts to attack the other. Lee directed Longstreet to flank the Union line and establish a rear cover for the Confederate army which would drive through the Union position, recover the trains of equipment and continue its retreat to the west. The Confederate attack began just as Union reinforcements began to arrive. The fighting lasted for four hours during which time more Confederate prisoners and supplies were captured by the Union forces. While losses were relatively light the injuries were unusually severe as a result of the heavy artillery bombardments.

As a result of Custer's initiative, the Confederate escape was cut off and the Union army held the high ground west of the small town of Appomattox Court House. During the night Lee determined with his staff officers that the Union cavalry which blocked his retreat could be overpowered and so planned an assault in the morning. However, more Union reinforcements arrived during the night to strengthen the Union line and, by morning the situation had changed.

The Confederate attack occurred at dawn on April 9 and it carried the Union lines to the top of the ridge above Appomattox Court House. However, as the Confederate soldiers followed the retreating Union line over the crest they were confronted with the massed forces of two Union army corps. Rather than smash into the Union line the Confederates pulled back and reported their situation to General Lee. The situation was indeed hopeless and Lee, upon hearing the report, told his staff;

> *"Then there is nothing left for me to do but to go and see General Grant and I would rather die a thousand deaths."*

At 8:00 a.m. with rifle fire breaking out sporadically, Lee rode out to meet Grant in order to petition for a cease-fire and a formal surrender of his army. In one of the great ironies of the Civil War, the location chosen for the surrender was the home of Wilmer McLean who had moved from his house located on the battlefield of the First Bull Run (the headquarters of General Pierre Beauregard) to the more serene country of Appomattox Court House. He could truly say that the Civil War had "started in his kitchen and ended in his parlour."

When the two generals met they were not immune to the pathos of the situation and Grant preferred to discuss personal trivia rather than get to the point of the meeting. At Lee's insistence Grant gave him the terms of surrender which were generous and consistent with the wishes of President Lincoln;

> "In accordance with the substance of my letter to you of the 8th inst., I propose to receive the surrender of the Army of N. Va. on the following terms, to wit: Rolls of all the officers and men to be made in duplicate. One copy to be given to an officer designated by me, the other to be retained by such officer or officers as you may designate. The officers to give their individual paroles not to take up arms against the Government of the United States until properly exchanged, and each company or regimental commander sign a like parole for the men of their commands. The arms, artillery and public property to be parked and stacked, and turned over to the officer appointed by me to receive them. This will not embrace the side-arms of the officers, nor their private horses or baggage. This done, each officer and man will be allowed to return to their homes, not to be disturbed by United States authority so long as they observe their paroles and the laws in force where they may reside."

In keeping with the solemnity of the occasion Grant did not allow any sign of jubilation within sight of the Confederate soldiers and immediately assigned 25,000 rations of food to Lee's men. On the following day, April 10, Lee addressed his army;

> "After four years of arduous service marked by unsurpassed courage and fortitude, the Army of Northern Virginia has been compelled to yield to overwhelming numbers and resources.

I need not tell the survivors of so many hard fought battles, who have remained steadfast to the last, that I have consented to the result from no distrust of them. But feeling that valour and devotion could accomplish nothing that could compensate for the loss that must have attended the continuance of the contest, I have determined to avoid the useless sacrifice of those whose past services have endeared them to their countrymen.

By the terms of the agreement, officers and men can return to their homes and remain until exchanged. You will take with you the satisfaction that proceeds from the consciousness of duty faithfully performed, and I earnestly pray that a merciful God will extend to you his blessing and protection.

With an unceasing admiration of your constancy and devotion to your Country, and a grateful remembrance of your kind and generous consideration for myself, I bid you an affectionate farewell."

The formal surrender took place on April 12 and was handled by Brigadier General Joshua Lawrence Chamberlain who recorded the event with an eloquence which typifies the written records of the Civil War;

"..... Before us in proud humiliation stood the embodiment of manhood: men whom neither toils and sufferings, nor the fact of death, nor disaster, nor hopelessness could bend from their resolve; standing before us now, thin, worn, and famished, but erect, and with eyes looking level into ours, waking memories that bound us together as no other bond;—was not such manhood to be welcomed back into a Union so tested

and assured? Instructions had been given; and when the head of each division column comes opposite our group, our bugle sounds the signal and instantly our whole line from right to left, regiment by regiment in succession, gives the soldier's salutation, from the "order arms" to the old "carry"—the marching salute. Gordon at the head of the column, riding with heavy spirit and downcast face, catches the sound of shifting arms, looks up, and, taking the meaning, wheels superbly, making with himself and his horse one uplifted figure, with profound salutation as he drops the point of his sword to the boot toe; then facing to his own command, gives word for his successive brigades to pass us with the same position of the manual,—honor answering honor. On our part not a sound of trumpet more, nor roll of drum; not a cheer, nor word nor whisper of vain-glorying, nor motion of man standing again at the order, but an awed stillness rather, and breath-holding, as if it were the passing of the dead!

On that day 27,800 Confederate soldiers stacked their arms, said their goodbyes and sadly parted company from men with whom they had shared an unimaginable adventure. Their lives, of course, had been dramatically altered as had those of their blue coated adversaries. After four long, bloody years they were countrymen again. It must have been an incredible event. It was repeated again on April 26 when General Joseph Johnson surrendered almost 90,000 men of the armies of the southeast to Major General William Tecumseh Sherman at Durham, North Carolina.

Several small battles broke out following these events and the final surrender of Confederate forces took place in the west. The last battle occurred on May 12 and 13 at Palmito Ranch in Texas and was considered a Confederate victory. It certainly was not a victory for the family and friends of Private John Williams of the Indiana Volunteers who was the last soldier to give his "last full measure" during the Civil War. On May 26 the Texas Confederate armies surrendered and on June 2 the army of General Edmund Kirby Smith surrendered.

It is interesting that General Lee remembered the generosity of Lieutenant General Grant for the remainder of his life and would not permit unkind words to be spoken about Grant in his presence. General Gordon who surrendered to Chamberlain considered him to be the "purest of knights" and General Johnson was a pall bearer at the funeral of the man to whom he surrendered – William Tecumseh Sherman.

The last major Civil War reunion was held at Gettysburg in 1937 and the last veteran to die was Confederate soldier, Walter Williams, on December 19, 1959.

The little war was finally over.

Afterward: What Makes America Great?

President Jefferson Davis, the man who had followed Mississippi out of the Union and led the often fractious members of the Confederate States of America, was captured on May 10, 1865 at Irwinville, Georgia. Due to pressure by a consortium of Northern and Southern businessmen he was paroled after two years in prison and traveled outside the United States until the case against him was dropped in 1869. He worked for a life insurance company and was re-elected to the US Senate but was unable to take his seat under the terms of the 14th Amendment. After writing his memoirs he died on December 6, 1889 and his funeral was the largest ever held in the South.

Father Abraham, the Great Emancipator

Abraham Lincoln, the self-taught rustic from Kentucky by way of Illinois, was, in the minds of many, a most unlikely president. Towering over most people, he appeared gaunt, awkward and ill at ease. Yet he was gentle, humorous and highly intelligent. It cannot be seriously questioned that he was the man for his hour and it is inconceivable that anyone else could have led his country through its four worst years. Whatever we might think of his religious inclinations it is undeniable that he was a man of deep faith which became more rooted as the terrible war bore him and his country to its inexorable destination. He knew that the war was about slavery and that the struggle was as much spiritual as it was physical. More than anyone else, President Lincoln pondered the implications of the spilt blood and the awful battlefields. How else to understand his ability to so succinctly encapsulate the horror and its meaning at Gettysburg and in his Second Inaugural Address?

As a politician he had been fighting slavery for many years prior to the Civil War. He saw it as an unspeakable horror which diminished the great work of the Founding Fathers. Nevertheless he was not a strict abolitionist and he appreciated the property law implications of emancipation. His policy was founded on gradual manumission with compensation paid to the former owners. Fearing the racist foundations of both North and South, he supported the transportation of the ex-slaves to a colony that would receive support from the United States as it (the colony) gradually become self-governing and self-reliant. His view was not widely supported and he came to the presidency with the Union already split by secessionist governments who were tired of looking for a compromise.

Secession meant that not only were the institutions of the country split but also the families of the country. Countless fathers would be firing on sons, brothers on brothers and cousins on cousins. It was to be a war and a national ordeal unlike any before seen. By its end, Lincoln declared himself to be the "most tiredest man I know." Throughout he had to face the disapprobation of the chattering classes, social elites, political opponents and even some in his cabinet. Daily he would face mothers and children bereaved of husbands and fathers. Many of his own relatives and friends were killed. The same faith that sustained the soldiers sustained their Commander-in-Chief and perhaps this is why they loved him as they did.

When the Civil War was over, the once-divided nation was faced with the prospect of reuniting and undoing the damage of the previous 4 years. President Lincoln, as the victorious Defender of the Union and Emancipator of four million slaves now was faced with reconstructing the nation.

However, within 6 days of the Union victory at Appomattox Court House, Lincoln himself lay dead – perhaps the costliest victim of the Civil War. The details of his death are well known. A dispirited and somewhat deranged Shakespearian actor named John Wilkes Booth decided to assuage his wounded pride by putting into action a plan to overthrow the hated Northern government. Using his intimate knowledge of the Ford Theatre he broke into the President's box during the April 14 staging of the British play, "Our American Cousin." It was Good Friday and the President was relaxing with his wife as well as Major Henry Rathbone and his fiancée Clara Harris. Lieutenant General Ulysses S. Grant and his wife had earlier decided not to attend the theatre with the Presidential party. Booth timed his attack to coincide with a burst of audience laughter and mortally wounded the President with a point blank shot to the back of his head. The bullet lodged behind President

Lincoln's right eye and he never regained consciousness, dying at 7:00 a.m. the following day. Booth, as he escaped from the theatre, called out the Virginia state motto, "Sic Semper Tyrannus," and was caught and died within the month. His accomplices were likewise caught and four died on the scaffold.

As monumental as were the events of the Civil War and as spiritually significant as was the massive shedding of blood to finally free the slaves, one must also give attention to the spiritual significance of the death of the President who was central to the story of emancipation. President Lincoln was so much larger than life that one wonders at the long term results of his death. His government did not have a written plan of Reconstruction but there can be little doubt that Lincoln had a clear idea of what he felt must be accomplished. It is inconceivable that the mess that followed the Civil War would have been permitted had Lincoln lived out his second term in office. He commanded immense moral and political allegiance and, as hinted at in his Second Inaugural Address, his approach to Reconstruction would have avoided many of the pitfalls of the partisan politics and outright avarice into which it sank. The slaves were free but their post bellum life was perhaps not an improvement over their antebellum life. It is difficult to believe that this would have been the case had Lincoln lived. But God measures time differently from humans and 143 years after the ratification of the 13th Amendment, the United States of America elected a black president. The last payment has been made; the wolf has been released.

In the final months of his life Abraham Lincoln was known as "Father Abraham" to more than just the slaves he had freed. The eulogies which were preached from many pulpits of the nation, at least in the North, spoke of him in reverential and patriarchal terms. But perhaps he was more of a "Father Moses." President Lincoln was the man for his times in the same fashion as Moses was for his. Both men led a rebellious people through bad times by following their understanding of God's will and neither lived to see the fruits of their hard labour. Both men were given a far reaching vision that others did not share. And both men had premonitions of their death prior to seeing the "Promised Land."

In President Lincoln's case, after his election in 1860 and prior to moving to Washington, in a dream he saw two visages of himself; one full-bodied and the other spectral. Weeks before his death he had a dream in which he awoke and, hearing the sound of loud lamentation, walked to the East Room of the White House to find a large gathering of people weeping around a coffin. When he looked into the coffin he saw himself. Lincoln himself put these two dreams together when discussing them with friends and correctly predicted his imminent demise. In fact, on the night of his visit to Ford's Theatre he did not take his usual body guard but merely said good bye, something which he had never before done. We cannot arrive at a spiritual conclusion and say, "This is what it means." But we can consider the circumstances surrounding the death of

President Lincoln and weigh the import of these circumstances in light of the profoundly important events of the Civil War. His job was done and Abraham Lincoln was both a man for and of "the ages" as Secretary Stanton said.

We will never know what the spiritual and physical consequences of the death of President Lincoln were because we cannot rewind history and play it back without John Wilkes Booth. But we can derive conclusions from the facts and even enter into a bit of metaphysical speculation. It is my conclusion that the freeing of four million slaves, irrespective of the need for another 100 years to pass before anything approaching equality could be achieved, was very pleasing to God and for four years there was a bitter struggle to align the constitutional affairs of the United States of America with the abiding spiritual truth that all men and women are created in the image of a loving God and thus have certain inalienable rights.

Did God require the blood of 620,000 men to atone for 250 years of slavery? We, on this side of Heaven, will never know the answer to that question. Does God intervene in the affairs of men? Again this is an imponderable. President Lincoln believed there was a good case to be made for this argument as he stated in his Second Inaugural Address;

> "...Fondly do we hope, fervently do we pray, that this mighty scourge of war may speedily pass away. Yet, if God wills that it continue until all the wealth piled by the bondsman's two hundred and fifty years of unrequit-

ed toil shall be sunk, and until every drop of blood
drawn with the lash shall be paid by another drawn
with the sword, as was said three thousand years ago,
so still it must be said "the judgments of the Lord are
true and righteous altogether.""

Surely the life of Abraham Lincoln suggests that God brings forth men and women who have caught a vision of His grace and love and are willing to act on that vision whatever the personal consequences. Did God will his death? Who knows but, even as a Canadian, I am grateful that Abraham Lincoln gave his last full measure to right such a horrible wrong. His was a spiritual battle and I am sure he was welcomed by his Saviour in the early morning hours of April 15 with, "Well done, good and faithful servant!"

***

So why is America great? I think it is because only in the United States has there been an understanding of the tremendous spiritual and creative energy that is released when bearing God's image is taken seriously and individual liberty and equality is valued at 620,000 lives. The men who returned from the war, including five future presidents, formed the corps of a new leadership which controlled the destiny of the United States until the early decades of the 20th Century and having lived through one of the most awful yet most spiritually significant episodes in human history they had many reasons to make good the horrible loss of life. Perhaps, like Private Ryan, they wanted that experience to count for something.

This is not to say that all Americans were or are individually great; some are and some aren't. And many decisions made by the government of the United States are just plain boneheaded. But nowhere on earth is there greater personal freedom and equality of opportunity. Nowhere on earth is there such security for those with differing opinions and ideas. And nowhere on earth is there such explosive creativity; in the arts, in business, in religion, in sports. And that creativity is a legacy from President Lincoln and the men who fought and sometimes died to bring a spiritual idea to life – we are all made in the image of God and we hold these truths to be self-evident, that all men are created equal, that they are endowed by their Creator with certain unalienable Rights, that among these are Life, Liberty and the pursuit of Happiness.

The history of the United States, as it has come to terms with the Civil War and the civil rights of its various communities, has, relative to other nations, been one of unrivalled blessing. Does this blessing derive directly from God? To the extent that citizens of the United States of America continue to embrace the God whose image they bear and grant equal freedoms and rights to all the image bearers, then yes. But perhaps it is not so much a question of "God blessing" as it is of a people redeeming a very ancient blessing that is available to any nation. But no other nation anywhere or at any time has been willing to pay the price to appropriate that blessing. And that is why the United States of America is the greatest nation ever. And that is why people from around the world come to Canada – so that they can more easily cross the border into the United States.

When people try to convince me that American economic hegemony is about to pass to India or China I smile and say, "Not while this one nation under God continues to respect and honour His image bearers. It just won't happen." However, I could be wrong. I am troubled by the denial of freedom for the million American children who are killed every year by abortion. At its most basic, abortion is a freedom issue every bit as important as slavery and Thomas Jefferson's words are no less appropriate today,

> *"Indeed I tremble for my country when I reflect that God is just: that his justice cannot sleep for ever . . . The Almighty has no attribute which can take side with us in such a contest."*

I have high hopes that the 44th President of the United States of America, who represents the highest achievement of American freedom, who has accepted the legacy of President Lincoln and the patience of generations of African-Americans, will be the president who launches a new, high energy wave of creativity by redeeming God's image and extending freedom of life to all American citizens. I believe this is the biggest issue which prevents the United States of America from realizing a greatness that has never before been seen.

Appendix 1: 1860 Census

Confederate States

State	Seceded	White	Free	Slave	Other	Total	Military
Alabama	Jan. 11	526.3	2.7	435.1	0.2	964.3	100.0
Arkansas	May. 6	324.1	0.1	111.1	-	435.3	65.2
Florida	Jan. 10	77.7	0.9	61.7	-	140.3	15.7
Georgia	Jan. 19	591.6	3.5	462.2	-	1,057.3	111.0
Louisiana	Jan. 26	357.5	18.6	331.7	0.2	708.0	83.5
Mississippi	Jan. 9	353.9	0.8	436.6	-	791.3	70.3
North Carolina	May. 20	629.9	30.5	331.1	1.2	992.7	115.4
South Carolina	Dec. 20	291.3	9.9	402.4	0.1	703.7	55.0
Tennessee	Jun. 8	826.7	7.3	275.7	0.1	1,109.8	159.4
Texas	Mar. 2	420.9	0.4	182.6	0.4	604.3	92.1
Virginia	Apr. 17	691.4	55.3	472.5	0.1	1,219.3	129.8
Total		5,091	130	3,503	2	8,726	997

Union States

State		White	Free	Slave	Other	Total	Military
California		323.2	4.1	-	52.7	380.0	170.0
Connecticut		451.5	8.6	-	-	460.1	94.4
Delaware		90.6	19.8	1.8	-	112.2	18.3
Illinois		1,704.3	7.6	-	-	1,711.9	375.0
Indiana		1,338.7	11.4	-	0.3	1,350.4	265.3
Iowa		673.8	1.1	-	0.1	675.0	139.3
Kansas		106.4	0.6	-	0.2	107.2	28.0
Kentucky		919.5	10.7	225.5	-	1,155.7	180.6
Maine		626.9	1.3	-	-	628.2	122.2
Maryland		515.9	83.9	87.2	-	687.0	102.7
Massachusetts		1,221.4	9.6	-	-	1,231.0	258.4
Michigan		736.1	6.8	-	6.2	749.1	164.0
Minnesota		169.4	0.3	-	2.4	172.1	41.2
Missouri		1,063.5	3.6	114.9	-	1,182.0	232.8
New Hampshire		325.6	0.5	-	-	326.1	63.6
New Jersey		646.7	25.3	-	-	672.0	132.2
New York		3,831.6	49.0	-	0.1	3,880.7	796.9
Ohio		2,302.8	36.7	-	-	2,339.5	459.5
Oregon		52.2	0.1	-	0.2	52.5	15.8
Pennsylvania		2,849.3	56.9	-	-	2,906.2	555.2
Rhode Island		170.6	4.0	-	-	174.6	35.5
Vermont		314.4	0.7	-	-	315.1	60.6
West Virginia		355.9	2.8	18.4	-	377.1	66.8
Wisconson		773.7	1.2	-	1.0	775.9	159.3
Union Total		21,564	347	448	63	22,422	4,538

* all numbers x 1000

Appendix 2: List of Battles

There were over 300 battles fought during the Civil War which ranged from minor skirmishes to full scale set-piece battles. They were fought in 29 states and territories and each produced unspeakable bravery and shed blood.

This appendix lists many of the battles with an assessment of who "won" the fight. The list is included more to give a sense of the continuity of the war rather than to be complete in the number of battles.

The Civil War produced famous battles such as Gettysburg and Antietam but it is well to remember that many died in the minor skirmishes as well as the great events. It was an all encompassing war and no one was left out. Black soldiers fought for their freedom under both flags and many Indian tribes were brought into the conflict as well.

The first table gives details of the ten largest battles and the second table attempts to list many of the lesser known affairs. The casualties shown on the first table are defined as killed, wounded and captured. One-sided casualty numbers generally indicate the surrender of one side to the other.

The 10 Most Significant Battles by Casualty Numbers

Battle	State	Dates	Forces		Victor	Casualties
			Conf.	Union		
Gettysburg	Pennsylvania	July 1–3, 1863	72,000	95,000	Union	U: 23,000 C: 28,000
Chickamauga	Georgia	Sep 19–20, 1863	75,000	62,000	Confederate	U: 16,000 C: 18,000
Chancellorsville	Virginia	May 1–4, 1863	61,000	134,000	Confederate	U: 17,000 C: 13,000
Spotsylvania Crt House	Virginia	May 8–21, 1864	52,000	100,000	Draw	U: 18,000 C: 12,000
Antietam	Maryland	Sep 17, 1862	65,000	83,000	Union	U: 12,000 C: 11,000
Wilderness	Virginia	May 5–7, 1864	61,000	102,000	Confederate	U: 18,000 C: 11,000
Second Bull Run	Virginia	Aug 29–30, 1862	49,000	80,000	Confederate	U: 16,000 C: 9,000
Stones River	Tennessee	Dec 31, 1862	44,000	54,000	Union	U: 13,000 C: 12,000
Shiloh	Tennessee	April 6–7, 1862	45,000	65,000	Union	U: 13,000 C: 11,000
Fort Donelson	Tennessee	Feb 13–16, 1862	12,000	20,000	Union	U: 3,000 C: 17,000

Appendix 2B: 1861 - 1865

DATE	NAME	DESCRIPTION
1861		
April 12	Fort Sumter	Confederate victory in Charleston Harbour
May 18/19	Sewell's Point	Union gunboats against land artillery
May 29-June 1	Aquia Creek	Union naval bombardment
June 3	Philippi Races	Union victory in western Virginia
June 10	Big Bethel	Union attack on Virginia peninsula
June 17	Boonville	Union victory in Missouri
June 19	Cole Camp	Confederate victory in Missouri
July 5	Carthage	Confederate victory in Missouri
July 11	Rich Mountain	Union victory
July 18	Blackburn's Ford	Confederate victory at Manassas
July 21	First Bull Run	Confederate victory
July 25	Mesilla	Confederates victory in N Mex Terr.
August 5	Wilson's Creek	Confederate victory west of Miss.
August 26	Kessler's Cross Lanes	Confederate victory
August 28/29	Hatteras Inlet	Union navy victory in No Carolina
September 2	Dry Wood Creek	Confederate victory in Missouri
September 10	Carnifex Ferry	Union victory

Sept. 12-15	Cheat Mountain	Union victory
Sept. 13-20	First Battle of Lexington	Confederate victory
September 17	Liberty	Confederate victory in Missouri
October 3	Greenbrier River	Union victory
October 9	Santa Rosa Island	Union victory
October 12	Head of Passes	Naval battle at mouth of Mississippi
October 21	Ball's Bluff	Confederate victory
October 21	Camp Wild Cat	Union victory
October 21	Fredericktown	Union victory
October 25	First Springfield	Union victory
November 7	Belmont	Union victory
November 7	Port Royal	Union naval victory
November 19	Round Mountain	Confederate victory
December 9	Chusto-Talasah	Confederate victory
December 13	Camp Alleghany	Confederate victory
December 20	Dranesville	Union victory
December 26	Chustenahlah	Confederate victory
December 28	Mount Zion Church	Union victory
1862		
January 3	Cockpit Point	Inconclusive result in Virginia
January 5/6	Hancock	Union victory in Maryland
January 8	Roan's Tan Yard	Union victory

January 10	Middle Creek	Union victory
January 19	Mill Springs	Union victory
February	Fort Henry	Union army/navy victory on Tennessee River
February 7/8	Roanoke Island	Union victory by Burnside
February 10	Elizabeth City	
Feb. 11-16	Fort Donelson	Union victory; Grant on Cumberland River
Feb. 20/21	Valverde	Confederate victory in New Mexico
March 7	Pea Ridge	Union victory in Missouri
March 9	Hampton Roads	Ironclad sea battle; draw
March 14	New Bern	Union victory
March 23	First Kernstown	Union victory over Stonewall Jackson
March 26-28	Glorieta	Union victory near Santa Fe
April 6/7	Shiloh	Union victory; A.S. Johnston killed
April 10/11	Fort Pulaski	Union victory
Feb 28/ Apr 8	Island #10	Union victory
April 15	Peralta	Union victory over Texas volunteers
April 15	Picacho Pass	Confederate victory
April 19	South Mills	Confederate victory
Mar 23/Apr 26	Fort Macon	Union victory by bombardment
Apr 25/ May 1	New Orleans	Union naval victory
Apr 5 / May 4	Yorktown	Union victory

May 5	Williamsburg	Draw McClellan vs Longstreet
May 7	Elthan's Landing	Draw
May 8/9	McDowell	Confederate victory by Jackson
May 15	Drewry's Bluff	Confederate victory of Union navy
May 19	Whitney's Lane	Union campaign in Arkansas halted
May 23	Front Royal	Confederate victory by Jackson
May 25	First Winchester	Confederate victory, Jackson over Banks
May 27	Hanover Courthouse	Union victory
Apr 29/ May 30	Corinth	Union victory; Beauregard escapes
May 31	Seven Pines	Draw; Joseph Johnston wounded
June 5	Tranter's Creek	Union victory
June 6	Memphis	Union victory to gain the city
June 7/8	First Chattanooga	Union bombardment of city
June 8	Cross Keys	Confederate Jackson over Fremont
June 9	Port Republic	Confederate victory
June 16	Secessionville	Confederate victory; Union court martial
June 17	St. Charles	Shore battery destroys Union gunboat
Jun 25 / July 1	Seven Days	Confederate victory
June 25	Oak Grove	Seven days; draw
June 26	Beaver Dam Creek	Seven days; Union victory
June 27	Gaine's Mill	Confederate victory

June 27/28	Garnett's Farm	Seven days; draw
June 29	Savage's Station	Seven days; Confederate victory
June 30	White Oak Swamp	Seven days; artillery duel leads to draw
June 30	Glendale	Seven days; Confederate victory
Jun 30/ Jul 1	Tampa	Union gunboat attack is a draw
July 1	Malvern Hill	Seven days; Union army withdraws
July 7	Hill's Plantation	Union victory in Arkansas
July 13	Stones River	Confederate victory
August 5	Baton Rouge	
August 6 - 9	Kirksville	Union victory
August 9	Cedar Mountain	Confederate victory
August 11	First Independence	Confederate victory in Kansas
August 15/16	Lone Jack	Confederate victory
August 21/22	Fort Ridgely	Santee Sioux attack Union fort
August 22 - 25	First Rappahannock	Confederate victory
August 27	Bull Run Bridge	Confederate victory at ManassasJunction
August 28	Thoroughfare Gap	Confederate victory
August 30	Second Bull Run	Confederate victory over Pope
August 30	Richmond	Confederate victory in Kentucky
September 1	Chantilly	Confederate victory
September 14	South Mountain	Union victory; McClellan over Lee

Sept. 12 - 15	Harper's Ferry	Confederate victory
September 17	Antietam	Union victory; bloodiest single day
Sept. 17/18	Munfordville	Confederate victory
Sept. 19/20	Shepherdstown	Confederate victory
September 30	First Newtonia	Confederate artillery victory
October 3/4	Second Corinth	Union victory
October 5	Hatchie's Bridge	Union victory
October 8	Perryville	Draw; Buell versus Bragg
November 7	Clark's Mill	Confederate victory
November 28	Cane Hill	Confederate escape
December 7	Prairie Grove	Union victory in Arkansas
December 7	Hartsville	Confederate victory
December 13	Fredericksburg	Confederate victory over Burnside
December 14	Kinston	Union victory
December 16	White Hall	Draw
December 17	Goldsboro Bridge	Union victory
December 19	Jackson	Confederate victory in Tennessee
Dec. 26- 29	Chickasaw Bayou	Confederate victory near Vicksburg
December 31	Parker's Cross Roads	Confederate victory
1863		
Dec 31/Jan. 2	Stones River	Draw
January 8	Second Springfield	Union victory

January 9	Arkansas Post	Vicksburg campaign
January 9 - 11	Hartville	Confederate victory
January 29	Bear River Massacre	Union massacre of Shoshone forces
February 3	Dover	Union victory
March 5	Thompson's Station	Confederate victory in Tennessee
March 13 - 15	Fort Anderson	Union victory
March 17	Kelly's Ford	Draw
March 20	Vaught's Hill	Union victory
March 25	Brentwood	Confederate victory
Mar 30/ Apr20	Washington	Union victory
April 1	First Franklin	Union victory
Apr 1 – May 4	Suffolk	Draw
April 26	Cape Girardeau	Union victory
April 29	Grand Gulf	Confederate victory
Apr 29/ May 1	Snyder's Bluff	Union maneuver
April 30	Day's Gap	Union victory
Apr 30/ May 6	Chancellorsville	Confederate victory, Jackson killed
May 1	Port Gibson	Union victory in Vicksburg campaign
May 1/2	Chalk Bluff	Confederate victory
May 3	Second Fredericksburg	Union victory
May 3/4	Salem Church	Confederate victory

May 12	Raymond	Union victory in Mississippi
May 14	Jackson	Union victory in Mississippi
May 16	Champion's Hill	Union victory in Mississippi
May 17	Big Black River Br.	Union victory in Mississippi
May 21	Plains Store	Union victory in Louisiana
June 7	Milliken's Bend	Union victory at Vicksburg
June 9	Brandy Station	Union victory over J.E.B. Stuart
June 13 - 15	Second Winchester	Confederate victory
June 17	Aldie	Draw (march to Pennsylvania)
June 17 - 19	Middleburg	Union victory (march to Pennsylvania)
June 21	Upperville	Draw (march to Pennsylvania)
June 24 - 26	Hoover's Gap	Union victory in Tennessee
June 29 - 30	Goodrich's Landing	Confederate victory
June 30	Hanover	Confederate cavalry deflected
July 1 - 3	Gettysburg	Union victory; Meade over Lee
July 4	Vicksburg	Grant's siege ends with Union victory
July 4	Helena	Union victory secures Arkansas
July 8	Boonsboro	Draw; battle during Lee's retreat
May 21 – Jul 9	Port Hudson	Union victory; control Miss. River
July 9	Croydon	Confederate raid kills civilians
July 11	Fort Wagner	Confederate victory

July 6 – 16	Williamsport	Draw
July 15/16	Apache Pass	Union battle with Apache Indians
July 17	Honey Springs	Union victory of black over Indian troops
July 18	Fort Wagner	Confederate victory
July 23	Manassas Gap	Confederate victory
July 24/25	Big Mound	Union victory over Indian forces
July 26	Dead Buffalo Lake	Union victory over Sioux forces
July 26	Salineville	Union victory in Ohio
July 28	Stony Lake	Union rout of Sioux forces
Aug.17/Sep.9	Second Fort Sumter	Confederate victory
Aug.21/ Sep.8	Second Chattanooga	Union victory
August 23	Lawrence	Confederate victory
September 1	Devil's Backbone	Union victory
September 3/5	Whitestone Hill	Union victory over Indian forces
September 8	Sabine Pass	Confederate shore battery shell Union fleet
September 10	Bayou Fourche	Union victory
Sept. 10/11	Davis' Cross Roads	Leadup to Chickamauga
September 19	Chickamauga	Confederate victory
September 22	Blountsville	Union victory
October 6	Baxter Springs	Confederate victory over black troops
October 10	Blue Springs	Union victory
October 13	First Auburn	Union chases J.E.B. Stuart

October 14	Second Auburn	Draw
October 14	Bristoe Station	Union victory
October 19	Buckland Mills	Confederate victory
October 25	Pine Bluff	Union victory
October 28/29	Wauhatchie	Union victory
November 3	Collierville	Union victory
November 7	#2 Rappahannock	Union victory
November 16	Campbell's Station	Union victory
Nov. 23-25	Third Chattanooga	Union victory; Grant over Bragg
November 27	Ringgold Gap	Confederate victory
November 29	Fort Sanders	Union victory
Nov.27/Dec. 2	Mine Run	Draw
December 14	Bean's Station	Union withdrawal
December 29	Mossy Creek	Confederate withdrawal
1864		
January 17	Dandridge	Union withdrawal
January 26	Athens	Union victory in Alabama
January 27	Fair Garden	Union victory
February 6/7	Morton's Ford	Union attack
Feb 14/ 20	Meridian	Union victory
February 20	Olustee	Confederate victory
March 2	Walkerton	

March 25	Paducah	Confederate victory by Forrest
April 3/4	Elkin's Ferry	Union victory
April 8	Mansfield	Confederate victory
April 9	Pleasant Hill	Union victory
April 9 - 13	Prairie D'Ane	
April 12	Fort Pillow	Confederate victory over black soldiers
April 17	Plymouth	Confederate victory in North Dakota
April 18	Poison Spring	Confederate victory Red River, Arkansas
April 23	Monett's Ferry	Union victory; Red River, Arkansas
April 25	Marks' Mills	Red River campaign, Arkansas
April 30	Jenkins' Ferry	Red River campaign, Arkansas
May 5	Wilderness	Draw between Grant and Lee
May 5	Albemarle	Draw in naval campaign
May 6/7	Port Walthall Junct.	Union victory
May 9	Cloyd's Mountain	Union victory
May 9	Swift Creek	Union victory
May 10	Cove Mountain	Union victory
May 10	Chester Station	Confederate victory
May 11	Yellow Tavern	Union cavalry victory, J.E.B. Stuart killed
May 7 - 13	Rocky Face Ridge	Draw near Atlanta
May 13	Resaca	Union victory over Johnston

May 15	New Market	Confederate victory
May 12 - 16	Proctor's Creek	Confederate victory
May 17	Adairsville	Union victory
May 20	Ware Bottom Church	Confederate victory
May 8 - 21	Spotsylvania Court House	Draw between Grant and Lee
May 24	Wilson's Wharf	Union victory
May 25/26	New Hope Church	Confederate victory
May 27	Pickett's Hill	Confederate victory
May 28	Haw's Shop	Confederate victory
May 28	Dallas	Union victory
May 28 - 30	Totpotomoy Creek	Confederate victory
May 30	Old Church	Union victory
May 31/Jun 12	Cold Harbor	Confederate victory
June 5	Piedmont	Union victory
June 9	First Petersburg	Confederate victory
June 10	Brices Crossroads	Confederate victory
June 11/12	Trevilian Station	Confederate victory
June 15 - 18	Second Petersburg	Confederate victory
June 17	Lynchburg	Confederate victory
June 19	Cherbourg, France	Union victory over CSS Alabama
June 22	Kolb's Farm	Union victory
June 21 - 24	Jerusalem Plank Road	Union lines extend

June 24	St. Mary's Church	Union delaying action
June 27	Kennesaw Mountain	Confederate victory
June 6 – July 3	Marietta	Union victory
July 9	Monocacy Junction	Union delaying action to save Washington
July 11/12	Fort Stevens	Union victory in Washington DC

Appendix 3: Selected Speeches of Abraham Lincoln

House Divided Speech (Cooperstown, NY; June 16, 1858)

Mr. President and Gentlemen of the Convention.

If we could first know where we are, and whither we are tending, we could then better judge what to do, and how to do it. We are now far into the fifth year, since a policy was initiated, with the avowed object, and confident promise, of putting an end to slavery agitation.

Under the operation of that policy, that agitation has not only, not ceased, but has constantly augmented. In my opinion, it will not cease, until a crisis shall have been reached, and passed.

"A house divided against itself cannot stand." I believe this government cannot endure, permanently half slave and half free. I do not expect the Union to be dissolved - I do not expect the house to fall - but I do expect it will cease to be divided. It will become all one thing or all the other. Either the opponents of slavery, will arrest the further spread of it, and place it where the public mind shall rest in the belief that it is in the course of ultimate extinction; or its advocates will push it forward, till it shall become alike lawful in all the States, old as well as new - North as well as South.

Have we no tendency to the latter condition? Let any one who doubts, carefully contemplate that now almost complete legal combination - piece of machinery so to speak - compounded of the Nebraska doctrine, and the Dred Scott decision. Let him consider not only what work the machinery is adapted to do, and how well adapted; but also, let him study the history of its construction, and trace, if he can, or rather fail, if he can, to trace the evidence of design and concert of action, among its chief architects, from the beginning.

But, so far, Congress only, had acted; and an indorsement by the people, real or apparent, was indispensable, to save the point already gained, and give chance for more. The new year of 1854 found slavery excluded from more than half the States by State Constitutions, and from most of the national territory by congressional prohibition. Four days later, commenced the struggle, which ended in repealing that congressional prohibition. This opened all the national territory to slavery, and was the first point gained.

This necessity had not been overlooked; but had been provided for, as well as might be, in the notable argument of "squatter sovereignty," otherwise called "sacred right of self government," which latter phrase, though expressive of the only rightful basis of any government, was so perverted in this attempted use of it as to amount to just this: That if any one man, choose to enslave another, no third man shall be allowed to object.

That argument was incorporated into the Nebraska bill itself, in the language which follows: "It being the true intent and meaning of this act not to legislate slavery into any Territory or state, not to exclude it therefrom; but to leave the people thereof perfectly free to form and regulate their domestic institutions in their own way, subject only to the Constitution of the United States."

Then opened the roar of loose declamation in favor of "Squatter Sovereignty," and "Sacred right of self-government."

"But," said opposition members, "let us be more specific - let us amend the bill so as to expressly declare that the people of the territory may exclude slavery." "Not we," said the friends of the measure; and down they voted the amendment.

While the Nebraska Bill was passing through congress, a law case involving the question of a negroe's freedom, by reason of his owner having voluntarily taken him first into a free state and then a territory covered by the congressional prohibition, and held him as a slave, for a long time in each, was passing through the U.S. Circuit Court for the District of Missouri; and both Nebraska bill and law suit were brought to a decision in the same month of May, 1854. The negroe's name was "Dred Scott," which name now designates the decision finally made in the case.

Before the then next Presidential election, the law case came to, and was argued in, the Supreme Court of the United States; but the decision of it was deferred until after the election. Still, before the election, Senator Trumbull, on the floor of the Senate, requests the leading advocate of the Nebraska bill to state his opinion whether the people of a territory can constitutionally exclude slavery from their limits; and the latter answers: "That is a question for the Supreme Court."

The election came. Mr. Buchanan was elected, and the indorsement, such as it was, secured. That was the second point gained. The indorsement, however, fell short of a clear popular majority by nearly four hundred thousand votes, and so, perhaps, was not overwhelmingly reliable and satisfactory. The outgoing President, in his last annual message, as impressively as possible, echoed back upon the people the weight and authority of the indorsement. The Supreme Court met again; did not announce their decision, but ordered a re-argument.

The Presidential inauguration came, and still no decision of the court; but the incoming President, in his inaugural address, fervently exhorted the people to abide by the forthcoming decision, whatever might be. Then, in a few days, came the decision.

The reputed author of the Nebraska Bill finds an early occasion to make a speech at this capital indorsing the Dred Scott Decision, and vehemently denouncing all opposition to it. The new President, too, seizes the early occasion of the Silliman letter to indorse and strongly construe that decision, and to express his astonishment that any different view had ever been entertained.

At length a squabble springs up between the President and the author of the Nebraska Bill, on the mere question of fact, whether the Lecompton constitution was or was not, in any just sense, made by the people of Kansas; and in that squabble the latter declares that all he wants is a fair vote for the people, and that he cares not whether slavery be voted down or voted up. I do not understand his declaration that he cares not whether slavery be voted down or voted up, to be intended by him other than as an apt definition of the policy he would impress upon the public mind - the principle for which he declares he has suffered much, and is ready to suffer to the end.

And well may he cling to that principle. If he has any parental feeling, well may he cling to it. That principle, is the only shred left of his original Nebraska doctrine. Under the Dred Scott decision, "squatter sovereignty" squatted out of existence, tumbled down like temporary scaffolding - like the mould at the foundry served through one blast and fell back into loose sand - helped to carry an election, and then was kicked to the winds. His late joint struggle with the Republicans, against the

Lecompton Constitution, involves nothing of the original Nebraska doctrine. That struggle was made on a point, the right of a people to make their own constitution, upon which he and the Republicans have never differed.

The several points of the Dred Scott decision, in connection with Senator Douglas's "care-not" policy, constitute the piece of machinery, in its present state of advancement. This was the third point gained. The working points of that machinery are:-

First, that no negro slave, imported as such from Africa, and no descendant of such slave, can ever be a citizen of any State, in the sense of that term as used in the Constitution of the United States. This point is made in order to deprive the negro, in every possible event, of the benefit of that provision of the United States Constitution, which declares that: "The citizens of each State shall be entitled to all privileges and immunities of citizens in the several States."

Second, that "subject to the Constitution of the United States, " neither Congress nor a Territorial legislature can exclude slavery from any United States Territory. This point is made in order that individual men may fill up the Territories with slaves, without danger of losing them as property, and thus to enhance the chances of permanency to the institution through all the future.

Third, that whether the holding a negro in actual slavery in a free State makes him free, as against the holder, the United States courts will not decide, but will leave to be decided by the courts of any slave State the negro may be forced into by the master. This point is made, not to be pressed immediately; but, if acquiesced in for a while, and apparently indorsed by the people at an election, then to sustain the logical conclusion that what Dred Scott's master might lawfully do with Dred Scott, in the free State of Illinois, every other master may lawfully do with any other one, or one thousand slaves, in Illinois, or in any other free State.

Auxiliary to all this, and working hand in hand with it, the Nebraska doctrine, or what is left of it, is to educate and mold public opinion, at least Northern public opinion, not to care whether slavery is voted down or voted up. This shows exactly where we now are; and partially, also, whither we are tending.

It will throw additional light on the latter, to go back, and run the mind over the string of historical facts already stated. Several things will now appear less dark and mysterious than they did when they were transpiring. The people were to be left "perfectly free," subject only to the Constitution. What the Constitution had to do with it, outsiders could not then see. Plainly enough now, it was an exactly fitted niche, for the Dred Scott decision to afterward come in, and declare the perfect free freedom of the people to be just no freedom at all. Why was the amendment, expressly declaring the right of the people, voted down? Plainly enough now: the adoption of it would have spoiled the niche for the Dred Scott decision. Why was the court decision held up? Why even a Senator's individual opinion withheld, till after the presidential election? Plainly enough now- the speaking out then would have damaged the perfectly free argument upon which the election was to be carried. Why the outgoing President's felicitation on the indorsement? Why the delay of a re-argument? Why the incoming President's advance exhortation in favor of the decision? These things look like the cautious patting and petting of a spirited horse, preparatory to mounting him, when it is dreaded that he may give the rider a fall. And why the hasty after-indorsement of the decision by the President and others?

We cannot absolutely know that all these exact adaptations are the result of preconcert. But when we see a lot of framed timbers, different portions of which we know have been gotten out at different times and places, and by different workmen- Stephen, Franklin, Roger, and James, for instance-and when we see these timbers joined together, and see they exactly matte the frame of a house or a mill, all the tenons and mortices exactly fitting, and all the lengths and proportions of the different l pieces exactly adapted to their respective places, and not a piece. too many or too few,-not omitting even scaffolding-or, if a single piece be lacking, we see the place in the frame exactly fitted and prepared yet to bring such piece in-in such a case we find it impossible not to believe that Stephen and Franklin and Roger and James all understood one another from the beginning and all worked upon a common plan or draft drawn up before the first blow was struck.

It should not be overlooked that, by the Nebraska Bill, the people of a State, as well as a Territory, were to be left "perfectly free," "subject only to the Constitution." Why mention a State? They were legislating for Territories, and not for or about States. Certainly the people of a State are and ought to be subject to the Constitution of the United States; but why is mention of this lugged into this merely Territorial law? Why are the people of a Territory and the people of a State therein lumped together, and their relation to the Constitution therein treated as being precisely the same? While the opinion of the court, by Chief-Justice Taney, in the Dred Scott case and the separate opinions of all the concurring judges, expressly declare that the Constitution of the United States neither permits Congress nor a Territorial legislature to exclude slavery from any United States Territory, they all omit to declare whether or not the same Constitution permits a State, or the people of a State, to exclude it.

Possibly this is a mere omission; but who can be quite sure, if McLean or Curtis had sought to get into the opinion a declaration of unlimited power in the people of a State to exclude slavery from their limits, just as Chase and Mace sought to get such declaration, in behalf of the people of a Territory, into the Nebraska Bill-I ask, who can be quite sure that it would not have been voted down in the one case as it ad been in the other?

The nearest approach to the point of declaring the power of a State over slavery is made by Judge Nelson. He approaches it more than once, using the precise idea, and almost the language, too, of the Nebraska Act. On one occasion, his exact language is, "except in cases where the power is restrained by the Constitution of the United States the law of the State is supreme over the subject of slavery within its g jurisdiction."

In what cases the power of the States is so restrained by the United States Constitution is left an open question, precisely as the same question, as to the restraint on the power of the Territories, was left open in the Nebraska Act Put this and that together, and we have another nice little niche which we may ere long see filled with another Supreme Court decisions declaring that the Constitution of the United States does not permit a State to exclude slavery from its limits. And this may especially be expected if the doctrine of "care not wether slavery be voted down or voted up," shall gain upon he public mind sufficiently to give promise that such a decision an be maintained when made.

Such a decision is all that slavery now lacks of being alike lawful in all the States. Welcome, or unwelcome, such decision is probably coming, and will soon be upon us, unless the power of the present political dynasty shall be met and overthrown. We shall lie down pleasantly dreaming that the people of Missouri. are on the verge of making their State free, and we shall awake to the reality instead, that the Supreme Court has made Illinois a slave State. To meet and overthrow the power of that dynasty is the work now before all those who would prevent that consummation. This is what we have to do. How can we best do it ? There are those who denounce us openly to their own friends and yet whisper us softly, that Senator Douglas is the aptest instrument there is with which to effect that object.

They wish us to infer all from the fact that he now has a little quarrel with the present head of the dynasty; and that he has regularly voted with us on a single point, upon which he and we have never differed. They remind us that he is a great man, and that the largest of us are very small ones. Let this be granted. But "a living dog is better than a dead lion." Judge Douglas, if not a dead lion, for this work, is at least a caged and toothless one. How can he oppose the advances of slavery? He does not care anything about it. His avowed mission is impressing the "public heart" to care nothing about it. A leading Douglas Democratic newspaper thinks Douglas' superior talent will be needed to resist the revival of the African slave trade. Does Douglas believe an effort to revive that trade is approaching? He has not said so. Does he really think so? But if it is, how can he resist it? For years he has labored to prove it a sacred right of white men to take negro slaves into the new Territories.

Can he possibly show that it is less a sacred right to buy them where they can be bought cheapest? And unquestionably they can be bought cheaper in Africa than in Virginia. He has done all in his power to reduce the whole question of slavery to one of a mere right of property; and as such, how can he oppose the foreign slave trade-how can he refuse that trade in that "property" shall be "perfectly free"-unless he does it as a protection to the home production? And as the home producers will probably not ask the protection, he will be wholly without a ground of opposition.

Senator Douglas holds, we know, that a man may rightfully be wiser today than he was yesterday-that he may rightfully change when he finds himself wrong. But can we, for that reason, run ahead, and infer that he will make any particular change, of which he, himself, has given no intimation? Can we safely base our action upon any such vague inference? Now, as ever, I wish not to misrepresent Judge Douglas's position, question his motives, or do aught that can be personally offensive to him. Whenever, if ever, he and we can come together on principle so that our cause may have assistance from his great ability, I hope to have interposed no adventitious obstacle. But clearly, he is not now with us-he does not pretend to be-he does not promise ever to be.

Our cause, then, must be intrusted to, and conducted by, its own undoubted friends-those whose hands are free, whose hearts are in the work-who do care for the result. Two years ago the Republicans of the nation mustered over thirteen hundred thousand strong. We did this under the single impulse of resistance to a common danger, with every external circumstance against us. Of strange, discordant, and even hostile elements, we gathered from the four winds, and formed and fought the battle through, under the constant hot fire of a disciplined, proud, and pampered enemy. Did we brave all them to falter now?-now, when that same enemy is wavering, dissevered, and belligerent? The result is not doubtful. We shall not fail-if we stand firm, we shall not fail. Wise counsels may accelerate, or mistakes delay it, but, sooner or later, the victory is sure to come.

Cooper Union Speech, New York City, (February 27 1860)

The Cooper Union Speech was intended to be a mild challenge to the front running Republican candidate, William Seward. Originally to be presented at the large church of Henry Ward Beecher in Brooklyn, the venue was moved, without telling Lincoln, to the newly opened Cooper Institute, causing Lincoln to make last minute changes. Rather than being a mild challenge, Lincoln's Cooper Union speech electrified the New England Republican party and launched the presidential bid of the lawyer from Springfield, Illinois.

Lincoln was not noted for his podium skills yet several eyewitnesses to his Cooper Union speech remarked on how skillfully he managed the audience with changes in his facial features and the tightness of his argument. Lest too much be made of the fact that Lincoln drew an audience of over 1500 it bears pointing out that there were 3 other political speeched in New York that night and at least one outdrew Lincoln. Political speeches were the professional sports of that day - and perhaps therein lies a lesson.

***

Mr. President and fellow citizens of New York: -

The facts with which I shall deal this evening are mainly old and familiar; nor is there anything new in the general use I shall make of them. If there shall be any novelty, it will be in the mode of presenting the facts, and the inferences and observations following that presentation.

In his speech last autumn, at Columbus, Ohio, as reported in "The New-York Times," Senator Douglas said:

"Our fathers, when they framed the Government under which we live, understood this question just as well, and even better, than we do now."

I fully indorse this, and I adopt it as a text for this discourse. I so adopt it because it furnishes a precise and an agreed starting point for a discussion between Republicans and that wing of the Democracy headed by Senator Douglas. It simply leaves the inquiry: "What was the understanding those fathers had of the question mentioned?"

What is the frame of government under which we live?

The answer must be: "The Constitution of the United States." That Constitution consists of the original, framed in 1787, (and under which the present government first went into operation,) and twelve subsequently framed amendments, the first ten of which were framed in 1789.

Who were our fathers that framed the Constitution? I suppose the "thirty-nine" who signed the original instrument may be fairly called our fathers who framed that part of the present

Government. It is almost exactly true to say they framed it, and it is altogether true to say they fairly represented the opinion and sentiment of the whole nation at that time. Their names, being familiar to nearly all, and accessible to quite all, need not now be repeated.

I take these "thirty-nine," for the present, as being "our fathers who framed the Government under which we live."

What is the question which, according to the text, those fathers understood "just as well, and even better than we do now?"

It is this: Does the proper division of local from federal authority, or anything in the Constitution, forbid our Federal Government to control as to slavery in our Federal Territories?

Upon this, Senator Douglas holds the affirmative, and Republicans the negative. This affirmation and denial form an issue; and this issue - this question - is precisely what the text declares our fathers understood "better than we."

Let us now inquire whether the "thirty-nine," or any of them, ever acted upon this question; and if they did, how they acted upon it - how they expressed that better understanding?

In 1784, three years before the Constitution - the United States then owning the Northwestern Territory, and no other, the Congress of the Confederation had before them the question of prohibiting slavery in that Territory; and four of the "thirty-nine" who afterward framed the Constitution, were in that Congress, and voted on that question. Of these, Roger Sherman, Thomas Mifflin, and Hugh Williamson voted for the prohibition, thus showing that, in their understanding, no line dividing local from federal authority, nor anything else, properly forbade the Federal Government to control as to slavery in federal territory. The other of the four - James M'Henry - voted against the prohibition, showing that, for some cause, he thought it improper to vote for it.

In 1787, still before the Constitution, but while the Convention was in session framing it, and while the Northwestern Territory still was the only territory owned by the United States, the same question of prohibiting slavery in the territory again came before the Congress of the Confederation; and two more of the "thirty-nine" who afterward signed the Constitution, were in that Congress, and voted on the question. They were William Blount and William Few; and they both voted for the prohibition - thus showing that, in their understanding, no line dividing local from federal authority, nor anything else, properly forbids the Federal Government to control as to slavery in Federal territory. This time the prohibition became a law, being part of what is now well known as the Ordinance of '87.

The question of federal control of slavery in the territories, seems not to have been directly before the Convention which framed the original Constitution; and hence it is not recorded that the "thirty-nine," or any of them, while engaged on that instrument, expressed any opinion on that precise question.

In 1789, by the first Congress which sat under the Constitution, an act was passed to enforce the Ordinance of '87, including the prohibition of slavery in the Northwestern Territory. The bill for this act was reported by one of the "thirty-nine," Thomas Fitzsimmons, then a member of the House of Representatives from Pennsylvania. It went through all its stages without a word of opposition, and finally passed both branches without yeas and nays, which is equivalent to a unanimous passage. In this Congress there were sixteen of the thirty-nine fathers who framed the original Constitution. They were John Langdon, Nicholas Gilman, Wm. S. Johnson, Roger Sherman, Robert Morris, Thos. Fitzsimmons, William Few, Abraham Baldwin, Rufus King, William Paterson, George Clymer, Richard Bassett, George Read, Pierce Butler, Daniel Carroll, James Madison.

This shows that, in their understanding, no line dividing local from federal authority, nor anything in the Constitution, properly forbade Congress to prohibit slavery in the federal territory; else both their fidelity to correct principle, and their oath to support the Constitution, would have constrained them to oppose the prohibition.

Again, George Washington, another of the "thirty-nine," was then President of the United States, and, as such approved and signed the bill; thus completing its validity as a law, and thus showing that, in his understanding, no line dividing local from federal authority, nor anything in the Constitution, forbade the Federal Government, to control as to slavery in federal territory.

No great while after the adoption of the original Constitution, North Carolina ceded to the Federal Government the country now constituting the State of Tennessee; and a few years later Georgia ceded that which now constitutes the States of Mississippi and Alabama. In both deeds of cession it was made a condition by the ceding States that the Federal Government should not prohibit slavery in the ceded territory. Besides this, slavery was then actually in the ceded country. Under these circumstances, Congress, on taking charge of these countries, did not absolutely prohibit slavery within them. But they did interfere with it - take control of it - even there, to a certain extent. In 1798, Congress organized the Territory of Mississippi. In the act of organization, they prohibited the bringing of slaves into the Territory, from any place without the United States, by fine, and giving freedom to slaves so bought. This act passed both branches of Congress without yeas and nays. In that Congress were three of the "thirty-nine" who framed the original Constitution. They were John Langdon, George Read and Abraham Baldwin. They all, probably, voted for it. Certainly they would have placed their opposition to it upon record, if, in their understanding, any line dividing local from federal authority, or anything in the Constitution, properly forbade the Federal Government to control as to slavery in federal territory.

In 1803, the Federal Government purchased the Louisiana country. Our former territorial acquisitions came from certain of our own States; but this Louisiana country was acquired from a foreign nation. In 1804, Congress gave a territorial organization to that part of it which now constitutes the State of Louisiana. New Orleans, lying within that part, was an old and comparatively large city. There were other considerable towns and settlements, and slavery was extensively and thoroughly intermingled with the people. Congress did not, in the Territorial Act, prohibit slavery; but they did interfere with it - take control of it - in a more marked and extensive way than they did in the case of Mississippi. The substance of the provision therein made, in relation to slaves, was:

First. That no slave should be imported into the territory from foreign parts.

Second. That no slave should be carried into it who had been imported into the United States since the first day of May, 1798.

Third. That no slave should be carried into it, except by the owner, and for his own use as a settler; the penalty in all the cases being a fine upon the violator of the law, and freedom to the slave.

This act also was passed without yeas and nays. In the Congress which passed it, there were two of the "thirty-nine." They were Abraham Baldwin and Jonathan Dayton. As stated in the case of Mississippi, it is probable they both voted for it. They would not have allowed it to pass without recording their opposition to it, if, in their understanding, it violated either the line properly dividing local from federal authority, or any provision of the Constitution.

In 1819-20, came and passed the Missouri question. Many votes were taken, by yeas and nays, in both branches of Congress, upon the various phases of the general question. Two of the "thirty-nine" - Rufus King and Charles Pinckney - were members of that Congress. Mr. King steadily voted for slavery prohibition and against all compromises, while Mr. Pinckney as steadily voted against slavery prohibition and against all compromises. By this, Mr. King showed that, in his understanding, no line dividing local from federal authority, nor anything in the Constitution, was violated by Congress prohibiting slavery in federal territory; while Mr. Pinckney, by his votes, showed that, in his understanding, there was some sufficient reason for opposing such prohibition in that case.

The cases I have mentioned are the only acts of the "thirty-nine," or of any of them, upon the direct issue, which I have been able to discover.

To enumerate the persons who thus acted, as being four in 1784, two in 1787, seventeen in 1789, three in 1798, two in 1804, and two in 1819-20 - there would be thirty of them. But this would be counting John Langdon, Roger Sherman, William Few, Rufus King, and George Read each twice, and Abraham Baldwin, three times. The true number of those of the "thirty-nine" whom I have shown to have acted upon the question, which, by the text, they understood better than we, is twenty-three, leaving sixteen not shown to have acted upon it in any way.

Here, then, we have twenty-three out of our thirty-nine fathers "who framed the government under which we live," who have, upon their official responsibility and their corporal oaths, acted upon the very question which the text affirms they "understood just as well, and even better than we do now;" and twenty-one of them - a clear majority of the whole "thirty-nine" - so acting upon it as to make them guilty of gross political impropriety and willful perjury, if, in their understanding, any proper division between local and federal authority, or anything in the Constitution they had made themselves, and sworn to support, forbade the Federal Government to control as to slavery in the federal territories. Thus the twenty-one acted; and, as actions speak louder than words, so actions, under such responsibility, speak still louder.

Two of the twenty-three voted against Congressional prohibition of slavery in the federal territories, in the instances in which they acted upon the question. But for what reasons they so voted is not known. They may have done so because they thought a proper division of local from federal authority, or some provision or principle of the Constitution, stood in the way; or they may, without any such question, have voted against the prohibition, on what appeared to them to be sufficient grounds of expediency. No one who has sworn to support the Constitution can conscientiously vote for what he understands to be an unconstitutional measure, however expedient he may think it; but one may and ought to vote against a measure which he deems constitutional, if, at the same time, he deems it inexpedient. It, therefore, would be unsafe to set down even the two who voted against the prohibition, as having done so because, in their understanding, any proper division of local from federal authority, or anything in the Constitution, forbade the Federal Government to control as to slavery in federal territory.

The remaining sixteen of the "thirty-nine," so far as I have discovered, have left no record of their understanding upon the direct question of federal control of slavery in the federal territories. But there is much reason to believe that their understanding upon that question would not have appeared different from that of their twenty-three compeers, had it been manifested at all.

For the purpose of adhering rigidly to the text, I have purposely omitted whatever understanding may have been manifested by any person, however distinguished, other than the thirty-nine fathers who framed the original Constitution; and, for the same reason, I have also omitted whatever understanding may have been manifested by any of the "thirty-nine" even, on any other phase of the general question of slavery. If we should look into their acts and declarations on those other phases, as the foreign slave trade, and the morality and policy of slavery generally, it would appear to us that on the direct question of federal control of slavery in federal territories, the sixteen, if they had acted at all, would probably have acted just as the twenty-three did. Among that sixteen were several of the most noted anti-slavery men of those times - as Dr. Franklin, Alexander Hamilton and Gouverneur Morris - while there was not one now known to have been otherwise, unless it may be John Rutledge, of South Carolina.

The sum of the whole is, that of our thirty-nine fathers who framed the original Constitution, twenty-one - a clear majority of the whole - certainly understood that no proper division of local from federal authority, nor any part of the Constitution, forbade the Federal Government to control slavery in the federal territories; while all the rest probably had the same understanding. Such, unquestionably, was the understanding of our fathers who framed the original Constitution; and the text affirms that they understood the question "better than we."

But, so far, I have been considering the understanding of the question manifested by the framers of the original Constitution.

In and by the original instrument, a mode was provided for amending it; and, as I have already stated, the present frame of "the Government under which we live" consists of that original, and twelve amendatory articles framed and adopted since. Those who now insist that federal control of slavery in federal territories violates the Constitution, point us to the provisions which they suppose it thus violates; and, as I understand, that all fix upon provisions in these amendatory articles, and not in the original instrument. The Supreme Court, in the Dred Scott case, plant themselves upon the fifth amendment, which provides that no person shall be deprived of "life, liberty or property without due process of law;" while Senator Douglas and his peculiar adherents plant themselves upon the tenth amendment, providing that "the powers not delegated to the United States by the Constitution" "are reserved to the States respectively, or to the people."

Now, it so happens that these amendments were framed by the first Congress which sat under the Constitution - the identical Congress which passed the act already mentioned, enforcing the prohibition of slavery in the Northwestern Territory. Not only was it the same Congress, but they were the identical, same individual men who, at the same session, and at the same time within the session, had under consideration, and in progress toward maturity, these Constitutional amendments, and this act prohibiting slavery in all the territory the nation then owned. The Constitutional amendments were introduced before, and passed after the act enforcing the Ordinance of '87; so that, during the whole pendency of the act to enforce the Ordinance, the Constitutional amendments were also pending.

The seventy-six members of that Congress, including sixteen of the framers of the original Constitution, as before stated, were pre- eminently our fathers who framed that part of "the Government under which we live," which is now claimed as forbidding the Federal Government to control slavery in the federal territories.

Is it not a little presumptuous in any one at this day to affirm that the two things which that Congress deliberately framed, and carried to maturity at the same time, are absolutely inconsistent with each other? And does not such affirmation become impudently absurd when coupled with the other affirmation from the same mouth, that those who did the two things, alleged to be inconsistent, understood whether they really were inconsistent better than we - better than he who affirms that they are inconsistent?

It is surely safe to assume that the thirty-nine framers of the original Constitution, and the seventy-six members of the Congress which framed the amendments thereto, taken together, do certainly include those who may be fairly called "our fathers who framed the Government under which we live." And so assuming, I defy any man to show that any one of them ever, in his whole life, declared that, in his understanding, any proper division of local from federal authority, or any part of the

Constitution, forbade the Federal Government to control as to slavery in the federal territories. I go a step further. I defy any one to show that any living man in the whole world ever did, prior to the beginning of the present century, (and I might almost say prior to the beginning of the last half of the present century,) declare that, in his understanding, any proper division of local from federal authority, or any part of the Constitution, forbade the Federal Government to control as to slavery in the federal territories. To those who now so declare, I give, not only "our fathers who framed the Government under which we live," but with them all other living men within the century in which it was framed, among whom to search, and they shall not be able to find the evidence of a single man agreeing with them.

Now, and here, let me guard a little against being misunderstood. I do not mean to say we are bound to follow implicitly in whatever our fathers did. To do so, would be to discard all the lights of current experience - to reject all progress - all improvement. What I do say is, that if we would supplant the opinions and policy of our fathers in any case, we should do so upon evidence so conclusive, and argument so clear, that even their great authority, fairly considered and weighed, cannot stand; and most surely not in a case whereof we ourselves declare they understood the question better than we.

If any man at this day sincerely believes that a proper division of local from federal authority, or any part of the Constitution, forbids the Federal Government to control as to slavery in the federal territories, he is right to say so, and to enforce his position by all truthful evidence and fair argument which he can. But he has no right to mislead others, who have less access to history, and less leisure to study it, into the false belief that "our fathers who framed the Government under which we live" were of the same opinion - thus substituting falsehood and deception for truthful evidence and fair argument. If any man at this day sincerely believes "our fathers who framed the Government under which we live," used and applied principles, in other cases, which ought to have led them to understand that a proper division of local from federal authority or some part of the Constitution, forbids the Federal Government to control as to slavery in the federal territories, he is right to say so. But he should, at the same time, brave the responsibility of declaring that, in his opinion, he understands their principles better than they did themselves; and especially should he not shirk that responsibility by asserting that they "understood the question just as well, and even better, than we do now."

But enough! Let all who believe that "our fathers, who framed the Government under which we live, understood this question just as well, and even better, than we do now," speak as they spoke, and act as they acted upon it. This is all Republicans ask - all Republicans desire - in relation to slavery. As those fathers marked it, so let it be again marked, as an evil not to be extended, but to be tolerated and protected only because of and so far as its actual presence among us makes that toleration and protection a necessity. Let all the guarantees those fathers gave it, be, not grudgingly, but fully and fairly, maintained. For this Republicans contend, and with this, so far as I know or believe, they will be content.

And now, if they would listen - as I suppose they will not - I would address a few words to the Southern people.

I would say to them: - You consider yourselves a reasonable and a just people; and I consider that in the general qualities of reason and justice you are not inferior to any other people. Still, when you speak of us Republicans, you do so only to denounce us a reptiles, or, at the best, as no better than outlaws. You will grant a hearing to pirates or murderers, but nothing like it to "Black Republicans." In all your contentions with one another, each of you deems an unconditional condemnation of "Black Republicanism" as the first thing to be attended to. Indeed, such condemnation of us seems to be an indispensable prerequisite - license, so to speak - among you to be admitted or permitted to speak at all. Now, can you, or not, be prevailed upon to pause and to consider whether this is quite just to us, or even to yourselves? Bring forward your charges and specifications, and then be patient long enough to hear us deny or justify.

You say we are sectional. We deny it. That makes an issue; and the burden of proof is upon you. You produce your proof; and what is it? Why, that our party has no existence in your section - gets no votes in your section. The fact is substantially true; but does it prove the issue? If it does, then in case we should, without change of principle, begin to get votes in your section, we should thereby cease to be sectional. You cannot escape this conclusion; and yet, are you willing to abide by it? If you are, you will probably soon find that we have ceased to be sectional, for we shall get votes in your section this very year. You will then begin to discover, as the truth plainly is, that your proof does not touch the issue. The fact that we get no votes in your section, is a fact of your making, and not of ours. And if there be fault in that fact, that fault is primarily yours, and remains until you show that we repel you by some wrong principle or practice. If we do repel you by any wrong principle or practice, the fault is ours; but this brings you to where you ought to have started - to a discussion of the right or wrong of our principle. If our principle, put in practice, would wrong your section for the benefit of ours, or for any other object, then our principle, and we with it, are sectional, and are justly opposed and denounced as such. Meet us, then, on the question of whether our principle, put in practice, would wrong your section; and so meet it as if it were possible that something may be said on our side. Do you accept the challenge? No! Then you really believe that the principle which "our fathers who framed the Government under which we live" thought so clearly right as to adopt it, and indorse it again and again, upon their official oaths, is in fact so clearly wrong as to demand your condemnation without a moment's consideration.

Some of you delight to flaunt in our faces the warning against sectional parties given by Washington in his Farewell Address. Less than eight years before Washington gave that warning, he had, as President of the United States, approved and signed an act of Congress, enforcing the prohibition of slavery in the Northwestern Territory, which act embodied the policy of the Government upon that subject up to and at the very moment he penned that warning; and about one year after he penned it, he wrote LaFayette that he considered that prohibition a wise measure, expressing in the same connection his hope that we should at some time have a confederacy of free States.

Bearing this in mind, and seeing that sectionalism has since arisen upon this same subject, is that warning a weapon in your hands against us, or in our hands against you? Could Washington himself speak, would he cast the blame of that sectionalism upon us, who sustain his policy, or upon you who repudiate it? We respect that warning of Washington, and we commend it to you, together with his example pointing to the right application of it.

But you say you are conservative - eminently conservative - while we are revolutionary, destructive, or something of the sort. What is conservatism? Is it not adherence to the old and tried, against the new and untried? We stick to, contend for, the identical old policy on the point in controversy which was adopted by "our fathers who framed the Government under which we live;" while you with one accord reject, and scout, and spit upon that old policy, and insist upon substituting something new. True, you disagree among yourselves as to

what that substitute shall be. You are divided on new propositions and plans, but you are unanimous in rejecting and denouncing the old policy of the fathers. Some of you are for
reviving the foreign slave trade; some for a Congressional
Slave-Code for the Territories; some for Congress forbidding
the Territories to prohibit Slavery within their limits; some for
maintaining Slavery in the Territories through the judiciary;
some for the "gur-reat pur-rinciple" that "if one man would
enslave another, no third man should object," fantastically
called "Popular Sovereignty;" but never a man among you is in
favor of federal prohibition of slavery in federal territories,
according to the practice of "our fathers who framed the Government under which we live." Not one of all your various
plans can show a precedent or an advocate in the century within
which our Government originated. Consider, then, whether your
claim of conservatism for yourselves, and your charge or
destructiveness against us, are based on the most clear and
stable foundations.

Again, you say we have made the slavery question more
prominent than it formerly was. We deny it. We admit that it is
more prominent, but we deny that we made it so. It was not we,
but you, who discarded the old policy of the fathers. We
resisted, and still resist, your innovation; and thence comes the
greater prominence of the question. Would you have that
question reduced to its former proportions? Go back to that old
policy. What has been will be again, under the same conditions.

If you would have the peace of the old times, readopt the precepts and policy of the old times.

You charge that we stir up insurrections among your slaves. We deny it; and what is your proof? Harper's Ferry! John Brown!! John Brown was no Republican; and you have failed to implicate a single Republican in his Harper's Ferry enterprise. If any member of our party is guilty in that matter, you know it or you do not know it. If you do know it, you are inexcusable for not designating the man and proving the fact. If you do not know it, you are inexcusable for asserting it, and especially for persisting in the assertion after you have tried and failed to make the proof. You need to be told that persisting in a charge which one does not know to be true, is simply malicious slander.

Some of you admit that no Republican designedly aided or encouraged the Harper's Ferry affair, but still insist that our doctrines and declarations necessarily lead to such results. We do not believe it. We know we hold to no doctrine, and make no declaration, which were not held to and made by "our fathers who framed the Government under which we live." You never dealt fairly by us in relation to this affair. When it occurred, some important State elections were near at hand, and you were in evident glee with the belief that, by charging the blame upon us, you could get an advantage of us in those elections. The elections came, and your expectations were not quite fulfilled. Every Republican man knew that, as to himself at least, your charge was a slander, and he was not much inclined by it to cast his vote in your favor. Republican doctrines and declarations are accompanied with a continual protest against any interference whatever with your slaves, or with you about your slaves. Surely, this does not encourage them to revolt. True, we do, in common with "our fathers, who framed the Government under which we live," declare our belief that slavery is wrong; but the slaves do not hear us declare even this. For anything we say or do, the slaves would scarcely know there is a Republican party. I believe they would not, in fact, generally know it but for your misrepresentations of us, in their hearing. In your political contests among yourselves, each faction charges the other with sympathy with Black Republicanism; and then, to give point to the charge, defines Black Republicanism to simply be insurrection, blood and thunder among the slaves.

Slave insurrections are no more common now than they were before the Republican party was organized. What induced the Southampton insurrection, twenty-eight years ago, in which, at least three times as many lives were lost as at Harper's Ferry? You can scarcely stretch your very elastic fancy to the conclusion that Southampton was "got up by Black Republicanism." In the present state of things in the United States, I do not think a general, or even a very extensive slave insurrection is possible. The indispensable concert of action cannot be attained. The slaves have no means of rapid communication; nor can incendiary freemen, black or white, supply it. The explosive materials are everywhere in parcels; but there neither are, nor can be supplied, the indispensable connecting trains.

Much is said by Southern people about the affection of slaves for their masters and mistresses; and a part of it, at least, is true. A plot for an uprising could scarcely be devised and communicated to twenty individuals before some one of them, to save the life of a favorite master or mistress, would divulge it. This is the rule; and the slave revolution in Hayti was not an exception to it, but a case occurring under peculiar circumstances. The gunpowder plot of British history, though not connected with slaves, was more in point. In that case, only about twenty were admitted to the secret; and yet one of them, in his anxiety to save a friend, betrayed the plot to that friend, and, by consequence, averted the calamity. Occasional poisonings from the kitchen, and open or stealthy assassinations in the field, and local revolts extending to a score or so, will continue to occur as the natural results of slavery; but no general insurrection of slaves, as I think, can happen in this country for a long time. Whoever much fears, or much hopes for such an event, will be alike disappointed.

In the language of Mr. Jefferson, uttered many years ago, "It is still in our power to direct the process of emancipation, and deportation, peaceably, and in such slow degrees, as that the evil will wear off insensibly; and their places be, pari passu, filled up by free white laborers. If, on the contrary, it is left to force itself on, human nature must shudder at the prospect held up."

Mr. Jefferson did not mean to say, nor do I, that the power of emancipation is in the Federal Government. He spoke of Virginia; and, as to the power of emancipation, I speak of the slaveholding States only. The Federal Government, however, as we insist, has the power of restraining the extension of the institution - the power to insure that a slave insurrection shall never occur on any American soil which is now free from slavery.

John Brown's effort was peculiar. It was not a slave insurrection. It was an attempt by white men to get up a revolt among slaves, in which the slaves refused to participate. In fact, it was so absurd that the slaves, with all their ignorance, saw plainly enough it could not succeed. That affair, in its philosophy, corresponds with the many attempts, related in history, at the assassination of kings and emperors. An enthusiast broods over the oppression of a people till he fancies himself commissioned by Heaven to liberate them. He ventures the attempt, which ends in little else than his own execution. Orsini's attempt on Louis Napoleon, and John Brown's attempt at Harper's Ferry were, in their philosophy, precisely the same. The eagerness to cast blame on old England in the one case, and on New England in the other, does not disprove the sameness of the two things.

And how much would it avail you, if you could, by the use of John Brown, Helper's Book, and the like, break up the Republican organization? Human action can be modified to some extent, but human nature cannot be changed. There is a judgment and a feeling against slavery in this nation, which cast at least a million and a half of votes. You cannot destroy that judgment and feeling - that sentiment - by breaking up the political organization which rallies around it. You can scarcely scatter and disperse an army which has been formed into order in the face of your heaviest fire; but if you could, how much would you gain by forcing the sentiment which created it out of the peaceful channel of the ballot-box, into some other channel? What would that other channel probably be? Would the number of John Browns be lessened or enlarged by the operation?

But you will break up the Union rather than submit to a denial of your Constitutional rights.

That has a somewhat reckless sound; but it would be palliated, if not fully justified, were we proposing, by the mere force of numbers, to deprive you of some right, plainly written down in the Constitution. But we are proposing no such thing.

When you make these declarations, you have a specific and well-understood allusion to an assumed Constitutional right of yours, to take slaves into the federal territories, and to hold them there as property. But no such right is specifically written in the Constitution. That instrument is literally silent about any such right. We, on the contrary, deny that such a right has any existence in the Constitution, even by implication.

Your purpose, then, plainly stated, is that you will destroy the Government, unless you be allowed to construe and enforce the Constitution as you please, on all points in dispute between you and us. You will rule or ruin in all events.

This, plainly stated, is your language. Perhaps you will say the Supreme Court has decided the disputed Constitutional question in your favor. Not quite so. But waiving the lawyer's distinction between dictum and decision, the Court have decided the question for you in a sort of way. The Court have substantially said, it is your Constitutional right to take slaves into the federal territories, and to hold them there as property. When I say the decision was made in a sort of way, I mean it was made in a divided Court, by a bare majority of the Judges, and they not quite agreeing with one another in the reasons for making it; that it is so made as that its avowed supporters disagree with one another about its meaning, and that it was mainly based upon a mistaken statement of fact - the statement in the opinion that "the right of property in a slave is distinctly and expressly affirmed in the Constitution."

An inspection of the Constitution will show that the right of property in a slave is not "distinctly and expressly affirmed" in it. Bear in mind, the Judges do not pledge their judicial opinion that such right is impliedly affirmed in the Constitution; but they pledge their veracity that it is "distinctly and expressly" affirmed there - "distinctly," that is, not mingled with anything else - "expressly," that is, in words meaning just that, without the aid of any inference, and susceptible of no other meaning.

If they had only pledged their judicial opinion that such right is affirmed in the instrument by implication, it would be open to others to show that neither the word "slave" nor "slavery" is to be found in the Constitution, nor the word "property" even, in any connection with language alluding to the things slave, or slavery; and that wherever in that instrument the slave is alluded to, he is called a "person;" - and wherever his master's legal right in relation to him is alluded to, it is spoken of as "service or labor which may be due," - as a debt payable in service or labor. Also, it would be open to show, by contemporaneous history, that this mode of alluding to slaves and slavery, instead of speaking of them, was employed on purpose to exclude from the Constitution the idea that there could be property in man.

To show all this, is easy and certain.

When this obvious mistake of the Judges shall be brought to their notice, is it not reasonable to expect that they will withdraw the mistaken statement, and reconsider the conclusion based upon it?

And then it is to be remembered that "our fathers, who framed the Government under which we live" - the men who made the Constitution - decided this same Constitutional question in our favor, long ago - decided it without division among themselves, when making the decision; without division among themselves about the meaning of it after it was made, and, so far as any evidence is left, without basing it upon any mistaken statement of facts.

Under all these circumstances, do you really feel yourselves justified to break up this Government unless such a court decision as yours is, shall be at once submitted to as a conclusive and final rule of political action? But you will not abide the election of a Republican president! In that supposed event, you say, you will destroy the Union; and then, you say, the great crime of having destroyed it will be upon us! That is cool. A highwayman holds a pistol to my ear, and mutters through his teeth, "Stand and deliver, or I shall kill you, and then you will be a murderer!"

To be sure, what the robber demanded of me - my money - was my own; and I had a clear right to keep it; but it was no more my own than my vote is my own; and the threat of death to me, to extort my money, and the threat of destruction to the Union, to extort my vote, can scarcely be distinguished in principle.

A few words now to Republicans. It is exceedingly desirable that all parts of this great Confederacy shall be at peace, and in harmony, one with another. Let us Republicans do our part to have it so. Even though much provoked, let us do nothing through passion and ill temper. Even though the southern people will not so much as listen to us, let us calmly consider their demands, and yield to them if, in our deliberate view of our duty, we possibly can. Judging by all they say and do, and by the subject and nature of their controversy with us, let us determine, if we can, what will satisfy them.

Will they be satisfied if the Territories be unconditionally surrendered to them? We know they will not. In all their present complaints against us, the Territories are scarcely mentioned. Invasions and insurrections are the rage now. Will it satisfy them, if, in the future, we have nothing to do with invasions and insurrections? We know it will not. We so know, because we know we never had anything to do with invasions and insurrections; and yet this total abstaining does not exempt us from the charge and the denunciation.

The question recurs, what will satisfy them? Simply this: We must not only let them alone, but we must somehow, convince them that we do let them alone. This, we know by experience, is no easy task. We have been so trying to convince them from the very beginning of our organization, but with no success. In all our platforms and speeches we have constantly protested our purpose to let them alone; but this has had no tendency to convince them. Alike unavailing to convince them, is the fact that they have never detected a man of us in any attempt to disturb them.

These natural, and apparently adequate means all failing, what will convince them? This, and this only: cease to call slavery wrong, and join them in calling it right. And this must be done thoroughly - done in acts as well as in words. Silence will not be tolerated - we must place ourselves avowedly with them. Senator Douglas' new sedition law must be enacted and enforced, suppressing all declarations that slavery is wrong, whether made in politics, in presses, in pulpits, or in private. We must arrest and return their fugitive slaves with greedy pleasure. We must pull down our Free State constitutions. The whole atmosphere must be disinfected from all taint of opposition to slavery, before they will cease to believe that all their troubles proceed from us.

I am quite aware they do not state their case precisely in this way. Most of them would probably say to us, "Let us alone, do nothing to us, and say what you please about slavery." But we do let them alone - have never disturbed them - so that, after all, it is what we say, which dissatisfies them. They will continue to accuse us of doing, until we cease saying.

I am also aware they have not, as yet, in terms, demanded the overthrow of our Free-State Constitutions. Yet those Constitutions declare the wrong of slavery, with more solemn emphasis, than do all other sayings against it; and when all these other sayings shall have been silenced, the overthrow of these Constitutions will be demanded, and nothing be left to resist the demand. It is nothing to the contrary, that they do not demand the whole of this just now. Demanding what they do, and for the reason they do, they can voluntarily stop nowhere short of this consummation. Holding, as they do, that slavery is morally right, and socially elevating, they cannot cease to demand a full national recognition of it, as a legal right, and a social blessing.

Nor can we justifiably withhold this, on any ground save our conviction that slavery is wrong. If slavery is right, all words, acts, laws, and constitutions against it, are themselves wrong, and should be silenced, and swept away. If it is right, we cannot justly object to its nationality - its universality; if it is wrong, they cannot justly insist upon its extension - its enlargement. All they ask, we could readily grant, if we thought slavery right; all we ask, they could as readily grant, if they thought it wrong. Their thinking it right, and our thinking it wrong, is the precise fact upon which depends the whole controversy. Thinking it right, as they do, they are not to blame for desiring its full recognition, as being right; but, thinking it wrong, as we do, can we yield to them? Can we cast our votes with their view, and against our own? In view of our moral, social, and political responsibilities, can we do this?

Wrong as we think slavery is, we can yet afford to let it alone where it is, because that much is due to the necessity arising from its actual presence in the nation; but can we, while our votes will prevent it, allow it to spread into the National

Territories, and to overrun us here in these Free States? If our sense of duty forbids this, then let us stand by our duty, fearlessly and effectively. Let us be diverted by none of those sophistical contrivances wherewith we are so industriously plied and belabored - contrivances such as groping for some middle ground between the right and the wrong, vain as the search for a man who should be neither a living man nor a dead man - such as a policy of "don't care" on a question about which all true men do care - such as Union appeals beseeching true Union men to yield to Disunionists, reversing the divine rule, and calling, not the sinners, but the righteous to repentance - such as invocations to Washington, imploring men to unsay what Washington said, and undo what Washington did.

Neither let us be slandered from our duty by false accusations against us, nor frightened from it by menaces of destruction to the Government nor of dungeons to ourselves. Let us have faith that Right makes Might, and in that faith, let us, to the end, dare to do our duty as we understand it.

First Inaugural Address (March 4, 1861)

Fellow-citizens of the United States:

In compliance with a custom as old as the government itself, I appear before you to address you briefly, and to take, in your presence, the oath prescribed by the Constitution of the United States, to be taken by the President *"before he enters on the execution of this office."* I do not consider it necessary at present for me to discuss those matters of administration about which there is no special anxiety or excitement.

Apprehension seems to exist among the people of the Southern States, that by the accession of a Republican Administration, their property, and their peace, and personal security, are to be endangered. There has never been any reasonable cause for such apprehension. Indeed, the most ample evidence to the contrary has all the while existed, and been open to their inspection. It is found in nearly all the published speeches of him who now addresses you. I do but quote from one of those speeches when I declare that "I have no purpose, directly or indirectly, to interfere with the institution of slavery in the States where it exists. I believe I have no lawful right to do so, and I have no inclination to do so." Those who nominated and elected me did so with full knowledge that I had made this, and many similar declarations, and had never recanted them. And more than this, they placed in the platform, for my acceptance, and as a law to themselves, and to me, the clear and emphatic resolution which I now read:

Resolved, That the maintenance inviolate of the rights of the States, and especially the right of each State to order and control its own domestic institutions according to its own judgment exclusively, is essential to that balance of power on which the perfection and endurance of our political fabric depend; and we denounce the lawless invasion by armed force of the soil of any State or Territory, no matter what pretext, as among the gravest of crimes."

I now reiterate these sentiments; and in doing so, I only press upon the public attention the most conclusive evidence of which the case is susceptible, that the property, peace and security of no section are to be in any wise endangered by the now incoming Administration. I add too, that all the protection which, consistently with the Constitution and the laws, can be given, will be cheerfully given to all the States when lawfully demanded, for whatever cause - as cheerfully to one section as to another.

There is much controversy about the delivering up of fugitives from service or labor. The clause I now read is as plainly written in the Constitution as any other of its provisions:

"No person held to service or labor in one State, under the laws thereof, escaping into another, shall, in consequence of any law or regulation therein, be discharged from such service or labor, but shall be delivered up on claim of the party to whom such service or labor may be due."

It is scarcely questioned that this provision was intended by those who made it, for the reclaiming of what we call fugitive slaves; and the intention of the law-giver is the law. All members of Congress swear their support to the whole Constitution - to this provision as much as to any other. To the proposition, then, that slaves whose cases come within the terms of this clause, "shall be delivered," their oaths are unanimous. Now, if they would make the effort in good temper, could they not, with nearly equal unanimity, frame and pass a law, by means of which to keep good that unanimous oath?

There is some difference of opinion whether this clause should be enforced by national or by state authority; but surely that difference is not a very material one. If the slave is to be surrendered, it can be of but little consequence to him, or to others, by which authority it is done. And should any one, in any case, be content that his oath shall go unkept, on a merely unsubstantial controversy as to how it shall be kept?

Again, in any law upon this subject, ought not all the safeguards of liberty known in civilized and humane jurisprudence to be introduced, so that a free man be not, in any case, surrendered as a slave? And might it not be well, at the same time to provide by law for the enforcement of that clause in the Constitution which guarantees that "the citizens of each State shall be entitled to all privileges and immunities of citizens in the several States"?

I take the official oath to-day, with no mental reservations, and with no purpose to construe the Constitution or laws, by any hypercritical rules. And while I do not choose now to specify particular acts of Congress as proper to be enforced, I do suggest that it will be much safer for all, both in official and private stations, to conform to, and abide by, all those acts which stand unrepealed, than to violate any of them, trusting to find impunity in having them held to be unconstitutional.

It is seventy-two years since the first inauguration of a President under our national Constitution. During that period fifteen different and greatly distinguished citizens, have, in succession, administered the executive branch of the government. They have conducted it through many perils; and, generally, with great success. Yet, with all this scope for precedent, I now enter upon the same task for the brief constitutional term of four years, under great and peculiar difficulty. A disruption of the Federal Union, heretofore only menaced, is now formidably attempted.

I hold, that in contemplation of universal law, and of the Constitution, the Union of these States is perpetual. Perpetuity is implied, if not expressed, in the fundamental law of all national governments. It is safe to assert that no government proper, ever had a provision in its organic law for its own termination. Continue to execute all the express provisions of our national Constitution, and the Union will endure forever - it being impossible to destroy it, except by some action not provided for in the instrument itself.

Again, if the United States be not a government proper, but an association of States in the nature of contract merely, can it, as a contract, be peaceably unmade, by less than all the parties who made it? One party to a contract may violate it - break it, so to speak; but does it not require all to lawfully rescind it?

Descending from these general principles, we find the proposition that, in legal contemplation, the Union is perpetual, confirmed by the history of the Union itself. The Union is much older than the Constitution. It was formed in fact, by the Articles of Association in 1774. It was matured and continued by the Declaration of Independence in 1776. It was further matured and the faith of all the then thirteen States expressly plighted and engaged that it should be perpetual, by the Articles of Confederation in 1778. And finally, in 1787, one of the declared objects for ordaining and establishing the Constitution, was "to form a more perfect Union." But if [the] destruction of the Union, by one, or by a part only, of the States, be lawfully possible, the Union is less perfect than before the Constitution, having lost the vital element of perpetuity.

It follows from these views that no State, upon its own mere motion, can lawfully get out of the Union, - that resolves and ordinances to that effect are legally void, and that acts of violence, within any State or States, against the authority of the United States, are insurrectionary or revolutionary, according to circumstances.

I therefore consider that in view of the Constitution and the laws, the Union is unbroken; and to the extent of my ability I shall take care, as the Constitution itself expressly enjoins upon me, that the laws of the Union be faithfully executed in all the States. Doing this I deem to be only a simple duty on my part; and I shall perform it, so far as practicable, unless my rightful masters, the American people, shall withhold the requisite means, or in some authoritative manner, direct the contrary. I trust this will not be regarded as a menace, but only as the declared purpose of the Union that will constitutionally defend and maintain itself.

In doing this there needs to be no bloodshed or violence; and there shall be none, unless it be forced upon the national authority. The power confided to me will be used to hold, occupy, and possess the property and places belonging to the government, and to collect the duties and imposts; but beyond what may be necessary for these objects, there will be no invasion - no using of force against or among the people anywhere. Where hostility to the United States in any interior locality, shall be so great and so universal, as to prevent competent resident citizens from holding the Federal offices, there will be no attempt to force obnoxious strangers among the people for that object. While the strict legal right may exist in the government to enforce the exercise of these offices, the attempt to do so would be so irritating, and so nearly impracticable with all, that I deem it better to forego, for the time, the uses of such offices.

The mails, unless repelled, will continue to be furnished in all parts of the Union. So far as possible, the people everywhere shall have that sense of perfect security which is most favorable to calm thought and reflection. The course here indicated will be followed, unless current events and experience shall show a modification or change to be proper; and in every case and exigency my best discretion will be exercised according to circumstances actually existing, and with a view and a hope of a peaceful solution of the national troubles, and the restoration of fraternal sympathies and affections.

That there are persons in one section or another who seek to destroy the Union at all events, and are glad of any pretext to do it, I will neither affirm nor deny; but if there be such, I need address no word to them. To those, however, who really love the Union may I not speak?

Before entering upon so grave a matter as the destruction of our national fabric, with all its benefits, its memories, and its hopes, would it not be wise to ascertain precisely why we do it? Will you hazard so desperate a step, while there is any possibility that any portion of the ills you fly from have no real existence? Will you, while the certain ills you fly to, are greater than all the real ones you fly from? Will you risk the commission of so fearful a mistake?

All profess to be content in the Union, if all constitutional rights can be maintained. Is it true, then, that any right, plainly written in the Constitution, has been denied? I think not. Happily the human mind is so constituted, that no party can reach to the audacity of doing this. Think, if you can, of a single instance in which a plainly written provision of the Constitution has ever been denied. If by the mere force of numbers, a majority should deprive a minority of any clearly written constitutional right, it might, in a moral point of view, justify revolution - certainly would, if such right were a vital one. But such is not our case. All the vital rights of minorities, and of individuals, are so plainly assured to them, by affirmations and negations, guaranties and prohibitions, in the Constitution, that controversies never arise concerning them. But no organic law can ever be framed with a provision specifically applicable to every question which may occur in practical administration. No foresight can anticipate, nor any document of reasonable length contain express provisions for all possible questions. Shall fugitives from labor be surrendered by national or by State authority? The Constitution does not expressly say. May Congress prohibit slavery in the territories? The Constitution does not expressly say. Must Congress protect slavery in the territories? The Constitution does not expressly say.

From questions of this class spring all our constitutional controversies, and we divide upon them into majorities and minorities. If the minority will not acquiesce, the majority must, or the government must cease. There is no other alternative; for continuing the government, is acquiescence on one side or the other. If a minority, in such case, will secede rather than acquiesce, they make a precedent which, in turn, will divide and ruin them; for a minority of their own will secede from them whenever a majority refuses to be controlled by such minority. For instance, why may not any portion of a new confederacy, a year or two hence, arbitrarily secede again, precisely as portions of the present Union now claim to secede from it? All who cherish disunion sentiments, are now being educated to the exact temper of doing this. Is there such perfect identity of interests among the States to compose a new Union, as to produce harmony only, and prevent renewed secession?

Plainly, the central idea of secession, is the essence of anarchy. A majority, held in restraint by constitutional checks and limitations, and always changing easily with deliberate changes of popular opinions and sentiments, is the only true sovereign of a free people. Whoever rejects it, does, of necessity, fly to anarchy or to despotism. Unanimity is impossible; the rule of a minority, as a permanent arrangement, is wholly inadmissible; so that, rejecting the majority principle, anarchy or despotism in some form is all that is left.

I do not forget the position assumed by some, that constitutional questions are to be decided by the Supreme Court; nor do I deny that such decisions must be binding in any case, upon the parties to a suit; as to the object of that suit, while they are also entitled to very high respect and consideration in all parallel cases by all other departments of the government. And while it is obviously possible that such decision may be erroneous in any given case, still the evil effect following it, being limited to that particular case, with the chance that it may be over-ruled, and never become a precedent for other cases, can better be borne than could the evils of a different practice. At the same time, the candid citizen must confess that if the policy of the government upon vital questions, affecting the whole people, is to be irrevocably fixed by decisions of the Supreme Court, the instant they are made, in ordinary litigation between parties, in personal actions, the people will have ceased to be their own rulers, having to that extent practically resigned their government into the hands of that eminent tribunal. Nor is there in this view any assault upon the court or the judges. It is a duty from which they may not shrink, to decide cases properly brought before them; and it is no fault of theirs if others seek to turn their decisions to political purposes.

One section of our country believes slavery is right, and ought to be extended, while the other believes it is wrong, and ought not to be extended. This is the only substantial dispute. The fugitive slave clause of the Constitution, and the law for the suppression of the foreign slave trade, are each as well enforced, perhaps, as any law can ever be in a community where the moral sense of the people imperfectly supports the law itself. The great body of the people abide by the dry legal obligation in both cases, and a few break over in each. This, I think, cannot be perfectly cured, and it would be worse in both cases after the separation of the sections, than before. The foreign slave trade, now imperfectly suppressed, would be ultimately revived without restriction, in one section; while fugitive slaves, now only partially surrendered, would not be surrendered at all, by the other.

Physically speaking, we cannot separate. We can not remove our respective sections from each other, nor build an impassable wall between them. A husband and wife may be divorced, and go out of the presence, and beyond the reach of each other; but the different parts of our country cannot do this. They cannot but remain face to face; and intercourse, either amicable or hostile, must continue between them. Is it possible, then, to make that intercourse more advantageous or more satisfactory, after separation than before? Can aliens make treaties easier than friends can make laws? Can treaties be more faithfully enforced between aliens than laws can among friends? Suppose you go to war, you cannot fight always; and when, after much loss on both sides, and no gain on either, you cease fighting, the identical old questions, as to terms of intercourse, are again upon you.

This country, with its institutions, belongs to the people who inhabit it. Whenever they shall grow weary of the existing Government, they can exercise their constitutional right of amending it, or their revolutionary right to dismember or overthrow it. I cannot be ignorant of the fact that many worthy and patriotic citizens are desirous of having the national Constitution amended. While I make no recommendation of amendments, I fully recognize the rightful authority of the people over

the whole subject to be exercised in either of the modes prescribed in the instrument itself; and I should, under existing
circumstances, favor rather than oppose a fair opportunity being
afforded the people to act upon it.

I will venture to add that to me the Convention mode seems
preferable, in that it allows amendments to originate with the
people themselves, instead of only permitting them to take or
reject propositions, originated by others, not especially chosen
for the purpose, and which might not be precisely such as they
would wish to either accept or refuse. I understand a proposed
amendment to the Constitution, which amendment, however, I
have not seen, has passed Congress, to the effect that the federal
government shall never interfere with the domestic institutions
of the States, including that of persons held to service. To avoid
misconstruction of what I have said, I depart from my purpose
not to speak of particular amendments, so far as to say that
holding such a provision to now be implied constitutional law, I
have no objection to its being made express and irrevocable.

The Chief Magistrate derives all his authority from the people,
and they have referred none upon him to fix terms for the
separation of the States. The people themselves can do this if
also they choose; but the executive, as such, has nothing to do

with it. His duty is to administer the present government, as it came to his hands, and to transmit it, unimpaired by him, to his successor.

Why should there not be a patient confidence in the ultimate justice of the people? Is there any better or equal hope, in the world? In our present differences, is either party without faith of being in the right? If the Almighty Ruler of nations, with his eternal truth and justice, be on your side of the North, or on yours of the South, that truth, and that justice, will surely prevail, by the judgment of this great tribunal of the American people.

By the frame of the government under which we live, this same people have wisely given their public servants but little power for mischief; and have, with equal wisdom, provided for the return of that little to their own hands at very short intervals. While the people retain their virtue and vigilance, no administration, by any extreme of wickedness or folly, can very seriously injure the government in the short space of four years.

My countrymen, one and all, think calmly and well, upon this whole subject. Nothing valuable can be lost by taking time. If there be an object to hurry any of you, in hot haste, to a step which you would never take deliberately, that object will be frustrated by taking time; but no good object can be frustrated by it. Such of you as are now dissatisfied still have the old Constitution unimpaired, and, on the sensitive point, the laws of your own framing under it; while the new administration will have no immediate power, if it would, to change either. If it were admitted that you who are dissatisfied, hold the right side in the dispute, there still is no single good reason for precipitate action. Intelligence, patriotism, Christianity, and a firm reliance on Him, who has never yet forsaken this favored land, are still competent to adjust, in the best way, all our present difficulty.

In your hands, my dissatisfied fellow countrymen, and not in mine, is the momentous issue of civil war. The government will not assail you. You can have no conflict without being yourselves the aggressors. You have no oath registered in Heaven to destroy the government, while I shall have the most solemn one to "preserve, protect, and defend it."

I am loath to close. We are not enemies, but friends. We must not be enemies. Though passion may have strained, it must not break our bonds of affection. The mystic chords of memory, stretching from every battle-field, and patriot grave, to every living heart and hearth-stone, all over this broad land, will yet swell the chorus of the Union, when again touched, as surely they will be, by the better angels of our nature.

Gettysburg Address (November 19, 1863)

Fourscore and seven years ago our fathers brought forth on this continent a new nation, conceived in liberty, and dedicated to the proposition that all men are created equal. Now we are engaged in a great civil war, testing whether that nation, or any nation so conceived and so dedicated, can long endure. We are met on a great battle-field of that war. We have come to dedicate a portion of that field as a final resting-place for those who here gave their lives that that nation might live. It is altogether fitting and proper that we should do this. But, in a larger sense, we cannot dedicate...we cannot consecrate...we cannot hallow...this ground. The bravemen, living and dead, who struggled here, have consecrated it far above our poor power to add or detract. The world will little note nor long remember what we say here, but it can never forget what they did here. It is for us, the living, rather, to be dedicated here to the unfinished work which they who fought here have thus far so nobly advanced. It is rather for us to be here dedicated to the great task remaining before us...that from these honored dead we take increased devotion to that cause for which they gave the last full measure of devotion; that we here highly resolve that these dead shall not have died in vain; that this nation, under God, shall have a new birth of freedom; and that government of the people, by the people, for the people, shall not perish from the earth.

Second Inaugural Address (March 5, 1865)

Fellow-Countrymen:

At this second appearing to take the oath of the Presidential office there is less occasion for an extended address than there was at the first. Then a statement somewhat in detail of a course to be pursued seemed fitting and proper. Now, at the expiration of four years, during which public declarations have been constantly called forth on every point and phase of the great contest which still absorbs the attention and engrosses the energies of the nation, little that is new could be presented. The progress of our arms, upon which all else chiefly depends, is as well known to the public as to myself, and it is, I trust, reasonably satisfactory and encouraging to all. With high hope for the future, no prediction in regard to it is ventured.   On the occasion corresponding to this four years ago all thoughts were anxiously directed to an impending civil war. All dreaded it, all sought to avert it. While the inaugural address was being delivered from this place, devoted altogether to *saving* the Union without war, urgent agents were in the city seeking to *destroy* it without war—seeking to dissolve the Union and divide effects by negotiation.

Both parties deprecated war, but one of them would *make* war rather than let the nation survive, and the other would *accept* war rather than let it perish, and the war came.   One-eighth of the whole population were colored slaves, not distributed generally over the Union, but localized in the southern part of it. These slaves constituted a peculiar and powerful interest. All knew that this interest was somehow the cause of the war. To strengthen, perpetuate, and extend this interest was the object for which the insurgents would rend the Union even by war, while the Government claimed no right to do more than to restrict the territorial enlargement of it. Neither party expected for the war the magnitude or the duration which it has already attained. Neither anticipated that the *cause* of the conflict might cease with or even before the conflict itself should cease.

Each looked for an easier triumph and a result less fundamental and astounding. Both read the same Bible and pray to the same God, and each invokes His aid against the other. It may seem strange that any men should dare to ask a just God's assistance in wringing their bread from the sweat of other men's faces, but let us judge not, that we be not judged. The prayers of both could not be answered. That of neither has been answered fully. The Almighty has His own purposes. "Woe unto the world because of offenses; for it must needs be that offenses come, but woe to that man by whom the offense cometh." If we shall suppose that American slavery is one of those offenses which, in the providence of God, must needs come, but which, having continued through His appointed time, He now wills to remove, and that He gives to both North and South this terrible war as the woe due to those by whom the offense came, shall we discern therein any departure from those divine attributes which the believers in a living God always ascribe to Him? Fondly do we hope, fervently do we pray, that this mighty scourge of war may speedily pass away.

Yet, if God wills that it continue until all the wealth piled by the bondsman's two hundred and fifty years of unrequited toil shall be sunk, and until every drop of blood drawn with the lash shall be paid by another drawn with the sword, as was said three thousand years ago, so still it must be said "the judgments of the Lord are true and righteous altogether."

With malice toward none, with charity for all, with firmness in the right as God gives us to see the right, let us strive on to finish the work we are in, to bind up the nation's wounds, to care for him who shall have borne the battle and for his widow and his orphan, to do all which may achieve and cherish a just and lasting peace among ourselves and with all nations.

Bibliography

The subject of the American Civil War is well tilled ground and there are thousands of very good reference sources. Following are those that were of most relevance to the writing of this book:

Lincoln Books:

Waugh, John, "Re-electing Lincoln: The Battle for the 1864 Presidency," Da Capo Press, 2001

Sandburg, Carl, "Abraham Lincoln," Harcourt Press, 1954 Civil War Books

Foote, Shelby, "The Civil War: A Narrative," Random House, 1958

Capt. Lee, Robert E., "The Recollections and Letters of Robert E.Lee," Konecky and Konechy, 1998

Grant, Ulysses S., "Personal Memoirs of Ulysses S. Grant," Cosimo Classics, 2006

Gozzens, Peter and Robert Girard editors, "The Military Memoirs of General John Pope," University of North Carolina Press, 1998

Symonds, Craig L., "Joseph E. Johnston: A Civil War Biography," W.W. Norton Books, 1992

Sears, Stephen, "Controversies and Commanders," Houghton Mifflin, 1999

Garrison Jr., Webb, "Strange Battles of the Civil War," Bristol Park Books, 2001

McPherson, James M., "What They Fought For 1861 - 1865," Anchor Books, 1995

Bierce, Ambrose, "Civil War Stories," Dover Publications, 1994

Olsen, Christopher J., "The American Civil War: A Hands On History," Hill and Wang, 2006

Miller, Rober J., "Both Prayed to the Same God: Religion and Faith in the American Civil War," Lexington Books, 2007

Websites:

www.civilwarphotos.net

www.archives.gov/research/military/civil-war

www.civilwar-pictures.com

www.civilwarphotography.org

About the Author

Murray Lytle is a professional mining engineer and economist who plies his trade throughout North and South America. Spending long periods away from home produces either a mild form of insanity or an ability to read prodigiously. In his case there are elements of both.

It was while struggling for breath high in the Andes Mountains that it occurred to him that there is something very unique about the United States. The ironic irrationality of a Canadian thinking about the United States while trekking in South America is not lost on him. But such are the effects of altitude sickness. His subsequent multi-year quest to understand why this is so and how it came to be led to an interest in the American Civil War. Murray is in the final throes of completing his PhD in Corporate Social Responsibility basing his research on an investigation of the role of world view in resource development conflict.

Mr. Lytle, a proud Centurion, is married to an unnaturally longsuffering wife and together they have three grown children and an increasing brood of grandchildren who exhibit every inclination of becoming blue-eyed sinners like their grandfather. When he is not on vocational walk-about he makes his home in Calgary, Alberta, Canada.

22843757R00236

Made in the USA
Lexington, KY
15 May 2013